Music and Human Flourishing

THE HUMANITIES AND HUMAN FLOURISHING

Series editor: James O. Pawelski, *University of Pennsylvania*

Music and Human Flourishing

Edited by

ANNA HARWELL CELENZA

OXFORD

UNIVERSITY PRESS

OXFORD
UNIVERSITY PRESS

Oxford University Press is a department of the University of Oxford. It furthers
the University's objective of excellence in research, scholarship, and education
by publishing worldwide. Oxford is a registered trade mark of Oxford University
Press in the UK and certain other countries.

Published in the United States of America by Oxford University Press
198 Madison Avenue, New York, NY 10016, United States of America.

Library of Congress Cataloging-in-Publication Data
Names: Celenza, Anna Harwell, editor.
Title: Music and human flourishing / [edited by] Anna Harwell Celenza.
Description: New York : Oxford University Press, 2023. |
Series: The humanities and human flourishing | Includes bibliographical references and index.
Identifiers: LCCN 2022042452 (print) | LCCN 2022042453 (ebook) |
ISBN 9780197646755 (paperback) | ISBN 9780197646748 (hardback) |
ISBN 9780197646779 (epub)
Subjects: LCSH: Music—Social aspects. | Music—Psychological aspects.
Classification: LCC ML3916 .M8607 2023 (print) | LCC ML3916 (ebook) |
DDC 306.4/842—dc23/eng/20220902
LC record available at https://lccn.loc.gov/2022042452
LC ebook record available at https://lccn.loc.gov/2022042453

DOI: 10.1093/oso/9780197646748.001.0001

1 3 5 7 9 8 6 4 2

Paperback printed by Marquis, Canada
Hardback printed by Bridgeport National Bindery, Inc., United States of America

Contents

PART III: COMMUNICATION

Series Editor's Foreword

Imagine being invited to a weekend meeting to discuss connections between the humanities and human flourishing. You talk about ways in which the humanities can help us understand what human flourishing is—and is not. You explore how the humanities can help increase human flourishing. And you consider whether human flourishing is an absolute good, or whether it comes with certain limits and even potential dangers. How do you imagine the conversation playing out? What contributions might you make to the discussion?

The volumes in this series were borne out of just such a meeting. Or rather a series of such meetings, each gathering including some dozen scholars in a particular discipline in the humanities (understood to be inclusive of the arts). These disciplines include philosophy, history, literary studies, religious studies and theology, theater, cinema and media, music, and the visual arts. Participants were asked to consider how their work in their discipline intersects with well-being (taken to be roughly synonymous with human flourishing), along with a series of specific questions:

- How does your discipline conceptualize, understand, and define well-being?
- What does your discipline say about the cultivation of well-being? How does it encourage the implementation of well-being?
- In what ways does your discipline support flourishing? Do some approaches within your discipline advance human flourishing more effectively than others? Are there ways in which certain aspects of your discipline could more effectively promote well-being?
- Does your discipline contribute to well-being in any unique ways in which other endeavors do not?
- Are there ways in which your discipline can obstruct human flourishing?

As might be expected, the conversations in these meetings were rich and wide-ranging. Some of them headed in expected directions; others were more surprising. Each of them yielded opportunities to question assumptions and deepen perspectives. The conversations were rooted in disciplinary contexts and questions but yielded many generalizable insights on how to conceptualize human flourishing more clearly, how to cultivate it more effectively, and how to avoid negative consequences of understanding it in incomplete or overblown ways. I cannot properly describe or even summarize the richness of the discussions here, but I would like to point out a few of the highlights included in each of the resulting volumes.

Philosophy and Human Flourishing, edited by John J. Stuhr, addresses a number of fundamental questions. What is the value of discussing human flourishing in a world that in so many ways is decidedly not flourishing? In what ways is flourishing similar to and different from happiness? What is the role of morality in human flourishing? How does it relate to systemic privilege and oppression? To what degree is flourishing properly the concern of individuals, and to what degree is it a function of communities and societies? What are key factors in the fostering of flourishing? In addressing these questions, philosophers explore concepts such as mattering, homeostasis, pluralism, responsibility, and values, and consider the roles of individuals, educational institutions, and governments.

History and Human Flourishing, edited by Darrin M. McMahon, centers on the question, What is the value of history for life? This core question leads to a number of further inquiries. Is history only about the past, or does it have important implications for the present and the future? If the latter, then how can historical inquiry most effectively contribute to well-being? Does such inquiry currently focus in an imbalanced way on ill-being—on prejudices, class struggles, and wars? Such work is doubtless of great importance, not least by investigating how claims about happiness can serve as propaganda for continued oppression. But would hope for the future be more effectively kindled and concrete steps toward its realization more adeptly guided by increased attention to what has actually gone well in the past and what we can learn from it or by more focus on how human beings have responded positively to adversity?

Literary Studies and Human Flourishing, edited by James F. English and Heather Love, focuses on the transformative power of literature. Scholars examine a range of topics, including the reparative possibilities of a literary encounter, the value of bibliotherapy and of therapeutic redescription, the genre of "uplit," and evolving methods for studying the activities and experiences of actual readers. A central question of this volume concerns the limits on transformations effected through literature. Several contributors worry that harnessing literary studies to the enterprise of human flourishing might lead readers merely to conform rather than to transform. To what extent might human flourishing serve as a palliative, enabling and encouraging readers to adapt to individual lives that lack moral depth and to social conditions that are rife with injustice, and thus obstruct the difficult and unsettling work of disruptive transformation needed for lasting individual and collective betterment?

Religious Studies, Theology, and Human Flourishing, edited by Justin Thomas McDaniel and Hector Kilgoe, explores ways in which individual and collective well-being can be increased through various religious perspectives and practices, including the Hindu concept of *sanmati* ("goodwill, wisdom, and noble-mindedness"), Buddhist meditation, and the cultivation of spiritual joy even while facing adversity. Scholars consider challenging questions concerning the proper contexts for learning *about* religion and for learning *from* religion, the right balance between the acknowledgment of suffering and the fostering of well-being, and the relationship between human flourishing and nonhuman worlds (including both natural and supernatural domains). A concern of some of these scholars is whether human flourishing entails a false universalism, one that seeks to reduce cultural diversities to one particular notion of what is desirable or even acceptable, and whether such a notion could be used to rate the value of different religions, or even ban religious practices (e.g., fasting, celibacy, or other ascetic austerities) that might be deemed misaligned with well-being.

Theater and Human Flourishing, edited by Harvey Young, considers the unique resources of theater and performance for imagining and enhancing well-being. Because theater involves both performers and audience members, it is inherently communal in ways many humanities disciplines and art forms are not. Theater allows groups of people—often strangers—to come together and experience the world in new ways. More than just an escape from ordinary life or a simple mirroring of reality, theater can provide opportunities for communal reimagining of the world, exploring new ways of thinking, feeling, and relating that can be experienced and then enacted to bring about a more flourishing future. Scholars examine connections between theater and human flourishing in more and less traditional spheres, looking at ways performance practices can be used to critique inadequate notions of human flourishing and to increase well-being in a wide variety of contexts, ranging from community theater to organizations serving soldiers with post-traumatic stress disorder (PTSD), and from oppressed groups to politically divided societies.

Cinema, Media, and Human Flourishing, edited by Timothy Corrigan, looks to film and a whole range of contemporary forms of digital media for what they can teach us about the nature of human flourishing and how it can be cultivated. These forms of communication have vast audiences and thus great power to support or subvert well-being. Contributors to this volume observe that human flourishing often seems to come piecemeal and as a hard-won result of conflict and struggle, and they explore ways in which well-being can be supported by collaborative practices for creating content, by the particular ways narratives are crafted, by certain genres, and by the various values that are embraced and transmitted. Contributors also consider how these popular forms can support individuals and groups on the margins of society by making more visible and sympathetic their struggles toward flourishing.

Music and Human Flourishing, edited by Anna Harwell Celenza, complements the commonly accepted and scientifically supported view that participating in music—as a listener, performer, or composer—can increase individual well-being. Instead of focusing on music as a performing art, this volume examines music as a humanities discipline, emphasizing the importance and value of music scholarship for fostering individual and collective human flourishing. How can music scholars (musicologists, ethnomusicologists, and music theorists) strengthen the effects of music on flourishing through a consideration of broader cultural, social, and political contexts? Contributors explore how processes of contemplation, critique, and communication within music scholarship can deepen the experience of music, resulting not just in the enhancement of individual well-being but in the more effective cultivation of wisdom and the greater realization of social justice.

Visual Arts and Human Flourishing, edited by Selma Holo, begins with the experience of artists themselves and the function of art in our society. If well-being is thought of as the happiness of self-satisfied complacency, then it would seem to be the antithesis of art, which is often disruptive, unnerving, and unsettling, asking viewers to question their assumptions and inviting them to see the world in new ways. But if well-being is understood more deeply as the flourishing that can arise from the full range of human experience, including the discomfort of contending forms of meaning and contested visions of reality, then it is difficult to think of it without art. Contributors to this volume consider the overwhelming personal necessity artists have to create, the role of well-being in art history, the increasing emphasis on human flourishing in architecture and public art, and salient questions of ethics, accessibility, and social justice in the context of art museums.

The Humanities and Human Flourishing, for which I serve as editor, is an interdisciplinary, capstone volume that contains contributions from the editors of the eight disciplinary volumes. After the disciplinary meetings were concluded, we gathered together to discuss what we had learned through the process. We considered both similarities and differences across the disciplinary discussions on human flourishing, identifying social justice and pedagogy as two common themes that emerged in the meetings. Like the other volumes in the series, this volume does not pretend to provide simple solutions or even unified answers to questions of how the humanities are or should be connected to the conceptualization and cultivation of human flourishing. Rather, it provides thoughtful questions and perspectives, distilled as it is from a deliberate process of extended engagement from diverse groups of scholars across eight different arts and humanities disciplines.

I would like to welcome you, the reader, to this book series. I hope you find it stimulating and even inspiring in its explorations into the complexities of the relationship between the humanities and human flourishing. And I hope you read across the volumes, as they are written in an accessible style that will yield valuable insights whether or not you have particular expertise in the discipline of the author whose work you are reading. To whatever degree you immerse yourself in this book series, though, I am sure of one thing: You will find it incomplete. As deep and as broad ranging as we tried to be in our explorations, none of the participants is under the illusion that the discussions and volumes brought it to a conclusion. We are keenly aware that a group of a dozen scholars, no matter how diverse, cannot speak for an entire discipline, and we realize that a focus on eight disciplines does not cover the entire domain of the humanities. Furthermore, our discussions and most of the writing were completed before the COVID-19 pandemic, which has made the nature and importance of flourishing all the more salient and has raised a host of new questions about well-being. Instead, we think of our work as an important beginning, and we would like to invite you to join the conversation. We hope a greater number and diversity of scholars, researchers, creators, practitioners, students, leaders in cultural organizations and creative industries, office holders in government, philanthropists, and members of the general public will bring their interests and expertise to the conversation, perhaps leading to new volumes in this series in the future. Investigations into human flourishing contribute to our knowledge and understanding of the human condition, and they have practical implications for the well-being of scholars, students, and societies. We hope our ongoing work together will enable the humanities to play a greater role in these investigations, effecting changes in scholarship, research, pedagogy, policy, and practice that will make them more supportive of human flourishing in academia and in the world at large.

Background and Rationale

For readers interested in more information on the background and rationale of this book series, I am happy to share further details on the perspectives, aims, and hopes that motivated it. A key catalyst for the development of this series was the dual observation that a growing number of individuals and organizations are focusing on human flourishing and that most of the headlines in this domain seem to be coming from the social sciences. Yale psychology professor Laurie Santos, for example, made the news when she developed a course on "Psychology and the Good Life"—and some 1,200 students (nearly a quarter of Yale's undergraduate population) signed up for it.[1] As of this writing, her subsequent podcast, "The Happiness Lab," has reached 65 million downloads.[2] On an international scale, dozens of countries around the world have adopted psychological measures of subjective well-being as a complement to economic indicators, and a growing number of nations have embraced well-being, happiness, or flourishing as an explicit governmental goal.[3] The Organisation for Economic Co-operation and Development (OECD), founded in 1961 to stimulate economic progress and world trade, has acknowledged the insufficiency of economic indicators

[1] David Shimer, "Yale's Most Popular Class Ever: Happiness." *New York Times*, January 26, 2018, https://www.nytimes.com/2018/01/26/nyregion/at-yale-class-on-happiness-draws-huge-crowd-laurie-santos.html.

[2] Lucy Hodgman and Evan Gorelick, "Silliman Head of College Laurie Santos to Take One-Year Leave to Address Burnout." *Yale News*, February 8, 2022, https://yaledailynews.com/blog/2022/02/08/silliman-head-of-college-laurie-santos-to-take-one-year-leave-to-address-burnout/.

[3] https://weall.org/; https://www.ons.gov.uk/peoplepopulationandcommunity/wellbeing/articles/measuresofnationalwellbeingdashboard/2018-04-25; https://www.gnhcentrebhutan.org/history-of-gnh/; https://www.worldbank.org/en/news/feature/2013/10/24/Bolivia-quiere-replicar-el-indice-de-felicidad-de-Butan; https://u.ae/en/about-the-uae/the-uae-government/government-of-future/happiness/.

alone for tracking progress. It launched its Better Life Initiative in 2011 to measure what drives the well-being of individuals and nations and to determine how countries can best support greater progress for all.[4] The United Nations publishes the World Happiness Report every year, releasing it on March 20, the UN International Day of Happiness.[5]

These are examples in the social sciences of what I have elsewhere called a "eudaimonic turn," an explicit commitment to human flourishing as a core theoretical and research interest and a desired practical outcome.[6] Over the last several decades, there has been a growing interest in human flourishing in economics, political science, psychology, and sociology, and in fields influenced by them, such as education, organizational studies, medicine, and public health. Perhaps the most well-known example of this eudaimonic turn in the social sciences occurred in psychology with the advent of positive psychology. Reflecting perspectives developed in humanistic psychology in the mid-twentieth century and building on increasing empirical work in self-efficacy, self-determination theory, subjective and psychological well-being, optimism, flow, passion, hope theory, positive emotions, and related areas, Martin Seligman and his colleagues launched the field of positive psychology. During a 1998 presidential address to the American Psychological Association, Seligman pointed out that mainstream psychology had become fixated on understanding and treating psychopathology. He argued that, although extremely important, healing mental illness is only part of psychology's mission. More broadly, he claimed, psychology should be about making the lives of all people better. He noted that this requires the careful empirical study of what makes life most worth living, including a deep understanding of flourishing individuals and thriving communities. Such study, he believed, would both increase well-being and decrease ill-being, since human strengths are both important in their own right and effective as buffers against mental illness. Known as "the scientific study of what enables individuals and societies to thrive,"[7] positive psychology has had a

---

[4] https://www.oecd.org/sdd/OECD-Better-Life-Initiative.pdf.

[5] https://worldhappiness.report/.

[6] James O. Pawelski, "What Is the Eudaimonic Turn?," in *The Eudaimonic Turn: Well-Being in Literary Studies*, ed. James O. Pawelski and D. J. Moores (Madison, NJ: Fairleigh Dickinson University Press, 2013), 3; and James O. Pawelski, "The Positive Humanities: Culture and Human Flourishing," in *The Oxford Handbook of the Positive Humanities*, ed. Louis Tay and James O. Pawelski (New York: Oxford University Press, 2022), 26.

[7] Constitution of the International Positive Psychology Association, Article 1, Section 2.

transformative effect on psychology and has deeply influenced many other fields of research and practice.

What role do the humanities play in all of this? What role could and should they play? How can the humanities help us conceptualize human flourishing more deeply, cultivate it more effectively, and critique it more insightfully? As a philosopher working in the field of positive psychology for more than twenty years, I have been concerned that there are not more voices from the humanities centrally involved in contemporary work in human flourishing. One of the core aims of this project and book series is to make a way for humanities scholars to play a larger role in this domain by inviting them to consider explicitly what contributions their work and their disciplines can make to the theory, research, and practice of human flourishing.

Historically, of course, human flourishing is at the root of the humanities.[8] The humanities were first defined and developed as a program of study by Renaissance scholars dissatisfied with scholasticism, which they perceived as leading to an overly technical university curriculum removed from the concerns of everyday life and unable to guide students toward human flourishing. They advocated, instead, a return to the Greek and Roman classics, reading them for insights and perspectives on how to live life well. Indeed, the Greeks and Romans had developed comprehensive programs of study (*paideia* and *artes liberales*, respectively) designed to teach students how to flourish individually and how to contribute to collective flourishing by participating effectively and wisely in civic life.

This emphasis on the understanding and cultivation of human flourishing that was so important to the Greeks and Romans was also of central concern to other philosophical and religious traditions that developed in the ancient world during what Karl Jaspers called the Axial Age.[9] Hinduism, Buddhism, Confucianism, Daoism, and Judaism, for example, along with the later Christianity and Islam, addressed the problem of human suffering and offered ways of promoting individual and collective flourishing. Although different in their cultural context and specific details, each of these traditions counseled against lives exclusively devoted to pleasure, wealth, power, or fame. They held that such lives only magnify suffering and that flourishing is actually fostered through a cultivation of virtue that allows

---

[8] Pawelski, "The Positive Humanities," 20–21; and Darrin M. McMahon, "The History of the Humanities and Human Flourishing," in *The Oxford Handbook of the Positive Humanities*, ed. Louis Tay and James O. Pawelski (New York: Oxford University Press, 2022), 45–50.

[9] Karl Jaspers, *The Origin and Goal of History* (Abingdon, UK: Routledge, 2011), 2.

for the transcendence of narrow, individual concerns in favor of a connection with the larger social world, the broader universe, or even the divine. Cultural forms such as literature, music, visual art, architecture, theater, history, and philosophical reflection were employed in the cultivation of virtue and the establishment of the broader and deeper connections valued for human flourishing.

Today, the humanities tend to be thought of less as a comprehensive program of study or means to cultivate virtue and more as a collection of academic disciplines. These disciplines are located largely within colleges and universities and are thus shaped by the values of these institutions. Much of higher education is driven more by the aim of creating knowledge than the goal of applying wisdom. To succeed in such an environment, scholars are required to become highly specialized professionals, spending most of their time publishing books and articles for other highly specialized professionals in their discipline. The courses they teach often focus more on the flourishing of their discipline than on the flourishing of their students, requiring students to learn *about* course content but not necessarily to learn *from* it. When human flourishing is addressed in the classroom, it is all too often done in a way that makes it difficult for students to apply it to their lives, and in many cases, it focuses more on obstacles to flourishing than on the nature and cultivation of well-being. It is important, of course, to understand and resist alienation, injustice, and malfeasance in the world and to expose corrosive ideologies that can permeate texts and other forms of culture. But it is also important to understand that flourishing is more than just the absence of languishing. And the argument has been made that "suspicious" approaches in the humanities need to be balanced by reparative approaches[10] and that critique needs to be complemented by a "positive aesthetics"[11] and a "hermeneutics of affirmation."[12] Meanwhile, students in the United States, at least, are reporting astonishingly high levels of anxiety, depression, and suicidality,[13] while at the same time coming under increasing economic

[10] Eve K. Sedgwick, "Paranoid Reading and Reparative Reading: Or, You're So Paranoid, You Probably Think This Introduction Is About You," in *Novel Gazing: Queer Readings in Fiction*, ed. Eve K. Sedgwick (Durham, NC: Duke University Press, 1997), 1–37.

[11] Rita Felski, *Uses of Literature* (Malden, MA: Blackwell, 2008), 22.

[12] D. J. Moores, "The Eudaimonic Turn in Literary Studies," in *The Eudaimonic Turn: Well-Being in Literary Studies*, ed. James O. Pawelski and D. J. Moores (Madison, NJ: Fairleigh Dickinson University Press, 2013), 27.

[13] Publications and Reports, National College Health Assessment, American College Health Association, accessed December 11, 2021, https://www.acha.org/NCHA/ACHA-NCHA_Data/Publications_and_Reports/NCHA/Data/Publications_and_Reports.aspx?hkey=d5fb767c-d15d-4efc-8c41-3546d92032c5.

pressure to select courses of study that will directly help them find employment. Students who in the past might have followed their interests in the humanities are now more likely to major in STEM fields or to enroll in pre-professional tracks. Consequently, the number of students earning bachelor's degrees in the humanities is decreasing significantly.[14]

Would a eudaimonic turn in the humanities be helpful in addressing these obstacles of narrow professionalism, imbalanced focus, and student pressure? Would it help with what Louis Menand has called a "crisis of rationale" in the humanities, with scholars unable to agree on the fundamental nature and purpose of the humanities and thus unable to communicate their value clearly to students, parents, philanthropists, policymakers, and the general public?[15] Could the eudaimonic turn provide a unifying rationale in the humanities? Of course, there is a sense in which such a turn would actually be a eudaimonic *return*. This return would not be a nostalgic attempt to recover some imagined glorious past. The human flourishing historically supported by the humanities was significant, as mentioned above, but it was also very far from perfect, often embracing perspectives that supported unjust power structures that excluded many people—including laborers, women, and enslaved persons—from participating in flourishing and that enabled the exploitation of these individuals to the advantage of those in power. Tragically, our society suffers from some of these same injustices today. Instead of a glorification of a problematic past, which could well reinforce these injustices, a eudaimonic re/turn would invite us to focus our attention on perennial questions about human flourishing, building on wisdom from the past, but committing ourselves to a search for more inclusive answers that are fitting for our contemporary world.[16]

Not surprisingly, there is disagreement among scholars in these volumes, with some contributors endorsing the eudaimonic turn in the humanities and working to advance it and others putting forward a variety of concerns about the limitations and potential dangers of such an approach—and some even doing both. Scholars supporting a eudaimonic turn believe it could

---

[14] Jill Barshay, "PROOF POINTS: The Number of College Graduates in the Humanities Drops for the Eighth Consecutive Year," *The Hechinger Report*, November 22, 2021, https://hechingerreport. org/proof-points-the-number-of-college-graduates-in-the-humanities-drops-for-the-eighth-cons ecutive-year.

[15] Louis Menand, "The Marketplace of Ideas," American Council of Learned Societies Occasional Paper No. 49 (2001), http://archives.acls.org/op/49_Marketplace_of_Ideas.htm.

[16] Pawelski, "What Is the Eudaimonic Turn?" 17; Pawelski, "The Positive Humanities," 26; and McMahon, "The History of the Humanities and Human Flourishing," 45, 54.

revitalize the humanities by encouraging deeper investigations into the eudaimonic hopes that initially gave rise to their disciplines and the various ways in which contemporary work can support and develop these hopes. They believe these investigations could bring together scholars across the various humanities disciplines to create a common understanding and language for an examination of questions of human flourishing appropriate for our times. To be successful, such a project would not require complete agreement among scholars on the answers to these questions. On the contrary, diverse perspectives would enrich the inquiry, opening up new possibilities for human flourishing that are more equitable and widespread and that support the flourishing of the nonhuman world as well. Some contributors see significant potential in collaborating with the social sciences in their eudaimonic turn, a process that can be facilitated through the Positive Humanities, a new, interdisciplinary field of inquiry and practice focused on the relationship between culture and human flourishing.[17]

Scholars endorsing a eudaimonic turn in the humanities believe it could also inform, inspire, and support the work of museums, libraries, performing arts centers, and even creative industries (in music, movies, publishing, and other domains) to advance human flourishing more broadly in our society. They see a eudaimonic turn as also being of potential value to the millions of students who study the humanities each year. Without expecting humanities teachers and professors to take on therapeutic roles, they see considerable possible benefits in a pedagogical focus on how human flourishing can be understood and cultivated, with resulting courses intentionally designed to promote and preserve students' well-being and mitigate and prevent their ill-being.[18] Indeed, these scholars believe the volumes in this series might serve as useful texts for some of these courses.

Scholars with misgivings about a eudaimonic turn, on the other hand, raise a number of important concerns. Some contributors wonder whether human flourishing is a proper ideal in a world with so much suffering. Would such an ideal raise false hopes that would actually contribute to that suffering? Furthermore, are there more valuable things than human flourishing

---

[17] For more information on the Positive Humanities, see Louis Tay and James O. Pawelski, eds., *The Oxford Handbook of the Positive Humanities* (New York: Oxford University Press, 2022), especially the first three foundational chapters. Also, visit www.humanitiesandhumanflourishing.org.

[18] Furthermore, would students who perceive real life value in humanities courses be more likely to make room for them in their schedules, as suggested by the students who enrolled in Laurie Santos's course on "Psychology and the Good Life" in such large numbers? If so, could a side benefit of the eudaimonic turn be greater numbers of students signing up for courses in the humanities?

(e.g., ethics, the environment), and should flourishing be limited in favor of these greater goods? Is human flourishing inextricably linked to problematic ideological perspectives, perhaps ones that place too much emphasis on the individual and downplay or ignore issues of systemic injustice, or perhaps ones that serve the interests of a small number of persons in power and encourage everyone else to conform to the status quo? Is human flourishing a false universalism that might result in a failure to see and acknowledge deep cultural differences—or worse, that might see these differences as deviances that need to be suppressed and punished? Could an emphasis on well-being be employed to exploit individuals or groups of people, as notions of happiness have sometimes been used in the past? Are there other unexpected harms that might arise from a eudaimonic turn?

The unresolved tensions among the various chapters are part of what makes these volumes compelling reading. Are there ways to overcome concerns about the eudaimonic turn by clarifying its nature and aims, avoiding the dangers raised? Or will these concerns always persist alongside efforts to achieve individual and communal betterment through a theoretical and practical emphasis on flourishing? I welcome you, the reader, to join this discussion. What are your views on the perspectives expressed in these volumes? What points might you contribute to the ongoing conversation?

Process and People

I would like to conclude with a fuller account of the process by which the various volumes were created and an acknowledgment of the individuals and institutions who have made this book series possible. With the desire to give contributors ample time to reflect on how their work and their discipline relate to human flourishing, as well as to create opportunities to discuss these ideas with colleagues, we put into place an extended process for the creation of these volumes. After deciding on the eight disciplines in the arts and humanities we would be able to include in the project, we invited a leading scholar to chair the work in each of these disciplines and asked them to bring together a diverse group of some dozen noted scholars in their discipline.[19] For each group, we provided participants with some background

---

[19] For a full list of project participants, visit www.humanitiesandhumanflourishing.org.

reading[20] and asked them to prepare a draft essay on how their scholarly work informs the conceptualization and cultivation of human flourishing. Many participants chose to address the background reading—appreciatively, critically, or both—in their papers, although none was required to address it at all. We then circulated these drafts to the entire group in preparation for a three-day, face-to-face meeting, during which the disciplinary chair led a discussion and workshopping of the drafts. These disciplinary consultations, held in 2018 and 2019, were also joined by a junior scholar (usually a graduate student) in the field, one or two social scientists with work on relevant topics, and the Core Team.

Following these meetings, participants were asked to revise their drafts in light of our discussion, with the chairs serving as editors for the resulting disciplinary volumes. Given the nature of the project, I also read each of the contributions, providing comments along the way. From beginning to end, the process for creating and editing each of the volume manuscripts took well over a year and allowed for deep engagement with the subject matter and with other scholars. The disciplinary chairs and I were careful to emphasize that these discussions were intended to be robust and the writing authentic, with no foregone conclusions about the nature of human flourishing or the value of exploring it, and we were pleased by the range and depth of thinking undertaken by each group.

As mentioned above, after we held the eight disciplinary consultations, we held a ninth meeting where we invited the chairs of each of the disciplinary groups to present and discuss drafts of essays for a ninth, interdisciplinary volume sharing what they and their colleagues had learned through the process. We also invited a few humanities policy leaders, including past National Endowment for the Humanities Chairman William Adams, to join us and help think about the broader implications of this work.

---

[20] Martin E. P. Seligman and Mihaly Csikszentmihalyi, "Positive Psychology: An Introduction," *American Psychologist* 55 (1) (2000): 5–14; Darrin M. McMahon, "From the Paleolithic to the Present: Three Revolutions in the Global History of Happiness," in *e-Handbook of Subjective Well-being*, ed. Ed Diener, Shigehiro Oishi, and Louis Tay (Champaign, IL: DEF Publishers, 2018); James O. Pawelski, "Defining the 'Positive' in Positive Psychology: Part I. A Descriptive Analysis," *The Journal of Positive Psychology* 11 (4) (2016): 339–356; James O. Pawelski, "Defining the 'Positive' in Positive Psychology: Part II. A Normative Analysis," *The Journal of Positive Psychology* 11 (4) (2016): 357–365; James O. Pawelski, "Bringing Together the Humanities and the Science of Well-Being to Advance Human Flourishing," in *Well-Being and Higher Education: A Strategy for Change and the Realization of Education's Greater Purposes*, ed. Donald W. Harward (Washington, D.C.: Bringing Theory to Practice, 207–216); and Louis Tay, James O. Pawelski, and Melissa G. Keith, "The Role of the Arts and Humanities in Human Flourishing: A Conceptual Model," *The Journal of Positive Psychology* 13 (3) (2018): 215–225.

The compiling of the volumes was organized and overseen by the Humanities and Human Flourishing (HHF) Project at the University of Pennsylvania. HHF was founded in 2014 to support the interdisciplinary investigation and advancement of the relationship between the humanities and human flourishing. As the founding director of HHF, I am pleased that it has developed into a growing international and multidisciplinary network of more than 150 humanities scholars, scientific researchers, creative practitioners, college and university educators, wellness officers, policy experts, members of government, and leaders of cultural organizations. In addition to the disciplinary consultations described above and the resulting book series, we have published a number of conceptual papers and systematic reviews, developed conceptual models to guide empirical research, and created and validated a toolkit of measures. Designated a National Endowment for the Arts Research Lab, HHF has developed ongoing programs of research (including on art museums and human flourishing and on narrative technologies and well-being) to understand, assess, and advance the effects of engagement in the arts and humanities on human flourishing. We have published *The Oxford Handbook of the Positive Humanities* to help establish the Positive Humanities as a robust field of inquiry and practice at the intersection of culture, science, and human flourishing. For more information on HHF, including each of these endeavors as well as its current undertakings, please visit www.humanitiesandhumanflourishing.org.

I am deeply grateful to all the individuals and institutions whose collaboration has made this book series possible. I would like to begin by thanking Chris Stewart and Templeton Religion Trust for the generous grants that have underwritten this work. Thanks also go to the University of Pennsylvania for their robust institutional and financial support. (Of course, the views expressed in these volumes are those of the authors and do not necessarily reflect the views of Templeton Religion Trust or of the University of Pennsylvania.) I am grateful to the more than 80 contributors to these volumes for accepting our invitation to be a part of this work and bringing more depth and richness to it than I could have imagined. I am especially grateful to the chairs of each of the disciplinary groups for their belief in the importance of this work and their long-term dedication to making it a success. I also wish to express my appreciation for the hard work of the entire HHF Core Team, including Research Director Louis Tay, postdoctoral fellows Yerin Shim and Hoda Vaziri, Research Manager Michaela Ward, and especially Assistant Director Sarah Sidoti, who meticulously planned and oversaw each of the disciplinary consultations and used her expertise in academic publishing to help shape this book series in countless crucial ways. Most of the disciplinary consultations took place on the beautiful grounds of the Shawnee Inn & Golf Resort along the banks of the Delaware River. I am grateful to Charlie and Ginny Kirkwood, John Kirkwood, and all the folks at Shawnee for their gracious support and hospitality. Additionally, I am grateful to Jonathan Coopersmith and the Curtis Institute for donating space for the music group to meet, and to Bill Perthes and the Barnes Foundation for similarly donating space for the visual arts group. Thanks to the Penn Museum for a beautiful setting for the first day of our Chairs consultation and to Marty Seligman and Peter Schulman for donating further space at the Positive Psychology Center. Finally, I am grateful to Peter Ohlin and all the staff and reviewers at Oxford University Press for their partnership in publishing the volumes in this book series. I hope these volumes inspire further conversation, welcoming more people from a larger number of disciplines and a greater range of nationalities and cultural and ethnic backgrounds to inquire into what human flourishing is, how its potential harms can be avoided, and how its benefits can be more deeply experienced and more broadly extended.

James O. Pawelski
February 19, 2022

List of Contributors

Michael Beckerman is Carroll and Milton Petrie Professor of Music, Collegiate Professor, at New York University and Chair of the Department of Music. He is author of seven books and more than a hundred scholarly articles on topics including Czech music, film studies, Mozart, form and meaning, orientalism, and music in the camps. His primary interest is in exploring connections between music and the rest of the world. Beckerman has been a regular contributor to *The New York Times*, has appeared on many episodes of PBS's Backstage at Lincoln Center, and has lectured throughout North America, Europe, Asia, and Australia. As a public musicologist he has given more than 250 pre-concert talks, and has organized more than fifteen conferences and music festivals. Beckerman has been the recipient of many prizes and honors, including two ASCAP Deems Taylor awards; an honorary doctorate from Palacký University in the Czech Republic; the Janáček medal and other awards from the Czech government; a Distinguished Alumni award from Hofstra University, and a Golden Dozen teaching award from NYU. In 2021 he was awarded the Harrison Medal from the Society for Musicology in Ireland and the Gratias Agit prize from the Czech government. He has taught at Columbia University, Washington University, the University of Chicago, the University of California, Santa Barbara, Central European University, and Charles University in Prague. During 2011–2015 he served as Distinguished Professor at Lancaster University in England; from 2016 to 2018 he was the Leonard Bernstein Scholar in Residence of The New York Philharmonic.

Melvin L. Butler is an associate professor of music at the University of Miami and the author of *Island Gospel: Pentecostal Music and Identity in Jamaica and the United States* (2019). An ethnomusicologist with broad interests in musical and religious practices of the African diaspora, he has conducted fieldwork on music in relation to charismatic Christianity in Caribbean and African American communities. In these transnational contexts, he interrogates the cultural politics of musical style and religion while attending to the role of musical performance in constructing collective identities. He has published articles and reviews in several scholarly journals, including *Ethnomusicology, Journal of the American Academy of Religion, Black Music Research Journal*, and *Journal of Popular Music Studies*. Much of his writing centers on the phenomenology of Pentecostal musical worship, how the transcendent becomes immanent through musical performance, and the intersections of faith, ritual, memory, gender, and power. These interests fuel his concern with ethnographic representation and the ways in which scholars negotiate their identities in relation to various fields of supernatural encounter. He earned his PhD in ethnomusicology from New York University and a bachelor's degree in saxophone performance from Berklee College of Music.

Joy H. Calico is Cornelius Vanderbilt Professor of Musicology and Professor of German Studies at Vanderbilt University. Her scholarship focuses on the interdisciplinary study of Cold War cultural politics, Schoenberg, and opera. She is the author of two monographs: *Arnold Schoenberg's* A Survivor from Warsaw *in Postwar Europe* (California, 2014), and *Brecht at the Opera* (California, 2008). Her Schoenberg book received the 2015 Award for an Exceptional Book in Jewish Studies and Music, as well as honorable mention for the 2016 Laura Shannon Prize in Contemporary European Studies. She is currently writing a book about operatic convention since *Salome* with a focus on Saariaho's *L'amour de loin*. Her research has been supported by fellowships and grants from the Gladys Krieble Delmas Foundation, the Sacher Stiftung, the ACLS, the American Academy in Berlin, the Berlin Program for Advanced German and European Studies, the DAAD, the Howard Foundation, and the NEH; she was also Gerstein Visiting Distinguished Professor at the Anne Tannenbaum Centre for Jewish Studies and Faculty of Music at the University of Toronto in winter 2019. Calico was co-founder and coordinator of the Music and Sound Studies Network of the German Studies Association (GSA) and served on the GSA Executive Board during 2013–2016, during which time she also directed Vanderbilt's Max Kade Center for European and German Studies. She has also served as Director-at-Large on the American Musicological Society's Board of Directors, and Editor-in-Chief of the *Journal of the American Musicological Society*.

Anna Harwell Celenza is a professor at Johns Hopkins University, where she holds a joint appointment in The Writing Seminars and the Musicology Department at Peabody Conservatory. She is the author of several scholarly books, including *Jazz Italian Style, from Its Origins in New Orleans to Fascist Italy and Sinatra* (2017), which won the Bridge Book Prize, and *The Cambridge Companion to George Gershwin* (2019). She has published numerous articles on a range of composers, from Franz Liszt and Gustav Mahler to Duke Ellington and Billy Strayhorn. Her current book project is titled *Music That Changed America*, which is under contract with W. W. Norton. In 2016 Celenza co-founded the *Music Policy Forum*, a nonprofit that advises local governments about how to create sustainable music ecosystems and build cross-sector networks between musicians, industry leaders, and policymakers. In addition to her scholarly and advocacy work, Celenza has published eight award-winning children's books. She is also an active curator, and her most recent exhibition catalogue, *Margaret Bonds and Langston Hughes: A Musical Friendship*, was awarded the 2018 Leab Exhibition Award by the American Library Association. Her work has been featured on nationally syndicated radio and TV programs, including the BBC's "Music Matters" and "Proms Broadcasts," and C-Span's "Book-TV."

Jonathan Coopersmith, a native of Princeton, New Jersey, is a highly regarded teacher, conductor, and lecturer on music theory and analysis, music history, and music's relationship to well-being. He has been on the Curtis Institute of Music faculty since 2005 and was appointed Chair of Musical Studies in 2010. He has served as the Associate Conductor for The Philadelphia Singers for twelve years and the Artistic Director of Nashirah for seven years, and has been a frequent guest chorus director of the Philadelphia Orchestra and the Pennsylvania Ballet. He has prepared choral ensembles for performances with Sir Simon Rattle, John Adams, Rafael Frühbeck de Burgos, Wolfgang Sawallisch, Christoph Eschenbach, Charles Dutoit, and Yannick Nézet-Séguin.

Since 2015, Mr. Coopersmith has been the festival host and a guest conductor at the world-renowned Music From Angel Fire summer music festival. In addition, he is a sought-after lecturer in the Philadelphia area, with recent lectures at the Philadelphia Chamber Music Society and the Philadelphia Museum of Art, and has been a regular guest lecturer in the Masters of Applied Positive Psychology program at the University of Pennsylvania, speaking about music and well-being.

Mr. Coopersmith holds a bachelor's degree in music theory and composition from the University of Pennsylvania, where he studied with George Crumb, and a master's degree in orchestral conducting from Mannes College of Music, where he studied Schenkerian analysis with Carl Schachter and Edward Aldwell. He has also studied at the Pierre Monteux School for conductors and orchestra musicians.

Todd Decker is the Paul Tietjens Professor of Music at Washington University in St. Louis. He has authored five books on American popular music and media: *Astaire by Numbers: Time & the Straight White Male Dancer* (Oxford, 2022); *Hymns for the Fallen: Combat Movie Music and Sound after Vietnam* (California, 2017, *Choice* Outstanding Academic Title); *Who Should Sing Ol' Man River?: The Lives of an American Song* (Oxford, 2015); *Show Boat: Performing Race in an American Musical* (Oxford, 2013, Honorable Mention, Woody Guthrie Award for Outstanding Book on Popular Music, International Association for the Study of Popular Music–US); and *Music Makes Me: Fred Astaire and Jazz* (California, 2011, Best First Book Award, Society for Cinema and Media Studies). Decker's journal articles and chapters in numerous essay collections consider a broad array of topics, including the 1930s operettas of Jeanette MacDonald and Nelson Eddy, Martin Scorsese's *Casino*, the twenty-first-century action franchise *The Fast and the Furious*, the post-9/11 envoicing of military men and families in country music, Christmas music in the pop marketplace, and the keyboard sonatas of Domenico Scarlatti. Decker has lectured on the stage and screen musical at the Library of Congress and London's Victoria and Albert Museum. In fall 2016, he was a visiting International Chair at Labex Arts-H2H, a humanities center at Université Paris 8. From 2020 to 2022, he served as editor of the journal *American Music*.

Annegret Fauser is the Cary C. Boshamer Distinguished Professor of Music and Adjunct Professor of Women's and Gender Studies at the University of North Carolina at Chapel Hill. She is a cultural musicologist whose work emphasizes how music intersects with its social, political, and artistic contexts. Her research focuses on music of the nineteenth and twentieth centuries, and in particularly that of France and the United States. She has published on French song and opera, women composers, exoticism, nationalism, reception history, and cultural transfer. She is author of *Der Orchestergesang in Frankreich zwischen 1870 und 1920* (1994), *Musical Encounters at the 1889 Paris World's Fair* (2005), *Sounds of War: Music in the United States during World War II* (2013)—for which she received both the Music in American Culture Award of the AMS and an ASCAP Deems Taylor Award— *The Politics of Musical Identity: Selected Writings* (2015), and *Aaron Copland's Appalachian Spring* (2017). The author of numerous articles and (co-)editor of five essay volumes, Fauser received the 2011 Edward J. Dent Medal of the Royal Musical Association. From 2011 to 2013, she was the Editor-in-Chief of the *Journal of the American Musicological Society*.

Wendy Heller, Scheide Professor of Music History specializes in the study of seventeenth- and eighteenth-century opera from interdisciplinary perspectives, with emphasis on gender and sexuality, art history, and the classical tradition. The winner of numerous grants and fellowships, her extensive publications include the award-winning *Emblems of Eloquence: Opera and Women's Voices in Seventeenth-Century Venice* (2004) and *Music in the Baroque* (2013). She is currently completing a book entitled *Animating Ovid: Opera and the Metamorphoses of Antiquity in Early Modern Italy*, as well as critical editions of Handel's *Admeto* and Francesco Cavalli's *Veremonda L'Amazzone d'Aragona*. She has been Chair of the Department of Music at Princeton since 2015.

Alejandro L. Madrid is a cultural theorist whose recent work explores questions of sound and masculinity, race and representation in Afro-Latinx communities, as well as historiography, narrative, archives, and alternative ways of knowledge production and circulation. Madrid is the author of more than half a dozen books, for which he has received numerous awards, including the Mexico Humanities Book Award from the Latin American Studies Association (2016); the Béla Bartók Award from the ASCAP Foundation (2014); the Robert M. Stevenson (2016 and 2014) and Ruth A. Solie (2012) awards from the American Musicological Society; the Woody Guthrie Award from the International Association for the Study of Popular Music (2009); and the Casa de las Américas Musicology Award (2005), among others. He is the recipient of the 2017 Dent Medal given by the Royal Musical Association for "outstanding contributions to musicology," being the only Ibero-Americanist who has received this prestigious honor since its inception in 1961. Madrid is editor of Oxford University Press's *Currents in Latin American and Iberian Music*, and co-editor of the journal *Twentieth-Century Music*. He is Professor of Musicology and Ethnomusicology at Harvard University; and he is frequently invited as an expert commentator by national and international media outlets, including *The Washington Post*, Agence France-Presse, Public Radio International, and Radio Uruguay. Recently, he acted as music advisor to acclaimed filmmaker Peter Greenaway, whose recent film, *Eisenstein in Guanajuato*, is set in early 1930s Mexico.

Nancy Yunhwa Rao is Professor of Music, Rutgers University. She is also affiliate faculty at Department of Asian Languages and Cultures and Department of Women's and Gender Studies. A specialist in American music, her work is multifaceted, bridging musicology, music theory, and scholarship on Chinese opera with gender and ethnic studies. Her research includes three areas: (1) American ultramodernism: the music of Ruth Crawford, Henry Cowell, and Elliott Carter, sketch studies, American composition theory of 1920–1950, and women composers; (2) exploration of global perspectives in contemporary Chinese music: historical context, cultural references, music gestures, vocal style, materiality, and percussion patterns of Beijing opera in contemporary music by composers of Chinese origin; (3) musical history of Chinese in North America: this has led to writings on analysis of opera arias, playbills, transnationalism, and gendered performance. Her research has led to writings on various transnational issues and the transpacific turn in the historiography of American music. Publications can be found in *Cambridge Opera Journal, Journal of the Society for American Music, Journal of 19th Century Music Review, Music Theory Spectrum*, and *Perspectives of New Music*, as well as collections of essays. Her article "Ruth Crawford's Imprint on Contemporary Composition" received the 2009 Lowens Award from the Society for American Music. Her book *Chinatown Opera Theater in North America* received the 2018 Music in American Culture Award from the American Musicological Society, as well as book awards from the Society of American Music and the Association for Asian American Studies.

Shana L. Redmond (she/her) is the author of *Everything Man: The Form and Function of Paul Robeson* (Duke University Press, 2020), which received prizes including the Walter and Lilian Lowenfels Award for Criticism from the Before Columbus Foundation and the Judy Tsou Critical Race Studies Award from the American Musicological Society, and *Anthem: Social Movements and the Sound of Solidarity in the African Diaspora* (New York University Press, 2014). Other scholarly and popular publications appear in periodicals such as *Race & Class, The Futures of Black Radicalism*, web and radio for NPR and the BBC, as well as the liner essay for the vinyl soundtrack of Jordan Peele's film *Us* (Waxwork Records, 2019). She is co-editor of "Phono: Black Music and the Global Imagination" book series with the University of California Press and Professor of English and Comparative Literature and the Center for the Study of Ethnicity & Race at Columbia University.

Introduction

Music and Human Flourishing

Anna Harwell Celenza

Notions of what constitutes human flourishing are numerous, and specific perceptions of the concept differ from one academic field to another. Various measures of subjective well-being have been proposed in the positive psychology literature. Some of the most widely used measures concern happiness conceived either as a brief, positive affective state, sometimes referred to as "hedonic happiness," or alternatively as overall life satisfaction, sometimes referred to as "evaluative happiness," both of which, over time and in combination, can contribute to eudaimonia or human flourishing (National Research Council). Regardless of the various approaches, it seems that most scholars who have engaged in the topic of human flourishing have described it as the attainment of a sense of wellness or contentment in one or more of the following five domains: mental and physical health; happiness and life satisfaction; meaning and purpose; character and virtue; and deep social relationships (VanderWeele).

In discussions of music's ability to facilitate human flourishing, the above-mentioned domains have each been covered in one way or another. It has long been accepted that participating in music, either as a performer, listener, and/or composer is good for the mind, body, and even society in general. More recently, work has been done on the behavioral, physiological, and psychological effects of engaging in music (Croom 2011). Neuroscience has shown the complex and demanding cognitive challenge that performing music presents (Zatorre et al.), and playing a musical instrument has been shown to be beneficial to all age groups (for example, MacRitchie et al.; Schneider et al.; Martins et al.). Music educators have explored the value of music studies among children and young adults (Sala and Gobert; Smith and Silverman; Cariotti et al.; Alsup; Schellenberg). Music has also been shown to be an active agent in the promotion of positive emotions, social engagement,

Anna Harwell Celenza, *Introduction* In: *Music and Human Flourishing*. Edited by: Anna Harwell Celenza,
Oxford University Press. © Oxford University Press 2023. DOI: 10.1093/oso/9780197646748.003.0001

the building of meaningful relationships, and the creation of a sense of accomplishment (Croom 2014). In all these areas, music has been defined *as a performing art*, and its role in contributing to human flourishing has been discussed within the confines of three categories of participants: listeners, performers, and composers. But as this volume demonstrates, describing the contribution of music *as a humanities discipline* to human flourishing requires a deepened sense of what human flourishing might entail. It also requires that we add a fourth category of music activity outside of listening, performing, and composing—namely, the act of *music scholarship*. For as important as listening, performing, and composing are to the human condition, their effectiveness in facilitating *human flourishing at its deepest level* is highly dependent on music scholars—those who engage with music as a humanistic discipline.

What exactly do we mean when we refer to "human flourishing at its deepest level"? In short, we mean the ability to attain wisdom and a sense of justice through the combined processes of contemplation, critique, and communication. To be clear, when we say "wisdom," we are not talking about the facts and data acquired through study, research, investigation, observation, or experience. That's knowledge. By wisdom we mean the ability to discern and judge which aspects of one's knowledge are true, right, lasting, and applicable to life. Wisdom involves the ability to apply one's knowledge to the greater scheme of things. Consequently, understanding the *value of music as a humanities discipline to human flourishing* requires a discussion of more than the ability of music as a performing art to affect one's mental state and/or life satisfaction. In the humanities, we must also consider music in the context of the cultural, social, and political practices within which it functions. Understanding these contexts can lead to a sense of wellness or contentment in the domains of wisdom and justice. And as this volume reveals, it is the role of music scholars, specifically, to engage with these ideas in a way that just listening, performing, and even composing cannot.

An overview of previous scholarship on music and human flourishing reveals that there has been little consideration of the contributions made by the fields of musicology, ethnomusicology, and music theory. Although there is a great deal of research on how performing and/or consuming music contributes to human flourishing, little to no discussion has occurred with regard to how contemplating music within the realms of cultural identity, social rituals, and political ideology can impact human flourishing. In creating this volume, the contributors were asked to apply their knowledge of a specific aspect of music scholarship to the greater scheme of things. In short, they were asked to mine their knowledge for a deeper sense of wisdom with regard to the humanities and human flourishing. The results were revelatory.

We can say from personal experience that contemplating music as a humanities discipline has brought us, and countless other music scholars, great fulfillment. Thinking deeply about music has helped us discern and judge which aspects of the knowledge we have previously gained as scholars are true, right, lasting, and applicable to life. It has also, at times, instilled the need to reassess assumptions from the past. This is especially true when it comes to discussions of the music canon. Whereas performers and composers often work within the established canon of their genre and generation, music scholars often thrive on challenging the canon. And these challenges, when they are most effective, engage with questions concerning identity, influence, appropriation, power, religious belief, social norms, cultural symbols, ritual, etc. Collectively, we can state as a group that our music scholarship has instilled in us a deeper sense of self-awareness, and as we hope to show in the chapters that follow, one of the values of music as a humanities discipline lies in its ability to engage with the real and imaginative realms that music performance can create. By keeping the goal of human flourishing in mind, music scholars can instill a level of wisdom that facilitates personal fulfillment and human flourishing, not only in themselves, but in their students and colleagues.

Music and Human Flourishing contains chapters by eleven contributors. Ten represent the fields of musicology, ethnomusicology, and music theory. The eleventh contributor is a conductor/composer from one of the nation's finest conservatories, who has dedicated much of his career to engaging audiences and expanding their awareness of Western classical music. In preparation for this volume, each contributor was asked to apply the topic of human flourishing to their own career in the field of music, and, without prompting, each demonstrated how the process of thinking and writing about music and human flourishing can lead to revelations about cultural identity, social rituals, political ideologies, and even spiritual transcendence. As one might imagine, the chapters contained in this volume cover a broad range of topics and music traditions. Most revelatory was the realization that within the realm of music, there is often an underlying divide between performers, composers, and conductors who feel charged with building and maintaining the canon and scholars who are committed to challenging it. This underlying divide in music practice can be detrimental to human flourishing. As a group, the contributors to *Music and Human Flourishing* came to the realization that, in general, there needs to be greater communication between creatives and scholars. Humanities programs need to embrace music performance as more than just entertainment, and conservatories should focus more consciously on the underlying messages, both positive and negative, imbedded in works preserved as part of the music canon. In short, music scholars are their most effective when they encourage listeners (including performers and composers) to engage deeply in the multifaceted meaning of music, to interrogate the rituals associated with performance, and to recognize that the benefits of music extend far beyond sensual pleasure. When done well, the work of music scholars facilitates a form of intellectual engagement that eventually leads to human flourishing, as embodied in the concepts of wisdom and justice.

The chapters in this volume are divided into three general categories: *Contemplation*, *Critique*, and *Communication*. These were terms that we felt reflect, in the broadest sense, the three stages that make up much of our activities as scholars. In Part I, *Contemplation*, contributors explore a specific facet of music's connection to human flourishing and contemplate new approaches for future action. Jonathan Coopersmith begins in Chapter 1, "Musical Flourishes: Lessons from a Conservatory," by describing the intellectual foundation upon which the concept of flourishing in music was built. He begins by describing music as one of our most basic and innate forms of expression and then goes on to explain the various parameters of music (e.g., consonance and dissonance, melody, musical rhythm, and later, harmony and instrumentation). As Coopersmith explains, music's unique properties contribute to its facility in promoting and supporting human flourishing. And as an accompaniment to other art forms (e.g., poetry, dance, film, and theater), music often enhances and amplifies the well-being effect of non-musical disciplines. But music does not *inherently* promote or obstruct well-being; rather, music has the power to cause positive and/or negative results for both listeners and performers.

Using Western classical music as his main point of reference, Coopersmith explores the ways in which music both supports and obstructs flourishing in the conservatory environment, especially when one achieves a high level of engagement, performance ability, or analytical knowledge. He concludes by offering effective strategies for the future, which correspond to Martin Seligman's PERMA (Positive emotions, Engagement, Relationships, Meaning, Achievement) model of well-being (Seligman).

Whereas Coopersmith focuses on the conservatory experience, Shana Redmond contemplates performance within the cultural realm of African American experiences in Chapter 2, "Jubilee: The (Positive) Science of Black Music." In an effort to understand the "positive" elements of human life, the question of "how?" looms large. How do people make themselves and each other happy? In distinction to Coopersmith's question of "why" music leads to human flourishing, Redmond's focus on "how" suggests that critical attention needs to be paid not simply to the context and conditions under which we live, but also to the imaginaries that make its improvement possible. In her chapter, Redmond explores the musical methods and techniques that make imagination real—the sometimes quotidian (yet unexpected) and sometimes spectacular musical utterances, performances, and habits grown from Black people's investment in the joys and possibilities of play(ing). As Redmond explains, "play" is not simply that which is performed unthinkingly, but also that which is studied, rehearsed, and intentional. Improvisation is but one element of this study, and in music performance, both live and recorded, it often reveals itself as a surprise for audiences and listeners. The concept of "Jubilee" lingers in these ephemeral moments, which open the opportunities for performers and witnesses to *be well* and make possible a realization of what was once imagined to be impossible.

While Coopersmith and Redmond focus on consonant, diatonic works that audiences regularly describe as pleasing to the ear, Joy Calico, in Chapter 3, "Post-Tonal Music and Well-Being," explores the importance of dissonant music to the process of human flourishing. Calico begins by discussing scientific investigations concerning the effect of music on the brain. In the past, experiments in the realm of neuroscience and music psychology have focused almost exclusively on consonant, diatonic music. Neuroscience that treats dissonance has tended to focus on cognition of isolated dissonant sounds rather than non-tonal music, and music psychology that focuses on non-tonal music has retained an orientation rooted in structural listening. Neither engages, as Calico does, in the question of well-being.

Building on the positive psychology model that Louis Tay, James O. Pawelski, and Melissa G. Keith have proposed for the humanities and human flourishing, and expanding their model to accommodate a mindset of openness as a prerequisite, Calico posits three modes of engaging with non-tonal music that could contribute to human flourishing: consumption, study, and critique (Tay, Pawelski, and Keith). As Calico explains, focusing on listening as a mode of consumption is the most fraught of the three modes, and it aligns most closely with existing research on music. The modes of study and critique engage directly with music as a humanities discipline, and in so doing, expand our perceptions of flourishing through music and introduce the importance of "stretch" to establishing long-term well-being. Calico's chapter also engages with Rita Felski's positive aesthetics, which was developed for literature but, as Calico reveals, is equally applicable to music (Felski). Overall, Calico engages in two central questions that expand perceptions of how neuroscience and psychology might be effectively used in the study of human flourishing: (1) Are there ways to test and think about sensory responses to non-tonal music that do not focus on hearing? (2) How can the synthesis of musicology and positive psychology help us move beyond questions of perception and cognition to human flourishing?

Michael Beckerman's Chapter 4, "Can 'Old-Fashioned' Approaches to Listening Contribute to Human Flourishing?," concludes Part I of the volume by investigating contemporary listening practices and thinking about their effectiveness with regard to mental health. Beckerman reassesses the importance of "deep listening," not with regard to discussions of pedagogical practices (where the term is often used), but rather around the topic of various mental disorders. As he explains, a simple "at-home" experiment reveals that most people cannot simultaneously follow the details of a musical composition and read at the same time. This reality makes it clear that certain parts of the mind are "shut off" when others are invoked. On the basis of this fact, Beckerman proposes that a certain kind of directed musical listening, which was an integral part of musicology pedagogy several decades ago, could be used more regularly today as a therapy to interrupt the patterns of obsessive thought at the core of many mental disorders that have been growing in prevalence recently among undergraduate and graduate students.

Part II, *Critique*, contains chapters that challenge past assumptions of the various roles of music in society, and in doing so, highlight the effects that unconscious bias and stereotyping have had on music's effectiveness to facilitate human flourishing. In Chapter 5, "Understanding Music Studies, Well-Being, and the Humanities in Times of Neoliberalism," Alejandro L. Madrid asserts that a transdisciplinary approach to the study of music that enables scholars to transcend the narrow sets of questions that musicology and music theory have traditionally privileged is essential in defining music studies as relevant to the topic of the humanities and human flourishing. Madrid is especially interested in addressing preconceptions of aesthetic value and intrinsic worthiness that are currently associated with the traditional canon of

Western classical music. Madrid focuses specifically on the performativity of musicking—on what happens when music happens—and the current need to transcend the boundaries in music scholarship and to establish more productive dialogues with other academic disciplines. Such a move emphasizes the importance of the affective and emotional experiences that give meaning to musicking and addresses questions of well-being central to the search for the significance of music as a human experience.

Madrid's transdisciplinary approach resonates with James Pawelski's call for an alliance between the humanities and positive psychology in an effort to make "humanities scholarship more informed and more relevant to contemporary debates" (Pawelski). Nevertheless, Madrid argues that Pawelski's definition of well-being in relation to "a society based on individual freedom and self-realization" and his suggestion that engaging quantitative evaluative methods and efficiency models to validate the effects of the humanities are plagued with neoliberal overtones that often overlook the identities of those outside the traditional "conservatory" eco-system. In response, Madrid offers an assessment of neoliberalism's take on human flourishing and proposes alternative well-being strategies that privilege collective realization as a way to avoid the demands of an economic, political, and philosophical model that thrives on human precarity and conflict.

In Chapter 6, "The Music Scholar as a Type of Non-Musician," Todd Decker directly addresses an identity predicament specific to music scholars: the loss of one's identity as a musician in the shift from the applied pursuit of music (making and performing musical sound) to the academic study of music as a humanities discipline (researching, writing, and speaking about musical sound). This loss can be located within an individual's life cycle. The musician identity of most music scholars is forged in childhood and youth in the pursuit of music as a nonverbal practice of bodily discipline, public accomplishment, and personal expression. This frequently foundational identity as a musician is set aside when career-defining choices concerning postgraduate education and professionalization are made in favor of the identity of music scholar and its different approach to human flourishing. And while this transition to a specific type of non-musician is felt most keenly by music scholars who are new to the academy, the tensions created by this loss might easily endure across an academic career spent thinking, writing, and speaking about, rather than making, music. Indeed, the music scholar's identity as a type of non-musician persists as a condition of the academic discipline of music studies. In this chapter, Decker seeks to describe the contours of this condition but does not attempt to offer solutions. Instead, he argues that the identities of musician and humanities scholar are incompatible. Once theorized, this incompatibility leads to both a questioning of the ultimate utility of music scholarship and a remediation of the music scholar's non-musician status in the possibility of escape from the fundamental ephemerality of musical sound and the musician's labor.

In Chapter 7, "They Say 'Music Should Be Seen but Not Heard': Performance and Flourishing in the Liberal Arts University," Wendy Heller continues the discussion of "musicians" versus "music scholars" by investigating the inequalities that often develop within the liberal arts university between faculty whose focus is on performance, and those in the fields of musicology/ethnomusicology and music theory/composition. "The English Department doesn't teach typing, why should the Music Department teach piano?" As Heller demonstrates, comments such as this reveal an attitude that once dominated elite liberal arts schools. While in decades past, musicology, ethnomusicology, theory, and (at some institutions) composition were regularly deemed fields sufficiently rigorous to earn advanced degrees (e.g., MA, PhD), performance was often relegated to the realm of extracurricular activities. Although this attitude has begun to change, there is still work to be done.

Using Princeton as a case study, Heller explores the ways in which the study of performance can benefit students in the elite liberal arts school. Studies show that by participating in the arts, students develop cognitive abilities and forms of intelligence that complement training in other disciplines, and in some cases, they discover talents and interests that shape their careers. In these ways, music performance leads to an increase in human flourishing among students, and faculty, at liberal arts universities. As Heller readily admits, however, the long-term consequences of studying music intensely in a liberal arts environment, rather than a music school/conservatory, still require further study. Although student reflections reveal a variety of viewpoints, more communication needs to take place among performers, music scholars, and members of other academic disciplines if continued change is to occur with regard to dispelling inequalities and preconceived notions about the value of music performance to the liberal arts education.

Part III of *Music and Human Flourishing* interacts broadly with the concept of *Communication* and features chapters that explore various ways in which ethnicity, gender, religion, and technology influence our ability to connect with others through music, be it as performers, scholars, or audience members.

In Chapter 8, "Interdisciplinary and Intercultural Artistic Collaboration," Nancy Yunhwa Rao reveals how collaboration among artistic groups with differing background experiences (be they visual artists, musicians, composers, dancers, dramaturges, or actors) increases the opportunities for human flourishing. At their best, such collaborations spark new levels of creativity among contributors, leading to an exalted mood and a feeling of betterment and fulfillment. As a means of demonstrating this phenomenon, Rao examines two types of collaborations—interdisciplinary and intercultural—in performing and visual arts, with a focus on the similarity between these two types of collaborations and the modes of human flourishing that they engender. For each type of collaboration, a case study is used as the point of departure for conceptual and theoretical exploration.

The first case study involves the creation of a course on interdisciplinary collaboration at the Mason Gross School of the Arts at Rutgers University. This course drew on faculty and students from five departments (music, dance, theater, visual arts, and filmmaking) and sought to inspire a sense of equality and shared experience among the participants by developing a communication practice that was not specifically associated with a single field. The second case study explores the idea of cultural merger through an analysis of an inter-Asia composition for Korean traditional ensemble by the Chinese American composer, Chou Wen-chung. Both cases provide a window on how collaboration in the arts, which requires deep engagement and learning about other arts, leads to new practices of communication and in so doing provides an extraordinary sense of fulfillment, excitement, and impetus among participants, that would otherwise be unattainable.

Annegret Fauser's Chapter 9, "Rethinking Women's Music-Making through the Lens of Human Flourishing," involves new approaches to thinking about and teaching topics related to feminist musicology. In Michelle Obama's memoir, *Becoming*, a significant section of her childhood recollections is dedicated to her piano lessons as a space where she could assert her individuality. Music-making—as feminist musicological inquiry has shown over the past decades—has been a uniquely empowering activity for women and girls in Western culture, even when it took place in an environment where other restrictions curtailed their flourishing along gendered, class, and racial boundaries. Yet, although musicological research has revealed the positive aspects of women's musicking, scholarly discourse and analyses often emphasize the restrictions that made individual women's achievements all the more exceptional. As Fauser proposes, rethinking women's music-making through the lens of human flourishing might provide a different narrative that emphasizes the empowering, creative, joyful, and affirmative quality of female musical achievement, without neglecting or denying the systemic oppression of gender inequality. Consequently, this chapter offers a different narrative framework through case studies that take into account not only professional musicians such as Wanda Landowska, but also women who flourished musically in their private or semi-private worlds of the salon. The focus is a historical and scholarly reflection, with examples drawn from French and American music of the mid-nineteenth to mid-twentieth centuries. Fauser also relates this discussion to her two decades of experience teaching introductory courses on female-identified musicians in the context of the general-education curriculum of a public university in the American South.

In Chapter 10, "Playful Transcendence: Paths to Human Flourishing in Black Music Research and Performance," Melvin L. Butler draws on the communication barriers occasionally created between the secular and sacred realms. Although notions of play and transcendence have long been used to explore music's capacity to shape and structure human experiences, few scholars explore how play and transcendence interrelate or facilitate human flourishing within and beyond ritual contexts. The concept of play is typically relegated to the realm of childlike "make-believe" activities, while transcendence, especially spiritual transcendence, is too often cast as a "serious" endeavor devoid of laughter and other "fun" aspects of social behavior. By exploring "play" and "transcendence" as complementary modalities, Butler uncovers how music—as sound, behavior, and concept—brings the connections between these two multivalent concepts into focus. He aims to interrogate how Black music-making, in particular, transcends ritual frames and accrues various meanings for audiences and "players"—especially in the face of social marginalization. Drawing on his fieldwork within African diasporic religious communities, and his professional work as a performer in sacred and secular contexts, Butler reflects on the following questions: How might ethnomusicological research on Black music-making stimulate fresh thinking about what it means to flourish in ritual contexts? What can music tell us about the human capacity to experience transcendence through play, and vice versa? Under what conditions does transcendence, religious and otherwise, become a playful phenomenon? To what extent might scholarly work in this area constitute a form of playful transcendence? This chapter touches on multiple forms of literal and symbolic expression while navigating the contested epistemological boundaries between work and play, scholarship and performance, and ritual and everyday life.

Music and Human Flourishing concludes with Anna Harwell Celenza's Chapter 11, "Music for the Masses: Finding a Balance between Emotional Labor and Human Flourishing." This chapter explores the connections between professional music performance and human flourishing, specifically the ways in which changes in technology have influenced, for good and for bad, the complex nature of performers' relationships with their audiences.

Celenza begins in the nineteenth century, when virtuoso performers connected with thousands of fans directly via extended, transcontinental concert tours. The discussion then moves to the rise of recording technology in the twentieth century and its impact on the performer/fan relationship. Finally, the appearance of social media and streaming services is considered. As Celenza demonstrates, with each technological advance, the role of the performer has changed, especially with regard to his/her/their participation in emotional labor.

"Emotional labor," a term coined by sociologist Arlie Hochschild, refers to the management of one's feelings and expressions based on the emotional requirements of a job (Hochschild). Hochschild did not list music performance among the service professions defined by emotional labor, but the requirements for such service-industry jobs, as she defined them, are applicable to professional musicians. They include: regular and direct contact with the consumer/public; producing an emotional state in the consumer/public; and adapting one's emotional activities in response to feedback from one's employer. The central question this chapter proposes to answer is: What happens to human flourishing when the performer/fan relationship is commodified?

Like any book with multiple contributors with various points of view, *Music and Human Flourishing* reveals a diversity of opinions that serve to elucidate the complexity of the topic. Yet, as the reader moves from one chapter to the next, a thread of commonality, linking one chapter to the next, slowly becomes visible. Running through the chapters in this book is a commitment to creativity. Creativity is the key to human flourishing in music. This has been demonstrated time and again in countless studies. But what is creativity in the realm of music as a discipline in the humanities, among music scholars? When the contributors to the *Music and Human Flourishing* volume were asked to ponder this question, two key concepts, each linked to a specific mental process emerged: *stretch* and *play*. Stretch is often difficult. It rarely leads to quick gratification or hedonic pleasure. Stretch is pushing beyond one's intellectual comfort level, challenging accepted norms, questioning what might seem obvious or universally accepted. Stretch eventually leads to a deeper respect and understanding of a topic. And as we have noted, this attainment of deeper respect and understanding, i.e., wisdom, with regard to a musical practice is a key component to human flourishing in music.

But human flourishing involves more than struggle and challenge. Equally important is the concept of play (not as to perform, but in the sense of joyful experimentation). Play often involves hedonic pleasure. As children, we play for the pure joy of discovering something new, delighting in the senses, and engaging the imagination. Play can often strengthen one's self-awareness, which in turn can eventually instill the confidence and desire to stretch.

Creativity also plays a role in distinguishing the difference between *hearing* and *listening*. Hearing music may offer hedonic pleasure: for example, when you hear a composition and automatically begin to move to the beat without even realizing it. But pleasure such as this passes once the music stops. Listening is different, especially listening closely, without distraction, which leads to creative thought or contemplation. One topic that arises again and again in this volume concerns the various rituals associated with listening. Over the last century, the cultural contexts defining listening have changed dramatically, largely as the result of evolving technology. Before the introduction of recording technology at the turn of the twentieth century, each music performance was a once-in-a-lifetime, unrepeatable event, and listening to it required either human interaction (between the performer and listener) or creative engagement with the music (as the performer or composer). But with the advent of recording technology, a non-musician could listen to the same performance over and over again in complete isolation.

The circumstances of these differing listening rituals have led to different expectations and listening habits. For example, in the nineteenth century, concert halls were not darkened during a concert, as they are today. Consequently, audience members came and went at their leisure during performances. They ate food and even played cards. They clapped and cheered when a musical phrase pleased them, and hissed when it did not. Today, audiences attending performances of Western classical music are expected to follow a markedly different set of rituals. They are encouraged to remain in their seats and listen attentively. An unexpected cough or the crinkling of a candy wrapper can attract sharp looks of condescension.

And heaven help the audience member who claps between movements or forgets to silence his cell phone. These new rituals have created a hierarchy between the performer(s) (on stage and in the spotlight) and the audience (silently observing from the darkened hall). They have also made the musical composition (and through association its composer) the focal point of the experience.

The rituals that enforce this concept have contributed to the applications of adjectives such as "elitist" and "highbrow" to classical music. Each genre has its own listening rituals, and with each ritual emerges different appellations: cool, avant-garde, lowbrow, urban, etc.

Of course, attaching such appellations to a musical genre is stereotyping. And such stereotyping occurs, for better or worse, with all genres of music. Take jazz, for example. Although performed in a variety of venues, including Lincoln Center and Carnegie Hall, the music is nonetheless perceived as less formal and more spontaneous than classical music. This stereotyping is largely tied to the rituals of performance in jazz and the impact such rituals have on the interactions between the performer(s) and audience. In jazz, the focus is not so much on the works themselves, but rather on the way they are performed. There is an intimacy to jazz that is tied to its reliance on improvisation. When attending a jazz performance, it is standard practice to listen attentively, but also to respond physically to the music as it is being performed—to applaud, or call out, when an improvised solo is especially good. The rituals of jazz encourage a dialogue of sorts, a call and response, not only among the musicians performing, but also between the musicians and listeners. Such interactions often create a deep sense of community and inclusion among listeners. Each genre has its own set of rituals, be it singing in unison during a church service or crowd surfing at a rock concert. For audience members, knowing the performance rituals of live music can create a sense of inclusion (if one is in the know) or exclusion (if one is experiencing the rituals for the first time). All of which is to say: listening to music as part of an audience can encourage or discourage human flourishing. It all depends on one's familiarity with the expected norms of behavior. Consequently, one of the key roles of music scholars is to engage creatively in discussions that both challenge and illuminate the practice and meaning of various music rituals—to encourage audiences to think deeply about the music ecosystems of the past and present and engage in creating rituals for the future that facilitate human flourishing. As the chapters in this volume demonstrate, creativity is a vital aspect of music scholarship, and the key to human flourishing in the humanities is a continued mix of stretch and play, the two-sided coin of achieving wisdom through music.

Finally, it should be noted that this volume contends that music is not simply the physical vibrations perceived by the ear. Those are sounds. True music is a complex of thoughts and ideas, conceived in the mind and experienced through the imagination. Music scholars, like the contributors to this volume, take listeners down a path of deeper thinking, which in turn can instill wisdom. By thinking *about* and *through* music, we gain a deeper understanding of issues like cultural identity, social rituals, political ideology, and our own place in the world. Music can instill a sense of empathy in listeners when presented as more than mere entertainment. It can serve as a tool for social justice and as a bridge between different cultures. It can help us understand and communicate the emotional and psychological characteristics that make us who we are. In short, the value of music as a humanities discipline is its ability to open our minds to new realms of understanding, which in turn can facilitate human flourishing. Most importantly, this volume contends that music is not a privilege, but rather a way of living, and in every society, it is critical to the healing, growing, and recovery processes of daily life.

Works Cited

Allsup, R. 2012. "Music Education and Human Flourishing: A Meditation on Democratic Origins." *British Journal of Music Education*, vol. 29, no. 2, 2012, pp. 171–179.

Carioti, Desiré, L. Danelli, M. Guasti, M. Gallucci, M. Perugini, P. Steca, N. Stucchi, Angelo Maffezzoli, M. Majno, M. Berlingeri, and E. Paulesu. "Music Education at School: Too Little and Too Late? Evidence From a Longitudinal Study on Music Training in Preadolescents." *Frontiers in Psychology*, vol. 10, December 18, 2019, pp. 1–14. https://doi.org/10.3389/fpsyg.2019.02704.

Croom, Adam M. "Music, Neuroscience, and the Psychology of Well-Being: A Précis." *Frontiers in Psychology*, vol. 2, 2011, pp. 1–15. https://doi.org/10.3389/fpsyg.2011.00393.

Croom, Adam M. "Music Practice and Participation for Psychological Well-Being: A Review of How Music Influences Positive Emotion, Engagement, Relationships, Meaning, and Accomplishment." *Musicae Scientiae*, vol. 19, 2014, pp. 44–64. https://doi.org/10.1177/1029864914561709.

Felski, Rita. *Uses of Literature*. Malden, MA: Blackwell, 2008.

Hochschild, Arlie R. *The Managed Heart: Commercialization of Human Feeling*. Berkeley: University of California Press, 1983.

MacRitchie, J., J. Breaden, A. J. Milne, and S. McIntyre, S. "Cognitive, Motor and Social Factors of Music Instrument Training Programs for Older Adults', Improved Wellbeing." *Frontiers in Psychology*, vol. 10. January 10, 2020, pp. 1–15. https://doi.org/10.3389/fpsyg.2019.02868.

Martins, Marta, Leonor Neves, Paula Rodrigues, Olga Vasconcelos, and São Luís Castro. "Orff-based Music Training Enhances Children's Manual Dexterity and Bimanual Coordination." *Frontiers in Psychology*, vol. 9, December 21, 2018, pp. 1–12. https://doi:10.3389/fpsyg.2018.02616.

National Research Council. *Subjective Well-Being*. Washington, DC: National Academies Press, 2013.

Pawelski, James O. "Bringing Together the Humanities and the Science of Well-Being to Advance Human Flourishing." *Well-Being and Higher Education: A Strategy for Change and the Realization of Education's Greater Purpose*, edited by Don Harward. Washington, DC: Bringing Theory into Practice, 2016, pp. 207–216.

Sala, G., and F. Gobet. "Cognitive and Academic Benefits of Music Training with Children: A Multilevel Meta-Analysis." *Memory and Cognition*, vol. 48, 2020, pp. 1429–1441.

Schellenberg, E. Glenn. "Long-Term Positive Associations between Music Lessons and IQ." *Journal of Educational Psychology*, vol. 98, 2004, pp. 457–468.

Schneider, C. E., E. G. Hunter, and S. H. Bardach. "Potential Cognitive Benefits from Playing Music among Cognitively Intact Older Adults: A Scoping Review." *Journal of Applied Gerontology*, vol. 38, December 2019, pp. 1763–1783.

Seligman, Martin E. P. *Flourish: A Visionary New Understanding of Happiness and Well-being*. New York: Free Press, 2011.

Smith, Gareth Dylan, and Marissa Silverman, editors. *Eudaimonia: Perspectives for Music Learning*. New York: Routledge, 2020.

Tay, Louis, James O. Pawelski, and Melissa G. Keith. "The Role of the Arts and Humanities in Human Flourishing: A Conceptual Model." *The Journal of Positive Psychology*, vol. 13, no. 3, 2018, 215–225.

VanderWeele, Tyler J. "On the Promotion of Human Flourishing." *Proceedings of the National Academy of Sciences of the United States of America*, vol. 14, no. 31, August 1, 2017, pp. 8148–8156. https://www.ncbi.nlm.nih.gov/pmc/articles/PMC5547610/#s4.

Zatorre, R. J., J. L. Chen, and V. B. Penhune. "When the Brain Plays Music: Auditory-Motor Interactions in Music Perception and Production." *Nature Reviews Neuroscience*, vol. 8, no. 7, July 2007, pp. 547–558.

PART I

CONTEMPLATION

1

Musical Flourishes

Lessons from a Conservatory

Jonathan Coopersmith

There is something special about music. That's why I dedicated my life to learning, analyzing, performing, and sharing as much of it as I can. Having spent close to two decades teaching at one of the world's leading classical conservatories, I've seen firsthand how music, particularly "classical music" in the Western European tradition, affects both performers and audiences. The courses I've taught over the years have tended to deal with how to understand and make sense of music—music theory, analysis, and conducting—so young professionals can comprehend what they are playing and can best communicate their musical interpretations to audiences. I have also sought, before and after (and sometimes during) concerts, to better understand the audience's perspective, asking questions about why they come to performances, how they benefit, what they like and don't like, and even why they think some people don't attend or enjoy the same concerts they do. In recent years, I've expanded my inquiry into music's effect on wellbeing to include non-classical concertgoers, family and friends, and students in the Masters of Applied Positive Psychology program at the University of Pennsylvania, and I've broadened the discussion to include music of other genres such as American popular music, musical theater, jazz, film soundtracks, and more. Participating in this book project extended further my points of reference with regard to music and human flourishing. Many of the insights that follow are a result of these extended conversations with students, audiences, individuals pre- and post-concert, and perhaps most importantly, my colleagues in this volume.

The most common observations to emerge from these interactions, despite such varied audiences across different genres, include music's "innateness" and its seemingly unique ability to influence one's emotions in real time, as well as one's character over the long term. These properties

Jonathan Coopersmith, *Musical Flourishes* In: *Music and Human Flourishing*. Edited by: Anna Harwell Celenza, Oxford University Press. © Oxford University Press 2023. DOI: 10.1093/oso/9780197646748.003.0002 define music as a stand-alone art form. They also facilitate music's ability to enhance the emotional content of extra-musical events such as special occasions, sports events, religious services, and so much more. Regardless of musical ability, many people derive great mental and spiritual benefits from music daily by listening to it, performing it, or creating it; however, music does not inherently promote well-being. One might think that professional musicians benefit the most from their musical abilities, but as a professional who has worked with some of the world's most talented performers, too often the opposite is true due to high expectations, competitiveness, and insecurity. Fortunately, there are things that everyone—professionals, experienced amateurs, and non-musicians alike—can do to increase their well-being by understanding and utilizing the power of music more effectively.

The "Innateness" of Music

In 1857, Herbert Spencer, the English philosopher, biologist, and sociologist, published "The Origin and Function of Music," in which he argued that speech and music evolved at the same time. He proposed that the tonal range and emotional ups and downs of excited speech gradually became uncoupled from words and evolved as its own language, the precursor of music. Words and speech evolved to convey information, while music evolved to communicate emotions. Leonard Bernstein supported the idea of music's innateness and universality in his six Harvard lectures from the early 1970s. In the first of those talks, entitled "Musical Phonology," Bernstein says, "if the theory of monogenesis is valid and speech indeed has common origins, and if the heightening of that speech produces music, then music may also be said to have common origins—and is therefore universal, whether the notes issue from the mouth of God or from [a] hungry infant" (*The Unanswered Question* 16). Charles Darwin proposed a different theory in *The Descent of Man* in 1871, arguing that music actually preceded speech and arose essentially as an elaboration of mating calls (Storr 11). Music—that is, notes and rhythms—came first, and speech came later. Marcel Proust writes in *Remembrance of Things Past*, Volume 5: "I asked myself if music were not the unique example of what might have been—if there had not come the invention of language, the formation of words, the analysis of ideas—the means of communication between one spirit and another. It is like a possibility which has ended in nothing; humanity has developed along other lines, those of spoken and written language."

If you subscribe to Spencer's theory or to Darwin's, it seems plausible that music and language originated and evolved organically as complementary forms of expression. Musical expressiveness may even be a *necessary* complement to speech for full and complete communication; that is, some things might best be conveyed using words, while other things might best—or only—be conveyed through music.

Some of the earliest theories and philosophies about music, such as Pythagoras's mathematical ratios, which form the foundation of music theory still in use today, are based on "natural phenomena." Aristoxenus, like his teacher Aristotle, set out to prove that "the voice follows a natural law in its motion, and does not place the intervals at random. And of our answers we endeavor to supply proofs that will be in agreement with the phenomena" (Tenney 11). The "rules" of counterpoint and composition associated with the Western European tradition have for centuries reflected a shared basic understanding of *consonance* and *dissonance*, terms that are generally poorly defined but which have tried to capture the essence of "what sounds good." As Alejandro Madrid notes later in this volume, this shared understanding of what is deemed "good" has at times narrowly focused on the traditional canon of Western classical music over other genres. Thus we should be careful not to fall victim to unconscious bias when discussing the aesthetic value and intrinsic innateness of music.

But what does it really mean to say that music is "innate" to human beings? Certainly, we are not born with the ability to play an instrument, read music, or articulate the differences between Bach and Beethoven, yet it seems clear that a certain basic musical ability resides within all of us from birth. Newborns (and younger) have an immediate, automatic, and strong physical response to music. Precursors to music and dance, such as rudimentary singing and rhythmic movement to music, are evident in newborns, who exhibit pronounced neural responses to changes in pitch, pitch direction, intervals, and consonance and dissonance (Trehub and Cirelli 225–242). There is also evidence that prelinguistic infants have an ability to perceive and distinguish differences in melodic contour, timing, and tempo similar to that of adults who have had years of informal exposure to music (Trehub 669–673).

The music theorist Eugene Narmour addresses the question of innateness by referring to some musical parameters as "bottom-up," those which we all tend to experience in a similar way, such as pitch sets, contours, timbres, durations, and meters. He defines "top-down" structures as those that are learned and culturally specific, such as voice leading, tonal strategies, harmonic progressions, form, etc. In *The Analysis and Cognition of Melodic Complexity: The Implication-Realization Model*, Narmour offers a specific explanation of how music's ability to move us works: its many parameters—melody, harmony, musical rhythm, tempo, dynamics, instrumentation, etc.—contribute to communicating emotion via a natural ability to create expectations in the listener, referred to as "implications," that are completely or partially "realized" (providing some degree of closure) or not (increasing tension). Narmour's model focuses on how music is perceived moment by moment, based on the idea that when one hears music, specifically a melody, the various musical implications lead to expectations about how it will continue, and when listeners hears something different from what they expect, they experience "arousal and tension." The idea that expectation plays a role in how we experience music was first suggested by the musicologist Leonard Meyer and has been supported by studies on the psychological nature of expectation itself (Meyer, *Emotion and Meaning*; Huron, *Sweet Anticipation*).

It is perhaps for these reasons that the composer and music theorist Paul Hindemith thought of composers as expert manipulators who know that "certain patterns of tone-setting correspond with certain emotional reactions on the listener's part" (36). While a composer cannot predict with certainty how a listener will respond to a complex work, "by experience and clever distribution of this material . . . he can reach a fairly close approximation to unanimity of all listeners' reactions" (Hindemith 44).

The Modes of Music Engagement

To understand the ways in which music might uniquely affect well-being, one needs to isolate the effect of music from the potential effect of words, visual images, drama, and other non-musical influences. The lyrics of a song, the beauty of movement in ballet, or the drama of musical theater will have their own effects on well-being, separate from the music alone. But this is not how most people experience music in their daily lives—that is, music uncoupled from visual images or the lyrics of popular songs. In fact, many of the people with whom I engage in this conversation find it extremely difficult to consider *only* the music itself—that which is played by an instrument, group of instruments, or sung without words—as distinct from the other art forms it often accompanies.

In reality, music is everywhere, providing an almost continuous sound-track to our lives. Whether it is the primary focus (e.g., instrumental jazz or a classical string quartet), an accompaniment or complement to other art forms (e.g., ballet, video game, or a film soundtrack), or background music (at parties, shopping malls, elevators, etc.), the most common mode of en-gagement with music is through listening. The powerful expressive and com-municative properties of music make it an art form worthy of primary focus, as Michael Beckerman explains in Chapter 4, but as an accompaniment to other art forms or even when played in the background, music exerts a strong impact on setting the mood. A movie scene without its music is much less emotionally intense. Adding music to almost anything tends to inflate the overall emotional dimension such that the whole is often greater than the sum of its parts.

How does listening to music affect well-being? On a musically quantum level, the implications of Narmour's "bottom-up" and "top-down" parameters, along with complete or partial realizations, provide unlim-ited combinations of tension and closure and infinite potential to affect (or manipulate) our emotions moment by moment as we listen. Music has the power to change one's mood, to validate or amplify feelings, to clarify un-known or confused feelings, and so much more, as measured by a forty-item scale known as Music in Mood Regulation, or MMR (Saarikallio 291–309). The scale was developed to measure how people (adolescents, specifically) use music to regulate their moods and includes categories such as entertain-ment, revival, diversion, mental work, and solace, among others. Another study asked 834 participants to rank 129 non-redundant functions of music in terms of importance, and the most common response was mood regu-lation, followed by achieving self-awareness, and third, as an expression of social relatedness (Schäfer, Sedlmeier, Städtler, and Huron 511). The right piece of music can also provide a way to confront and realize more extreme feelings that one might not otherwise experience, for example, inducing a state of euphoria or providing a safe form of relief from anger, aggression, or depression.

In a larger sense, listening consistently to the same style or genre of music over longer periods of time can have a profound effect on one's character and perhaps even can help inspire people to become more virtuous and moral human beings. As Aristotle wrote in *Politics*, "[Melodies] contain in themselves imitations of ethoses . . . it is plain that music has the power of producing a certain effect on the ethos of the soul, and if it has the power to do this, it is clear that the young must be directed to music and educated in it" (*Source Readings* 29). There is a large body of research across various disciplines, including the psychology, sociology, and anthropology of music, as well as cultural musicology, examining the direct influence of music on emotion and the connections between music and long-term character, such as increased empathy, to name just a few (Vuoskoski and Eerola 204–213; Schellenberg 324–338; Rabinowitch, Cross, and Burnard 484–498; Clarke, DeNora, and Vuoskoski 61–88).

Whether you are attending a live performance or simply listening to a music recording, enjoying music with family, friends, or even strangers can fulfill a need for shared experiences. Before recordings, listening to music was primarily a group activity, serving as a form of social entertainment or as a way to enhance feelings of unity in religious services and at public events. In group settings, music has the incredible ability to coordinate and align movement, as well as the emotional rise and fall of congregations and audiences. Sharing a moving experience with a room full of people can enhance one's emotions and feelings, make the entire experience more special, and provide an opportunity for discussion, deeper bonds, longer-lasting memories, and stronger relationships.

Music tends to stay with us over long periods of time, making it an ideal tool for learning and remembering. The alphabet is set to music to help children remember it and to make learning more fun. Corporations rely on marketing jingles to help consumers remember their products. I'm amazed at how often I remember the lyrics of songs I learned as a child or as a teen, even if I haven't heard those songs in decades. I was part of a generation that learned (and can still sing) the preamble to the U.S. Constitution because of a song on School House Rock in the mid-1970s. There's a strong nostalgic element to music, as well, capturing moments in time and creating long-lasting associations to people, places, and events. Hearing music from one's past can help recall memories once thought to be lost, as well as conjure up feelings from that earlier time.

Since music may act as an emotional complement of speech, engagement through performance—that is, singing or playing an instrument—could have a potentially deeper effect on well-being by providing an outlet for a wider range of expression. In addition, developing the skills and overcoming the technical challenges necessary to play an instrument can foster feelings of pride and accomplishment, building confidence and self-esteem while instilling discipline and humility. Research has shown that children who rise to this challenge report an increase in self-identity and self-expression, and an alternative means of communicating feelings (Hallam 269–289).

Performers of music can derive the same mood-regulating and long-term character benefits as do listeners, but in a self-expressive and potentially more cathartic way. With the exception of professionals under someone else's direction or students working with a teacher, performers choose the music they wish to perform and shape the emotional content with full control over interpretation. Learning how to sing or to play an instrument also builds appreciation for those who might be further along the path, leading to a higher level of engagement, enjoyment, and fulfillment when listening to music.

The collaborative aspect of performing, especially in small groups, requires an awareness of when to take the lead versus when to play a supporting role. In an ensemble, it's fulfilling to be a part of the creative process and of the greater whole. The presence of an audience adds yet another social dimension—a great sense of satisfaction in sharing music with and affecting the lives of other people, bringing joy and even emotional and spiritual healing to others.

Beyond listening to and performing music, perhaps an even more personally expressive method of musical engagement is through composition, from the most basic improvisations and musical utterances by untrained musicians to the written orchestrations of highly skilled professional composers. My informal talks with family, friends, and audiences reveal that even self-conscious non-musicians enjoy making up songs and humming to themselves when they think no one is listening. This type of improvised singing is a form of composition, too, frequently used by music therapists and in community music outreach and education programs as a way to get beginners to engage with music. In this way, learning to "compose" and improvise is like learning a language; it doesn't take any education or experience to start, but only through more formal education, along with much practice and trial and error, will a coherent and personal style emerge. To extend the analogy, the art of composition is similar to creative writing—in order to fully, succinctly, and artistically express oneself, one needs a more developed vocabulary in addition to knowledge of things like structure and balance, often learned through formal training.

The composer creates something new, something that exists outside of him/herself. Formal composition—music that is written down or recorded and intended to be played by others—necessarily involves collaboration in order to bring the music to life. Each performance might involve a slightly different interpretation, which can be extremely gratifying and humbling, especially when a performance includes a welcome interpretation that the composer hadn't considered.

Employing music's full potential to address the well-being and therapeutic needs of individuals is the domain of music therapy. Using the three modes of engagement described above—listening, performing, and composing—therapists and their patients, individually and in groups, listen to recordings, perform music at various levels, play musical games, and improvise and compose songs. Music therapy is an effective method to calm and relieve stress; provide social and cognitive stimulation; enhance concentration, self-reflection, creativity, and subjective well-being; improve focus, attention span, and frustration tolerance; help with pain management and mood regulation; and strengthen memory.

Music and Well-Being: For Better or for Worse?

Despite its potential to deliver substantial positive benefits, music, as with other arts, does not inherently promote flourishing; rather, it may enhance well-being in one case and weaken it in another. While music can be used to fully express one's feelings, trigger positive memories, or celebrate life's milestones, loud or aggressive music can trigger post-traumatic stress disorder (PTSD) or validate negative or violent feelings (Carlson, Saarikallio, Toiviainen, Bogert, Kliuchko, and Brattico 466). Unwanted music, the repetition of an incessant melody, or unresolved melodic material can be distracting, even torturous. Involuntary musical imagery—the spontaneous recall and repetition of music often referred to as an "earworm"—has been associated with heightened emotional responses, as compared to the voluntary or deliberate recall of the same music (Jakubowski, Bashir, Farrugia, Stewart 741–756). Where music therapists might employ a slow beat, melody, or harmonic rhythm in order to calm someone's breathing, music could just as easily be used to increase a person's heart rate or agitation. If music has the power to coordinate and inspire religious feelings in large congregations, it also has the power to facilitate a destructive mob mentality.

Ironically, the positive effects of music seem to be lost on many professional classical musicians, even though they are surrounded by beautiful music played at a high level on almost a daily basis. While they may have a greater capacity for musical self-expression, these professionals often lose sight of the joy and fulfillment that caused them to fall in love with music in the first place, and they may instead come to see music as just a competitive struggle. As Aristotle warned in *Politics*: "Since, as we have seen, that actual performance is needed to make good judgements, one should while young do much playing and singing, and then, when they are older, give up performing. . . . Musical exercises . . . should be pursued only up to the point at which the pupil becomes capable of appreciating good melodies and rhythms. . . . We reject as education a training in material performance which is professional and competitive" (Aristotle, *The Politics*, trans. T. A. Sinclair 307–316).

Many years of dedication and training are required to become a professional classical performer, which can lead to a lack of balance when it comes to hobbies and relationships outside of music. For many, playing at a high level becomes an obsession, and practicing becomes an addiction (Ahrends 191–202). Like some professional athletes, musicians at the top of their game may find it difficult to maintain their level of excellence, and diminishing returns can cause anxiety and frustration. Professionals, or those on a professional track, tend to create unrealistic expectations for themselves, leading to unnecessary or unfair comparisons. In fact, as I was writing this section, a colleague actually posted this on Facebook:

> I often forget how much joy the piano used to bring me, before my pure and honest love of making music became inextricably entangled in a painful web of manipulation, doubt, fear, guilt, jealousy, and the staggering weight of other people's expectations. It's a real mess I've been working slowly and surely to forgive and release. Tonight, I spent some time with an old friend of a piece, and my fingers remembered a bit of the joy. My heart felt it too, I think. And it was sweet.

Performers and especially composers tend to be vulnerable and insecure, exposing their artistic expressions and creations to criticism. Composers might have hopes and dreams for a new piece of music, but what if it is only performed once, or never? What if audiences, critics, or publishers don't like it? What if a conductor or performer has a different interpretation, but the composer does not approve of it?

Students at the top conservatories who aspire to be soloists might end up having to join a professional orchestra as their second choice for a career.

Others join orchestras they feel are beneath them or end up having to teach or freelance to earn a living. After so much time and dedication to their craft, these performers often feel they have no artistic control, as they are forced to play music they don't always like, under guest or even principal conductors they don't respect. The emotional labor connected with these careers can be overwhelming, as Anna Celenza explains at the end of this volume. Consequently, many musicians become jaded, even in the best orchestras.

Experienced or educated audience members are also susceptible to missing out on music's positive effects on well-being. Those who have achieved a high level of engagement, performance ability, or analytical knowledge might have unrealistic expectations of perfection or historical accuracy when attending a performance. The notion that a performance must always live up to a favorite recording or interpretation inevitably leads to disappointment. Worse, it can be upsetting to see performances that are insincere or poorly executed. Sometimes new music is meant to be challenging, provocative, or even anxiety-inducing. Even with an open mind and the best of intentions, not every performance experience will be enjoyable.

Flourishing on a Larger Scale

When I first started teaching and giving pre-concert talks, I prepared and presented information on academic topics like historical context and under-standing and following form and structure. In the past five years, however, I've turned my pre- and post-concert lectures and audience development events into conversations about music and well-being, facilitating discussions and capturing audiences' thoughts and impressions before and immediately after each performance. These conversations typically focus on classical music in the Western European tradition. But I have also had conversations with family, friends, and students at the University of Pennsylvania that focus more on popular music and musical theater. The topic of well-being has made its way into my classroom and even into the curriculum at the conservatory where I teach. I have become focused on plumbing the emotional depths of each piece of music, irrespective of genre, and getting the most out of every performance no matter which side of the stage (or music streaming device) you are on. So, regardless of musical training, what can one do to utilize music more effectively to promote flourishing? The following suggestions, organized according to Seligman's PERMA (Positive emotions, Engagement,

Relationships, Meaning, Achievement) model of happiness, are based on the aforementioned formal and informal conversations and may suggest areas for further research and testing.

Positive Emotions

Plan ahead to regulate emotions throughout the day with music. Listening to music can provide an effective way to regulate emotions in one's daily life (Saarikallio, Nieminen, Brattico 27–39). Much thought might go into selecting the right music playlist for a party or for a group exercise class, but what about the rest of life? Given strong emotional and physical reactions to music and a tendency to imitate music's ethos in both the short and long term, one should carefully and purposefully select music based on predicted or possible emotional needs throughout the day. Instead of turning on the news or a streaming music service in the morning, one should choose a specific piece of music that can help create the right mood and set the tone for the day. The right music can help alleviate midday feelings of frustration or anxiety, while calming, reflective, or meditative music could help settle the mind before going to bed. Playlists curated in advance, when in a clear state of mind, might include music that generates joy, for example, to be played during times when a depressed mood strikes. Taken to an extreme, in 2010, Donna Chadwick and Karen Wacks, both music therapists and musicians themselves, advocated what they called an Advance Music Directive (AMD), similar to a living will, which includes a "lifespan music review" detailing a person's music and sound preferences and possibly a treatment plan. The AMD would include pieces that were known to influence a person's physical and emotional condition should a life-altering event occur. The same could be done on a smaller scale for everyday or weekly listening.

Conversely, one should try to avoid music that triggers negative emotions in the short term or that leads to long-term unhappiness. Sometimes listening to sad music when you're sad can be validating, and music can help express those feelings in a way that words cannot. Wallowing in sad music for extended periods of time, however, is different. In the same way that watching too much TV has been shown to be related significantly to long-term unhappiness, perhaps too much of one type of music, especially music that triggers or reinforces negative emotions, could have the same effect (Robinson and Martin 74–86). Some of my closest friends and relatives suffer from a mild form of depression, and I have noticed that many of them tend to listen to dark and depressing music most of the time, almost on a loop. But after switching to what could be considered a more positive and upbeat genre for just a month, they reported beneficial effects, including a more positive mood. Could it be that switching to a different genre or simply adding music of a different genre to one's regular mix could change one's general outlook in the long term? Perhaps this experiment could be done in a more scientific way on a larger scale.

Redefine what it means to have a "positive" musical experience. A positive musical experience is one that promotes overall personal growth, not just one that leaves you feeling good. Music doesn't need to be happy or result in a good mood for it to have a long-term positive effect. Accepting this and being open to experiencing challenging music or music that expresses and allows one to work through a range of emotions might lead to a better personal balance in the long run.

Listen to as much music as possible and accept that not every musical experience will be transformative. This includes listening to new music in a variety of genres, both recorded and in live performance. When listening to a new recording or live performance of a favorite piece, high expectations can lead to disappointment. Realistically, there will be music, performances, and performers you don't like. When that happens, it is important to reflect on your opinion and identify the good as well as the bad. Just as real-world, non-musical experiences often have both pros and cons, there's almost always something moving or positive to be found in every performance—a melody, rhythm, or simply the fact that there were performers doing their best to bring that music to life. Each new performance is a chance to enjoy someone else expressing themselves or to witness others being moved by it, even if you dislike the piece or disagree with the performer's version, interpretation, or artistic choices.

Engagement

The art historian Wilhelm Worringer suggests two possibilities when engaging with a piece of art: *stay engaged by being in the moment, completely absorbed emotionally* or, as an alternative to engaging on simply an emotional level, *stay somewhat distanced by thinking and observing analytically.* In his 1908 book *Abstraction and Empathy*, Worringer summarized the way people relate to art: "Aesthetic enjoyment is objectified self-enjoyment. To enjoy aesthetically means to enjoy myself in a sensuous object diverse from myself, to empathize myself into it" (4). He goes on to argue that this is not sufficient for modern works of art and offers "abstraction" as an equal but mutually exclusive alternative, recognizing that in some cases we must think analytically when engaging with contemporary art in order to understand and appreciate it. When applied to music in any genre from any era, this model recognizes two distinct modes of engagement: complete emotional immersion and emotional detachment. The latter is a conscious focus on form, structure, and other non-musical parameters such as movement, or the recognition and appreciation of skill, originality, or creativity. Music causes increased physical and emotional arousal in those who allow themselves to become emotionally engrossed, but abstraction is also a valid and appropriate way of appreciating music. Even though abstraction may not produce the same emotional effects, it can be intellectually engaging and satisfying in other ways.

Stay engaged in the long-term process of changing and expanding styles by encouraging innovation and new repertoire. The great music of the past that we still listen to today has already stood the test of time. When these classics were composed, though, there were many more pieces written that for various reasons did not go on to become classics. Today, while new genres and repertoires are being created, audiences need to show patience and understanding, and they should keep an open mind. Experimentation in musical expression should be encouraged and is necessary for the field of music to grow. Therefore, don't be so quick to dismiss a new piece of music! Pundits and critics have declared many times that "the era of good music is over" or that "the music of today is no good," but what seems like an outrage today might actually be ahead of its time and could possibly become tomorrow's classic. Audiences have reacted negatively to changes in music throughout history, from criticism of Monteverdi's use of dissonance in "Cruda Amarilli" in 1605 and the "Quarrel of the Comic Actors" pamphlet wars in Paris in the 1750s, to Schoenberg's use of atonality in 1908 and the riots caused by Stravinsky's *The Rite of Spring* in 1913. Stay open to new music and to new and different musical experiences so that you can be present when, in those rare moments, something truly excellent or transformative happens.

Relationships

Attend more live performances. Recordings are static, whereas live music is different every time. If you hear various live performances of the same piece, or even recordings of the same piece by various performers, you may start to have a relationship to the music, noticing the differences between performances and interpretations. In this way, a given piece of music can develop a life of its own.

Attend more performances with family and friends. In today's world of solitary online interactions, being in the same space, hearing the same music at the same time, and sharing an experience with others can be a welcome connection. Looking around at an audience, just knowing that everyone ordered tickets in advance and then arranged their day to be there might be enough to make you feel more connected with tens, hundreds, or thousands of other listeners. Even though audiences can be distracting sometimes—there's extraneous noise, and many will not be engaged in the same way you are—the benefits are well worth it. Music's ability to coordinate and align emotions within a group is powerful, and experiences can end up being more memorable and more rewarding when shared with others.

Meaning

Seek out and listen to music of greater depth, which will develop the capacity for deeper meaning down the road. Popular music tends to be short and far less complex than classical music, where there is a learning curve for the average listener. Most people speak the language of popular music; it's familiar and easy to understand. There's an unending stream of new popular songs, but most won't be around after a few months or even a few weeks. Even popular music that survives for decades tends to be repetitive and relatively simple musically and rhythmically, carried more by its lyrics and nostalgia than the music itself. The language of contemporary classical music, by comparison, is often too complicated or too abstract for those with little exposure, and it's hard to find meaning when you don't understand (or *feel like* you don't understand) how to listen. Even more accessible classical music may require an investment of time for the novice listener, but it's worth it. Choosing music with the potential for greater meaning, even if challenging at first, is an important step toward greater well-being.

Prime yourself. If the musical language is unfamiliar, preparing in advance can help. If the music is meant to tell a story, reading the program notes ahead of time can help you follow along, as with Berlioz's *Symphonie Fantastique*, Mussorgsky's *Pictures at an Exhibition*, or Prokofiev's *Peter and the Wolf*.

Learning about the non-musical aspects surrounding a piece of music—e.g., its history, the context of its creation, or the life story of the composer—can bring you closer to it, increase its accessibility and relatability, and enhance your enjoyment and connection to the music during a performance.

Even people who are engaged and attend concerts on a regular basis often complain that some works written within the last century are not accessible or relatable. Worse, they feel like it's their fault for not understanding them. (In this case, I encourage these regular concertgoers to give themselves permission to not like a piece of music, but also to stay engaged and not let it stop them from coming back!) Even without elaborate program notes, a composer's music should be able to stand on its own. Musical abstractions— thought experiments like John Cage's 4′33″, or some of Iannis Xenakis's stochastic music, like *Pithoprakta*, where the instruments are conceived as molecules, and the music itself is based on the statistical mechanics of gases—can be interesting intellectually, but they tend to ignore the aforementioned more innate aspects of melody and melodic expectation and the effects of consonance and dissonance on musical tension and resolution, which play a large and important role in music's ability to communicate emotion and encourage well-being. To be clear, even these types of experimental works can stimulate curiosity and appeal to more open-minded and novelty-seeking personalities, but the average conservatory students and music consumers with whom I regularly engage have a hard time putting these works in the same category as other contemporary, non-tonal, or non-Western pieces that retain at least some connection to the most fundamental (and possibly innate) properties of music. Today's composers could do their part to help close this "musical language gap" with a return to writing music that is *mimetic*—an ancient Greek concept that the arts represent and interpret human reality, and specifically with regard to music, metaphorically reflect human emotional experiences—if they want the average audience member to feel a more immediate connection to their works (Borstlap, "Killer Myth"). Many of the composers with whom I work feel this way and are already doing this.

For professional musicians, great meaning can be found in knowing that you've touched or affected someone else's life. While it's sometimes difficult for professional performers or composers to remain connected to their reasons for becoming musicians, learning that they have moved someone with their music is a powerful realization. It often creates a profound sense in them that their work is meaningful. Conservatories and music teachers everywhere must help their students better understand the flourishing aspects and healing potential of music-making.

Accomplishment

Learn to play an instrument, but heed Aristotle's warning and avoid becoming competitive. In addition to becoming capable of appreciating good melodies and rhythms, learning to play an instrument leads to a sense of accomplishment. Unfortunately, far too many people have never had the opportunity to learn an instrument and have little to no confidence when it comes to singing. By contrast, most people begin to express themselves in words and through language in early infancy, slowly mimicking the sounds and grammar of the people around them. A small vocabulary gradually emerges, and toddlers and elementary school students begin to recognize letters, to read, and eventually, to write. Even starting from a young age, most people don't master the ability to write clearly and creatively until their late teens or twenties. This is even more so when it comes to learning music. There's great pride in being able to play an instrument or sing well, and immense satisfaction and fulfillment in being able to express oneself musically. No doubt, human flourishing would increase exponentially if greater attention were given to formal music education.

The question of exactly which properties or parameters of music, if any, are innate to human beings across cultures is a question for science. Until we know more, the creators and consumers of music will have to rely on their personal and anecdotal experiences in deciding how best to engage as listeners, performers, and composers in order to increase their well-being. While humans may be born with a certain degree of musicality, there is still a great deal of musical knowledge that must be learned, and that requires an investment of time. Listening to a variety of genres, attending live concerts, learning to play an instrument, and reading about music history and theory are all investments that have the potential to pay off in greater happiness through deeper engagement. The careful selection of specific pieces of music can increase both positive feelings in the short term and can help cultivate moral character in the long term. Music can strengthen relationships and give a deeper meaning to life's most important events. Even professionals who have dedicated their lives to practicing and performing music could benefit from a greater awareness of their own competitiveness and insecurities, as well as music's ability to increase their personal well-being and the well-being of others. Learning the language of music and appreciating its importance and power is a lifelong process, though, and like anything that's good for us, the extent to which music increases our well-being may come down to the choices we make and our commitment to self-improvement.

Works Cited

Ahrends, Christine. "Does Excessive Music Practicing Have Addiction Potential?" *Psychomusicology: Music, Mind, and Brain*, vol. 27, no. 3, September 2017, pp. 191–202. https://doi.org/10.1037/pmu0000188.

Aristotle. *The Politics* 8.5, translated by Harris Rackham. *Source Readings in Music History*, rev. ed., edited by Oliver Strunk, general editor Leo Treitler. New York: W. W. Norton, 1998, 29. Quoted in J. Peter Burkholder, Donald Jay Grout, and Claude V. Palisca, *A History of Western Music*. 9th ed. New York: W. W. Norton, 2014, p. 14.

Aristotle, *The Politics*, translated by T. A. Sinclair, revised and re-presented by Trevor J. Saunders. Harmondsworth: Penguin Classics, rev. ed., 1981, pp. 307–316. Quoted in Piero Weiss and Richard Taruskin, ed., *Music in the Western World: A History In Documents*. 2nd ed. Australia: Thomson/Schirmer, 2008, p. 9.

Bernstein, Leonard. *The Unanswered Question: Six Talks at Harvard*. Cambridge, MA: Harvard University Press, 1976.

Borstlap, John. "The 'Killer Myth': The Fallacy of Progress in the Arts." John Borstlap, Composer (website), September 15, 2013, accessed July 1, 2019, http://johnborstlap.com/the-killer-myth-the-fallacy-of-progress-in-the-arts/#more-761.

Carlson, Emily, Suvi Saarikallio, Petri Toiviainen, Brigitte Bogert, Marina Kliuchko, and Elvira Brattico. "Maladaptive and Adaptive Emotion Regulation through Music: A Behavioral and Neuroimaging Study of Males and Females." *Frontiers in Human Neuroscience*, vol. 9, August 2015, pp. 1–13. https://doi.org/10.3389/fnhum.2015.00466.

Clarke, Eric, Tia DeNora, and Jonna Vuoskoski. "Music, Empathy, and Cultural Understanding." *Physics of Life Reviews*, vol. 15, December 2015, pp. 61–88. https://doi.org/10.1016/j.plrev.2015.09.001.

Hallam, Susan. "The Power of Music: Its Impact on the Intellectual, Social and Personal Development of Children and Young People." *International Journal of Music Education*, vol. 28, no. 3, August 2010, pp. 269–289. https://doi.org/10.1177/0255761410370658.

Hindemith, Paul. *A Composer's World: Horizons and Limitations*. Cambridge, MA: Harvard University Press, 1952.

Huron, David. *Sweet Anticipation: Music and the Psychology of Expectation*. Cambridge, MA: MIT Press, 2006.

Jakubowski, Kelly, Zaariyah Bashir, Nicolas Farrugia, and Lauren Stewart. "Involuntary and Voluntary Recall of Musical Memories: A Comparison of Temporal Accuracy and Emotional Responses." *Memory & Cognition*, vol. 46, no. 5, July 2018, pp. 741–756. https://doi.org/10.3758/s13421-018-0792-x.

Meyer, Leonard. *Emotion and Meaning in Music*. Chicago: University of Chicago Press, 1956.

Narmour, Eugene. *The Analysis and Cognition of Melodic Structures: The Implication Realization Model.* Chicago: University of Chicago Press, 1990.

Proust, Marcel. *The Captive, Remembrance of Things Past,* vol. 5, translated by C. K. Scott Moncrieff. London: Chatto & Windus, 1929, reprint Project Gutenberg Australia, 2003, vol. 2, chap. 2, http://gutenberg.net.au/ebooks03/0300501h.html.

Rabinowitch, Tal-Chen, Ian Cross, and Pamela Burnard. "Long-Term Musical Group Interaction Has a Positive Influence on Empathy in Children." *Psychology of Music,* vol. 41, no. 4, July 2013, pp. 484–498. https://doi.org/10.1177/0305735612440609.

Robinson, John P., and Steven Martin. "Of Time and Television." *The Annals of the American Academy of Political and Social Science,* vol. 625, no. 1, September 2009, pp. 74–86. https://doi.org/10.1177/0002716209339275.

Saarikallio, Suvi H. "Music in Mood Regulation: Initial Scale Development." *Musicae Scientiae,* vol. 12, no. 2, July 2008, pp. 291–309. https://doi.org/10.1177/10298649080 1200206.

Saarikallio, Suvi, Sirke Nieminen, and Elvira Brattico. "Affective Reactions to Musical Stimuli Reflect Emotional Use of Music in Everyday Life." *Musicae Scientiae,* vol. 17, no. 1, March 2013, pp. 27–39. https://doi.org/10.1177/1029864912462381.

Schäfer, Thomas, Peter Sedlmeier, Christine Städtler, and David Huron. "The Psychological Functions of Music Listening." *Frontiers in Psychology,* vol. 4, 2013, pp. 1–33. https://doi.org/10.3389/fpsyg.2013.00511.

Schellenberg, E. Glenn. "Cognitive Performance after Listening to Music: A Review of the Mozart Effect." *Music, Health, and Wellbeing,* edited by Raymond AR MacDonald, Gunter Kreutz, and Laura Mitchell. Oxford: Oxford University Press, 2012, pp. 325–338. https://doi.org/10.1093/acprof:oso/9780199586974.003.0022.

Seligman, Martin E. P. *Flourish: A Visionary New Understanding of Happiness and Well-being.* New York: Free Press, 2011.

Spencer, Herbert. "The Origin and Function of Music." *Fraser's Magazine,* October 1857, pp. 396–408.

Storr, Anthony. *Music and the Mind.* New York: Ballantine Books, 1933.

Tenney, James. *A History of "Consonance" and "Dissonance."* Excelsior Music, 1988.

Trehub, Sandra. "The Developmental Origins of Musicality." *Nature Neuroscience,* vol. 6, no. 7, 2003, pp. 669–673. https://doi.org/10.1038/nn1084.

Trehub, Sandra, and Laura K. Cirelli. "Precursors to the Performing Arts in Infancy and Early Childhood." *Progress in Brain Research,* vol. 237, 2018, pp. 225–242. https://doi.org/10.1016/bs.pbr.2018.03.008.

Vuoskoski, Jonna, and Tuomas Eerola. "Can Sad Music Really Make You Sad? Indirect Measures of Affective States Induced by Music and Autobiographical Memories." *Psychology of Aesthetics Creativity and the Arts,* vol. 6, no. 3, August 2012, pp. 1–10. https://doi.org/10.1037/a0026937.

Worringer, Wilhelm. *Abstraction and Empathy,* translated by Michael Bullock. Chicago: Ivan R. Dee, 1997.

2

Jubilee

The (Positive) Science of Black Music

Shana L. Redmond

Her performance provides too many surprises to name. You listen from the edge of your seat, attempting to know what will come from that song or that set that you've heard over and over again, but her technique reveals no easy answers or predictable steps in your listening. The whine, the wail, the response to the audience is unlike anything you've ever heard before, and you smile. You cry. You respond in ways that transgress the lonely isolation of consumption and enter into ecstatic transcendence.

I watched much of the film with baited breath: Aretha Franklin's 1972 performance at the New Temple Missionary Baptist Church in Los Angeles, which resulted in the live album *Amazing Grace*, was cinematic. Its 2018 turn in film showed that, even though the sanctuary and its patrons were beautiful in their period-specific earth and jewel tones, it was Franklin's voice that developed the picturesque scenes of mountains and heavens. In some ways, her performance was what you'd expect from the luminary: extended and penetrating riffs of exaltation, runs of melodic and antiphonal intimacy with the Reverend James Cleveland and the backing Southern California Community Choir, revealing and personal moments in song at the piano. Yet there were moments in which what she gave was nothing of what could have been expected. One in particular struck *the* chord. It was during "Amazing Grace." It wasn't the composition itself; it was what she made of it. She hummed. I crossed over. Nothing more could or should have been said or sung. In that moment, she'd done all that could be asked of her. She made me feel.

What *the* chord was that connected me so deeply to her is unknown. What I do know is that I've had that experience with musicians dozens of times in my life, and each time I learn something new about them, myself, and the world. Music does this. It's an experience that, in its recorded and popular form, often lasts less than five minutes but is dense with possibilities

Shana L. Redmond, *Jubilee* In: *Music and Human Flourishing*. Edited by: Anna Harwell Celenza, Oxford University Press.
© Oxford University Press 2023. DOI: 10.1093/oso/9780197646748.003.0003

for change. Our emotions, knowledges, and politics are ripe for adjustment through the act of listening, which positions us in conversation with the performers. Indeed, while we may often understand our affective responses as individualized emotion, recent literatures document that "emotional feelings and displays are not considered to represent internal states of an individual (whether innate or acquired through learning and experience) which result in physiological reactions to environmental stimuli. Rather, they are meaningful displays that are taken as emotional when they are embodied expressions of judgements, and in many cases, ways of accomplishing certain social acts" (Sloboda and O'Neill 415). This layered experience and *future* of music, in which one engagement (listening) inspires another ("social acts"), is both the genealogy of Black musics and the methodology by which it is advanced. It is, as Alejandro Madrid later explains, the type of layered experience that can free music aesthetics from the preconceived notions of the past.

The sociality of music-making is pronounced in vocal musics, which predominate in popular culture. Building on the work of scholar and sound artist Mendi Obadike, Nina Sun Eidsheim refigures the racialized voice through the "acousmatic question" (Who is this?) and argues that "Voice is not singular; it is collective. Voice is not innate; it is cultural." Indeed, the receiver holds a significant position in the performative event; so much so that Eidsheim ends her tripartite intervention with the provocation, "Voice's source is not the singer; it is the listener" (Eidsheim 9). We, the audience, make sense and meaning of the voice. Our responses to the experience of music, which are revealed in audible and inaudible ways—from shallow breathing and tears to complete stillness or dancing—transform us with the potential to be like or near the sounds and their makers. When we know the performance well, we can participate in anticipated ways, which brings its own joys of familiarity and comfort. Yet beyond the performances that we know line for line, measure by measure, are those that take us off guard, disarming us in the process. From this vulnerability comes unexpected and potentially transformative experiences like mine with Aretha.

I'd like to sit a while in these moments of unanticipated musical revelation in order to examine how Black musical sciences (as I define them) animate human flourishing.[1] I'm concerned with the intrigue of the

---

[1] The unconventional use of the word "science" as a description for Black musical creation is a nod to the educated and repetitive nature of the form(s). I am interested in thinking of Black composition and performance as studied experiments with indeterminate results. Each performance is a new trial, yielding new results. While the ends may be envisioned or even hoped for, it is the process—the experimentation and improvisation—that better marks the rigors of this science.

impossible—those performances within popular Black musical cultures that go off script and are rarely, perhaps never otherwise, achieved. It is the departure that defines the journey in this musicking; at the "crossroads" of performance, unforeseen feelings and ways of being are accomplished (Small). The science of this reveal is not invested as much in the conclusion or the result as in the process: the experimentation, rehearsal, and practice that makes improvisation possible. "A human response to necessity," improvisation is, as a number of jazz artists contend, educated and perfected, even if it is impromptu and different with every single performance.[2] Part of the intrigue of these moments is precisely their function as a deviation from what we know or expect, meaning that our collective beliefs and understanding are challenged even if we experience the results singularly. These elements of educated play make possible the surprise genius of ecstatic emotion by bringing us closest to our human potential. As play theorist Michael Ellis argues, "To the extent that we unfetter individuals from the demands of work or duty, we allow them leisure or opportunities to play and we commit those individuals to be themselves. Thus, ideologically a human is most human, as defined by our culture, when at play" (Ellis 9). Later in this volume (Chapter 10), Melvin Butler expands on the importance of play and its ability to transcend the present. That this play in Black communities is also indelibly tied to a horrific past does nothing to undermine its spirit or innovation; indeed, one derives great resource from the other.

Being our most knowledgeable and expressive selves (human) is the first step toward the happiness that human flourishing is meant to advance—a topic discussed at length in Chapter 1 by Jonathan Coopersmith. This positive science is one background to my discussion of the science of Black music, which also seeks to understand and express the highest ideals and potential of meaningful being. I hesitate to call this being "human" in light of the deep and necessary challenges that scholars have brought to bear on that very term and its ideologies in relation to racial bodies and subjects who, as Alexander Weheliye argues, are "afforded . . . no easy passage to the sign of the human" (Weheliye, "Feenin'" 24). Sylvia Wynter, Saidiya Hartman, Hortense Spillers, and others have carefully mapped the traditions, both philosophical and material, that dispossess African peoples—especially Black women—from the

---

[2] This concise and stunning insight is from composer-musician Muhal Richard Abrams, quoted in Miller and Vijay, "Improvising Digital Culture." Musician Yusef Lateef refused to use the word "improvisation," arguing that "every note I play on my saxophone has over six decades of preparation." Quoted in written communication with professor Michael Dessen, January 18, 2019.

claims of autonomy and freedom that have defined the (post)Enlightenment human (re: "man").[3] With this reality in view, I am working toward an articulation of the "multifarious ways" in which Black people have performed a dimensional and emotionally complex "human" through the science of Black music, which may be understood as the greatest antidote to its producers' dehumanization (Weheliye, "Feenin'" 26). Indeed, as many scholars and musicians have documented, the music is the evidence of not only the lives and struggles of these communities, but their triumph as well.[4]

The constitution of this elastic, living science is, like our emotions, context-specific, taking shape multiply over time and space, yet there are elements that broadly mark its methods and performances. Antiphony is regularly cited as indicative of Black musics and is, in this formulation, an opportunity for communication that can be improvisatory and impromptu; it brings people together and, sometimes, brings people back.[5] Experimentation, rehearsal, and practice are additional strategies in this science, and also lend themselves to relation with improvisation. These forms of educated play are practically and conceptually collaborative; even if one practices alone, the play is in service of or in relation to someone(s) else, whether it be other musicians, sounds, or environments. This sightedness as one plays is also a cue to the emotional register of the task, which, as I'll demonstrate, can be filled with exhilarating and impactful victories that produce the final, speculative element of Black music's science: Jubilee.

Drawn from a biblical passage in Leviticus and described as "a cyclical time of liberation, of abolition, and of mechanisms of redress," Jubilee is the language of self-emancipation by the enslaved. Emancipation was considered impossible in its time; its success reveals the unexpected and incredible feats for which its actors daily trained. I argue that this training for the impossible that became possible in Black history is also musical. A unique addition to historian David Roediger's "broad politics of Jubilee," this science appears singular but is always collective and advances the study of the human

---

[3] See, for example: Hartman, *Scenes of Subjection*; Spillers, *Black, White, and in Color*; Wynter, "'No Humans Involved'" 42–73, and Wynter, "Unsettling" 257–337.

[4] A perfect example of this duality in Black music is found in the Negro National Anthem, "Lift Ev'ry Voice and Sing," the text of which reads (in part): "Sing a song, full of the faith that the dark past has taught us. Sing a song, full of the hope that the present has brought us" (1899).

[5] In *Everything Man*, I develop the language of "antiphonal life" to describe the longevity of Paul Robeson and his influence. This method is a response to calls for assistance and solidarity in and beyond living.

and human emotion through the alchemies of its improbable performance (*Seizing Freedom*).

Training for Jubilee

> For my people everywhere singing their slave songs repeatedly:
> their dirges and their ditties and their blues and jubilees. . . .
> —Margaret Walker, "For My People" (1989)

Margaret Walker wrote her own praise song for those who sing repeatedly, daily, hourly. These people are embattled and fighting, thinking and praying, learning to live in a world that is not of their creation and in which they are uniquely vulnerable. The variety of forms in which they sing are numerous, and while there is genius there, it's the performance of the songs that offers a correction and new way of living. So much is revealed in the singing: the causes, the information, the futures that impact and transform our realities. These visions are important; while Walker ends her poem with a wish for the end of dirges, she recognizes still that the conditions that produce them are numerous. The continuous "and . . . and . . . and" in her litany of commas and missing commas tell us that the histories of Black life are deep and dense and their sounds produce their own reveal. There is no way to make sense of the insensible or to make brutality humane, yet the histories of enslavement provide evidence of the *possibility* that radical violence is not a totality—if struggled against and forged collectively, it can ripen alternative worldviews grounded by the genius of those most vulnerable. Enslavement was a genocidal institution that produced some of the most fantastic human displays of creativity and flight that the world has ever known. From capoeira and spirituals to ocean mutinies and underground escape, captivity was made to mean something new and, invariably, different in the hands of African-descended peoples. That beauty would come from devastation is but one of the paradoxes of the institution. And yet another: bondage was the training ground for the impossible. These maneuvers set the stage for more popular and musical feats by postbellum generations.

The impossible under slavery's regime is best understood by looking at the struggle for its end on a number of different registers and how they together built what eminent sociologist W. E. B. Du Bois termed a "counter-revolution of property" (*Black Reconstruction in America*). This counter-revolution was global and occurred at various scales. At its most profound, we might first consider abolition, which was monumental in its task and the futures that might be because of its success. Centuries of enslavement around the world rehearsed its permanence through the constant evolution of de jure and de facto practices that worked diligently to produce a forever system. Its end was imagined first by those who lived under its yoke: enslaved men and women who, through acts large and small, chipped away at its foundation daily. The preparation for abolition included activities unique to bondage, such as arson, poisoning, feigned illness, and sabotage. Other techniques were studied and deployed over the long struggle for freedom—well into and beyond the twentieth century—and became an art. Learned and refined under enslavement, communal experimentation and improvisation were strategies of survival foundational to the traditions and innovations of Black music.

It is not an exaggeration to say that efforts to survive became muscle memory within Black communities. We know this, notably, through their sounds. Training for the (im)possibility of freedom is revealed amply in the musical performances of African-descended peoples on both sides of Emancipation. The Negro spirituals were the bridge between the two moments; they served as salve and inspiration, code and instruction for those enslaved as well as those newly freed, for neither the memory nor structures of enslavement were gone.[6] The spirituals spoke to both conditions—unfreedom and freedom—as artifact and living document and allowed their bards to produce new associations while carrying on the techniques of improvisation, communalism, and close listening that defined survival under the institution. Performers of the spirituals in the years following Emancipation had to contend with not only the reality of enslavement, but also its rise as popular entertainment. Blackface minstrelsy was built from caricatures of enslaved and newly freed peoples. Zip Coon and the pickaninnies, Sambo, and Nigger Jim marked U.S. popular culture in the 1850s. In order to contend with these repulsive portrayals, freed Black

---

[6] "Slavery had established a measure of man and a ranking of life and worth that has yet to be undone. If slavery persists as an issue in the political life of black America, it is not because of an antiquarian obsession with bygone days or the burden of too-long memory, but because black lives are still imperiled and devalued by a racial calculus and a political arithmetic that were entrenched centuries ago. This is the afterlife of slavery—skewed life chances, limited access to health and education, premature death, incarceration, and impoverishment" (Hartman, *Lose Your Mother* 6).

women and men took to the concert stage in order to sing the songs that
these characters mocked: the spirituals.

In the wake of the Civil War (1861–1865), it was the Fisk Jubilee Singers
who most defined the popular performance of the spirituals. Founded
in 1871, the Singers—all of them students at the historically Black Fisk
University in Nashville, Tennessee—became ambassadors for their fiscally
precarious school and for the spirituals that quickly became the answer to
that precarity. Tours of the eastern United States and, eventually, Europe
brought the financial returns to sustain and expand the University, making
the Singers famous both locally and abroad. Prior to the successes of famed
concert singers of the spirituals Roland Hayes, Paul Robeson, and Marian
Anderson, and arrangers Lawrence Brown and Harry T. Burleigh, the Fisk
Jubilee Singers trained for the new, post-Emancipation world by singing
and allowing others to do the same. Within a year of their public launch,
the Singers were so proficient in their craft that they were able to publish
arrangements of their concert spirituals.

Composed of two dozen songs, including the classics "Didn't My Lord
Deliver Daniel," "Swing Low," and twenty-four verses of "Go Down,
Moses," the collection entitled *Jubilee Songs: As Sung by the Fisk Jubilee
Singers* mirrors the form of many other Black texts of the period. Like the
testimonials of the (formerly) enslaved, *Jubilee Songs* comes with prefa-
tory and concluding remarks by authenticating figures—religious and
critical alike. In his contribution, composer Theo Seward argues: "It is certain that the critic stands completely disarmed in [the spirituals'] presence." According to him, the listener's vulnerability stems from the songs'
unique origin and its relationship to live performance. "They are never
'composed' after the manner of ordinary music," he writes, "but spring
into life, ready-made, from the white heat of religious fervor during some
protracted meeting in church or camp" (*Jubilee Songs* 2.) This language
suggests atavism or religious possession as the wellspring of genius among
the singers, when it's more accurate to understand these performers as
highly educated—not through formal musical literacies (Western nota-
tional systems) necessarily, but through a deep relation to the songs and
their performance, which stem from long genealogies of shared vision and
rehearsal.

The insider knowledges formed through this repertoire are suggested
in the brief comments that precede the first selection, "Nobody Knows the
Trouble I See, Lord!": "In some of the verses the syllables do not correspond

exactly to the notes in the music. The adaptation is so easy that it was thought best to leave it to the skill of the singer rather than to confuse the eye by too many notes" (*Jubilee Songs* 5). Critics and cynics of the spirituals throughout the nineteenth and twentieth centuries would comment on what they perceived as their childish, simplistic nature; here we find an assertion of their rigor and the talents that they require in performance. The "skill of the singer" is given a moment of consideration, even if only briefly, and in perfect syncopation with the coming songs that distill the past while looking, with hope and inspiration, forward. A reviewer from *The Newark Courier* described that the "sensation produced" by listening to the Singers "was one of joy and sadness combined" (*Jubilee Songs*, 32). This duality also lived in the singers and developed into a type of endurance as it was carried into and beyond the twentieth century.[7]

Along with the author's praise for the skilled singer is a cautionary note: beware those whose eyes might be confused by the true nature of these sounds. The complicated chords, polyvocals, and bending that the notes request are not for the faint of heart. For those who might be overwhelmed, the notation in *Jubilee Songs* has been stripped and simplified, not for the initiated singer, but for the sake of those whose reading practices and skill sets are not complex enough to hear or perform the songs as they need be sung. The fear or concern with "too many notes" in Black music is ongoing, producing a dilemma for its performers. As theorist-musician George Lewis argues, "virtually every extant form of black music has been characterized as 'noise'" due to its aesthetic traditions of "multidominance," which he, drawing from artist and critic Robert Douglas, identifies as an intense abundance beyond the scope of Western taxonomies and knowledges. These features are linked to improvisation and other culture-specific conditions that are recognizable "not with timbre alone, but with the expression of personality, the assertion of agency, the assumption of responsibility and an encounter with history, memory and identity" (Lewis 37). Black vocalists' inheritance of too much, of abundance, of musical virtuosity that exceeds the page and the concert hall is the evidence of the impossible, and it transcends the moment of legal freedom. Honed and refined over time, Jubilee is still possible and present today.

---

[7] The blues is one of the best examples of the expression of "joy and sadness" within Black musics.

"... total elation"

In human behavior, what is most intriguing is not the average but the improbable.

—Martin E. P. Seligman and Mihaly Csikszentmihalyi (2000)

If we step away from the violence and consider all of the creative energies that too animate knowledges of Blackness, we might conclude that "impossibility" is *the* keyword for Black life in the New World. Spectacular feats often mark these pasts and how the future is imagined in recognition of the fact that the forces stacked against these communities are numerous and committed. These tremendous acts and sounds are embodied and inherited, drawing upon both latent and explicit pedagogies of music making and survival. Intrigue is developed and sustained by the successful performance of the many improbable—and select impossible—sonic maneuvers that narrativize the relationship between inspiration and tribute, teacher and student, parent and child.

Singer Lalah Hathaway lives and works in the long shadow cast by her father, Donny Hathaway. A multi-instrumentalist and composer/arranger, the elder Hathaway had a voice and musical mind to be envied. In addition to composing for Curtis Mayfield and Quincy Jones and hitting the charts in collaboration with Roberta Flack, his solo projects include iconic soul ballads "The Ghetto" (1970) and "Someday We'll All Be Free" (1973), as well as the holiday classic, "This Christmas" (1971). His fantastic career and unexpected death at the age of thirty-three set a formidable tone for Lalah, whose popular career was launched in 1990 with her self-titled debut. This album produced "It's Somethin'," the third and final single that, though failing to chart at the moment of its release, is the song that now indelibly marks her career. An opening of keyboard leads us to the upbeat brightness of the song, which is solidly in the vein of urban adult contemporary (UAC) music. An admixture of R&B and soul with radio-friendly crossover instrumentation, hooks, and length, UAC was hugely successful in the moment of release for *Lalah Hathaway*. Groups like Boyz II Men set a high bar for success in the 1990s and Hathaway's "It's Somethin'" approached that sound, while more deeply echoing the jazz influences of contemporary Black women singers, including Anita Baker. Hathaway's foundation in jazz is present throughout her oeuvre and remarkably so in her off-script runs. The "ooohs" and lyrical adlibs are perfectly matched to her contralto voice and improvisational training, which allows her to embellish and bring sophistication to an otherwise straightforward composition.

While the original recording of "It's Somethin' " offers some evidence of her budding talents, it is far from the song that it would become almost twenty-five years later. In 2013 Hathaway was contacted by Grammy Award–winning drummer and producer Robert "Sput" Searight, then working with the band Snarky Puppy. Described as "a joyous large ensemble that draws on jazz, fusion, funk, and rock," Snarky Puppy is a Brooklyn-based collective that typically records in front of live audiences (Micallef). This element sets the scene for Hathaway's performance and the science that she reveals therein. She was asked to select a song from her repertoire that the group might collectively reimagine and improvise, which provoked her return to "It's Somethin.'" Retitled "Something" and arranged by Searight, Snarky Puppy bandleader Michael League, and three other band members, the song offers Hathaway double the original length of tape, with just over seven minutes in which to play with the thirteen musicians who improvise alongside her.[8] With an intimate audience of two or three dozen listeners, all wearing individual headphones and lounging in arm chairs and comfy couches on stage, Hathaway opens the song with her now-characteristic hum to open vowel transition. The rich, deep tones lead to a slow build alongside the electric piano with the guitar, muted horns, woodwinds, percussion and drums, and bass following in sequence as the verse builds and the chorus returns.

> You and I have something.
> How I long to be around when
> when you can see that
> you and I have something in common.

From the slow accumulation of musicians over an R&B groove develops a funk break at the 4:39 mark, which also introduces three backup singers. Throughout, Hathaway improvises her line in between her lyrics, which are sparse and spread out, but it is at this moment that her jazz chops take center stage as she scats across the bass licks and organ vamp. At 5:57 the musicians quiet, leaving only the organ, a few taps of the high hat, and a barefoot

---

[8] Information about the arrangement and participating musicians as well as all footage for the performance is drawn from "Snarky Puppy feat. Lalah Hathaway—Something (Family Dinner—Volume One)," *YouTube.com*, https://www.youtube.com/watch?v=0SJIgTLe0hc. Accessed December 13, 2018.

Hathaway, who continues to improvise her runs. For thirty-eight seconds everyone is still but her. As the other musicians watch and listen, she shows her vocal range, exceeding the lows for which she is best known. At 6:25 the backup singers sway and giggle. League smiles widely and, while holding his electric bass, begins to jump up and down. Searight, who has otherwise been keeping time on the high hat, abruptly walks away from his drum kit with a look of ecstatic disbelief. The cheers from band members and audience alike follow and are a part of the final record(ing). She's done it. In the still of an organ chord, Hathaway has just added her own. She accomplishes the final and most successful of her four maneuvers for multiphonic clarity: she sings a chord.

Prior to the live recording, Hathaway rehearsed this song with Snarky Puppy twice and on neither occasion did she perfect her delivery of the chords. It was in the stakes of a rehearsal (that became a recording) that new opportunities and a new method were revealed to her. She recalled:

> The hook was that I was able to sing multiple chords at once. On the YouTube video you can see me realizing, in the moment, how to control that process. It took six minutes to get to that point, but it was an incredible, expansive experience. I went to a different place vocally to be able to manipulate those chords. People are still trying to figure out how I'm doing it. And I don't even know. It's just something I've been doing since I was 12–13 years old.

Rehearsal revealed new stakes and new talents. Though Hathaway knew of this skill for some time, it was through the collaborative and experimental space of the live recording that she came to trust her own ability. She knew that her talent was specialized and, for fear of listeners questioning its authenticity, she saved it only for live performances. That she waits for six minutes to attempt the feat and moves through four distinct efforts at "control[ing] that process" suggests that revision and rehearsal were ongoing, even as all worked toward a final product (the recording). The song *as process* revealed the unanticipated genius of her labors.

Present here are the characteristics that compose Black music's science. The antiphony shared between Hathaway and the musicians, as they set the tonal structure that she followed in kind, is also present as she works her way through the four chords. With each she is gauging her comfort as well as the reception from her collaborators and audience. Indeed, as

Hathaway explained: "The organist, Cory Henry, and I decided before we got to that vamp that he would go wherever he was going and I'd follow him," she said. "His playing really encouraged me to come to that space. The great part of the performance is it's a real conversation between musicians." This conversation may have had an outline, but it was only fleshed out in the live performance. She is experimenting throughout and taking seriously the educated maneuvers that inform her improvisation. "Every music lesson [I] ever took, all the scales [I] ever learned, the people happy for [me] sitting in that room—[it was] total elation" (Hathaway as told to Roy Trakin, "Making 'Something' "). This the final element of this unfinished science, the Jubilee that forced the drummer away from his drums and moved the bassist up into the air. Elation was the happiness of her being and those around her; the collaborative risks and rewards of play; the smiles (and tears) of those who heard and continue to hear her possible impossible.

I knew that it was joy when the teardrop traced my jawline. My inability to inhale made more space for Aretha's voice, which continued to swell in size and impact. She again entered a rollcall of musicians who created a moment—an experience—from air. Their sounds are not born of a rigid formula but rather an experiment in which the highs and lows of success or failure are mutually designed. Their talents facilitate this encounter, but they do not define it. We are all participating, bringing the expectations and energies that might cause a change in the program or a vocal leap where it otherwise would have been still. She/they coax us into alternative affective registers where we might forget that our heartache or trouble is not the only evidence of our being. They convince us that beauty exists and that the impossible of Black life is achievable, even if it may announce itself in ways unanticipated or wayward. Indeed, Hartman theorizes that term in counterpoint with sound. "Wayward," she posits,

> is a *beautiful experiment* in how to live. . . . a practice of possibility at a time when all roads, except the ones created by *smashing out*, are foreclosed. It obeys no rules and abides no authorities. It is unrepentant. It traffics in occult visions of other worlds and dreams of a different kind of life. Waywardness is an ongoing exploration of *what might be*; it is an improvisation with the terms of social existence. (*Wayward Lives*, 228 [emphasis in original])

In these choice moments when wayward musicians experiment and improvise—when they take risks—new knowledges of self, environment, and community are revealed. We willingly follow in the adventures and detours that compel us to welcome the unexpected because it is there that impossible futures are heard, seen, and felt.

Works Cited

DuBois, W. E. B. *Black Reconstruction in America, 1860–1880*. New York: Harcourt, Brace, 1935.

Ellis, M. J. *Why People Play*. Englewood Cliffs, NJ: Prentice-Hall, 1973.

Eidsheim, Nina Sun. *The Race of Sound: Listening, Timbre and Vocality in African American Music*. Durham, NC: Duke University Press, 2019.

Hartman, Saidiya V. *Lose Your Mother: A Journey along the Atlantic Slave Route*. New York: Farrar, Straus and Giroux, 2008.

Hartman, Saidiya V. *Scenes of Subjection: Terror, Slavery, and Self-Making in Nineteenth-Century America*. New York: Oxford University Press, 1997.

Hartman, Saidiya V. *Wayward Lives, Beautiful Experiments: Intimate Histories of Social Upheaval*. New York: W. W. Norton, 2019.

Hathaway, Lalah (as told to Roy Trakin). "Making 'Something': Learn Lalah Hathaway's Special Talent." *Grammy.com*, https://www.grammy.com/interview/the-making-of-lalah-hathaway-and-snarky-puppys-something. Accessed October 6, 2022.

Jubilee Songs: As Sung by the Fisk Jubilee Singers, of Fisk University (Nashville, Tenn.). Under the Auspices of the American Missionary Association. New York: Biglow & Main, 1872.

Lateef, Yusuf. Written communication with professor Michael Dessen, January 18, 2019.

Lewis, George E. "Too Many Notes: Computers, Complexity and Culture in *Voyager*." *Leonardo Music Journal*, vol. 10, 2000, pp. 33–39.

Micallef, Ken. "Features: Robert 'Sput' Searight." *ModernDrummer.com*, November 2015, pp. 46–50. https://www.moderndrummer.com/article/november-2015-robert-sput-searight/. Accessed February 7, 2019.

Miller, Paul D., and Vijay Iyer. "Improvising Digital Culture." *Critical Studies in Improvisation*, vol. 5, no. 1, 2009, pp. 225–243.

Redmond, Shana L. *Everything Man: The Form and Function of Paul Robeson*. Durham, NC: Duke University Press, 2020.

Roediger, David R. *Seizing Freedom: Slave Emancipation and Freedom for All*. New York: Verso, 2014.

Sloboda, John A., and Susan A. O'Neill. "Emotions in Everyday Listening to Music." *Music and Emotion: Theory and Research*, edited by Patrik N. Juslin and John A. Sloboda. Oxford: Oxford University Press, 2001, pp. 415–429.

Small, Christopher. *Musicking: The Meanings of Performing and Listening*. Middletown, CT: Wesleyan University Press, 1998.

"Snarky Puppy Feat. Lalah Hathaway—Something (Family Dinner—Volume One)," *YouTube.com*, https://www.youtube.com/watch?v=0SJIgTLe0hc. Accessed December 13, 2018.

Spillers, Hortense J. *Black, White, and in Color: Essays on American Literature and Culture.* Chicago: University of Chicago Press, 2003.

Weheliye, Alexander. "'Feenin': Posthuman Voices in Contemporary Black Popular Music." *Social Text*, vol. 20, no. 2, Summer 2002, pp. 21–47.

Wynter, Sylvia. "'No Humans Involved': An Open Letter to my Colleagues" [1992]. *Forum N.H.I.: Knowledge for the 21st Century*, vol. 1, no. 1 (repr., 1994), pp. 42–73.

Wynter, Sylvia. "Unsettling the Coloniality of Being/Power/Truth/Freedom: Towards the Human, After Man, Its Overrepresentation—An Argument." *CR: The New Centennial Review*, vol. 3, no. 3, 2003, pp. 257–337.

3

Post-Tonal Music and Well-Being

Joy H. Calico

The modern university requires that humanists demonstrate their relevance, which is often determined according to metrics designed primarily for professional schools and STEM disciplines. For music scholars, collaborating with neuroscientists represents one solution to this quandary, in part because neuroscience includes music cognition, the rare area of STEM research that takes music seriously as a line of scientific inquiry. Furthermore, and unlike the humanities, the sciences traffic in data, which is the coin of the neoliberal university realm. If humanists participate in research that generates scientific data, and then use those data in some meaningful way, so goes the argument, we will bolster the credentials of our own grant proposals, legitimize our work, and justify our continued existence on campus.

This was in the back of my mind several years ago, when I observed that music cognition always seemed to use diatonic Western music as the basis for experiments, and I mentioned this to a couple of neuroscientists working in that area. I asked if they knew anyone investigating questions of genuine scholarly interest to me: Why do some people like post-tonal music, and what happens in the body and brain when individuals engage it? Not isolated instances of discrete dissonant *simultaneities*, but segments of post-tonal *music*. My colleagues did not know anyone doing that work at the time and were already committed to other projects. I was incapable of carrying out such an investigation on my own, so I pursued other research interests. From time to time, I perused music cognition scholarship in search of substantial work on post-tonal music, with limited results.

I therefore welcomed the opportunity to address these questions about post-tonal music as part of the Human Flourishing Project. I based my hypothesis not on neuroscientific data, but on decades of experience as a practicing musician, audience member, listener, scholar, and educator: scholarly engagement with post-tonal music can contribute to human flourishing. Positive studies offers a useful framework for my claim. I began theorizing

Joy H. Calico, *Post-Tonal Music and Well-Being* In: *Music and Human Flourishing*. Edited by: Anna Harwell Celenza, Oxford University Press. © Oxford University Press 2023. DOI: 10.1093/oso/9780197646748.003.0004 my position by using several of its concepts: a model for the role of the arts and humanities in human flourishing; positive aesthetics; and eudaimonia.[1] I augmented those with two ideas of my own that I refer to as "openness" and "stretch." I used the relatively small body of music psychology research on *cognition* and post-tonal music as a point of departure for research on *well-being* and post-tonal music, hoping to find a niche at the intersection of positive psychology and musicology. This approach provided some initial traction.

Then Elvira Brattico introduced me to the field of neuroaesthetics, in which some scientists are already working with post-tonal music. Wikipedia describes neuroaesthetics variously as "a relatively recent sub-discipline of empirical aesthetics," and "a field of experimental science that aims to combine (neuro-) psychological research with aesthetics by investigating the 'perception, production, and response to art, as well as interactions with objects and scenes that evoke any intense feeling, often of pleasure.'" (https://en.wikipedia.org/wiki/Neuroesthetics). It is certainly new to North America; the first Neuroaesthetics Research Center in the United States opened at the University of Pennsylvania in 2018.

In a 2019 article, Brattico and her colleagues provided rationales for their neuroaesthetic research that confirmed my impressions as outlined above: most studies use Western tonal art music and exclude other kinds of music (non-Western, atonal) and therefore the data are necessarily incomplete.[2] Increased scientific interest in "the cognitive, affective, and neural correlates of music listening" has focused on the role of emotions or on the similarities between music and language, but not on questions of aesthetics (Mencke, Omigie, Wald-Fuhrmann, and Brattico 2). They based their work on excerpts of atonal music rather than discrete dissonant sonorities, and generated the all-important scientific data. It seems, then, that the fault lay not with music cognition, but with me. I had been seeking interlocutors in the wrong subfield of neuroscience.

Although the arts and humanities are frequently lumped together, this chapter distinguishes between music-*making* (the arts), also known as musicking, and the academic study of music (the humanities), although the

---

[1] Positive psychology's argument in favor of collaboration between the humanities and sciences is articulated in James O. Pawelski, "Bringing Together the Humanities and the Science of Well-Being" (207–216). Regarding the three concepts listed, see Tay, Pawelski, Keith (215–225); Felski, *Uses of Literature*; and Pawelski, "What Is the Eudaimonic Turn?" (1–26).

[2] See Mencke, Omigie, Wald-Fuhrmann, and Brattico (1). Expanding the types of music used in experiments could also support attempts to decolonize musicology's methods and objects of study.

former may be a constituent of the latter.[3] The notion that musicking can contribute to general human flourishing has become conventional wisdom, as noted in various chapters of this volume, and as outlined most succinctly by Jonathan Coopersmith. Advocates of music performance, like Wendy Heller (see Chapter 7), have successfully leveraged the eudaimonic argument, touting the cognitive benefits of playing an instrument and the social benefits of performing in an ensemble as factors in lifelong learning and holistic well-being, to say nothing of the fact that most humans seem to derive pleasure from listening to one kind of music or another. Even parents who have economic anxieties about children majoring in music may be supportive of extracurricular musical activities, or pay tuition to fulfill a general education arts requirement by playing in an ensemble.

The idea that rigorous intellectual engagement with music (the humanities) might also contribute to general human flourishing, as described in this volume's Introduction, is less commonplace, but equally important. The notion that humanistic engagement with *post-tonal music* could be beneficial in its own way is probably even less widespread, for reasons I will examine below. This engagement may take the form of consumption, study, and critique in activities like reading, listening, writing about, analyzing, watching, and playing music. Since experiments in music cognition and neuroaesthetics tend to treat sensory perception in the form of conventional hearing, one advantage to emphasizing the benefits of humanistic engagement with music is that it offers a less ableist entrée into well-being via music.[4] This chapter draws on my own experience and uses scholarship from music cognition, positive studies, and neuroaesthetics to argue that humanistic engagement with post-tonal music can contribute to well-being.

Challenges

There are several challenges in bringing together the humanities and the sciences. There are very real, systemic obstacles that prohibit genuine research partnerships in which humanists and scientists contribute and benefit

---

[3] See Small, *Musicking*. My distinction in no way minimizes the intellectual demands and benefits of musicking, nor does it imply that there is no overlap between musicking and humanistic engagement with music. The distinction serves to focus the scope of this particular chapter.

[4] On music, ableism, and hearing, see Holmes, "Expert Listening beyond the Limits of Hearing: Music and Deafness" (171–220).

equally. These obstacles are endemic to the disciplinary training, tenure criteria, and funding models of academic institutions. The peril facing the author who goes it alone and fails to master both the humanistic and scientific literature is evident in a piece like "Schoenberg, Serialism and Cognition: Whose Fault if No One Listens?" by science writer Philip Ball. His opening gambit is to attribute the notorious title of the article "Who Cares if You Listen," to the author, composer Milton Babbitt, without acknowledging Babbitt's claim that the editor was responsible for changing the title from "The Composer as Specialist" in hopes of generating the 1958 equivalent of clickbait (Babbitt 38–40, 126–127).[5] The lack of nuance undermines Ball's credibility with music scholars. As a humanist, I fear similar scientific missteps in the present chapter.

Another potential obstacle is the usage of key terminology. Mencke et al. are primarily concerned with distinguishing the music that has long dominated psychological and neurological scientific research (which they refer to as "tonal music," or TM) from "atonal music" (AM), the term they use to describe music without a tonal center composed since "around 1911" (Mencke et al., n1, 2). I refer to the plethora of non-diatonic Western musical styles that have proliferated since 1908 as *post-tonal* rather than atonal, as this term is more inclusive and less encumbered by some of the baggage of the latter, although I suspect that many of their findings will still apply.[6]

Why Post-Tonal Music?

Much of the music I research and teach as a musicologist is post-tonal. So is a lot of the music I listen to and perform for fun (but by no means all). I have had an affinity for post-tonal music since I was a teenager and bonded with kindred spirits over that at university. That said, I recognize that my experience is far from universal, even among classically trained musicians. Many are reluctant to study, listen to, and perform this repertoire. I am particularly sympathetic to vocalists, as those of us without perfect pitch can find this repertoire quite daunting to sing. Yet I frequently have the sense

---

[5] Regarding his claim that his editor was responsible for the title, see Anthony Tommasini, "Finding Still More" (H39).

[6] Some music theorists define post-tonality more narrowly; see Joseph N. Straus, *Introduction to Post-Tonal Theory*. Others take a more capacious view closer to my own, such as Stefan Kostka, *Materials and Techniques of Post-Tonal Music*.

that, even among some quarters of the academy, the resounding (re)turn to diatonicism in American contemporary art music is perceived as confirmation that the tyrannical reign of atonality in the academy has ended,[7] and evidence that the long arc of music history bends ineluctably toward tonality as the natural sonic world order.[8] It is beyond the scope of this chapter to address the potential cultural bias inherent in the assumption that tonality is natural and universal when many non-Western musics use other scales and compositional systems.[9] Some scientists argue that culturally specific musics are in fact all rooted in a few universal traits, including a preference for consonance, but consonance is not equivalent to tonality (Carterette and Kendall 725–791; Fritz et al. 573–576).[10]

In 1896 the physician and physicist Hermann von Helmholtz wrote that "the modern system [of tonality] was developed not from a natural necessity, but from a *freely chosen* principle of style; that beside it, and before it, other tonal systems have been developed from other principles" (quoted in translation in Steege 284). Nevertheless, variants of the theory that "because tonality is natural atonality must be unnatural" are remarkably persistent. Andrew Timms summarizes Brian K. Etter's metaphysical interpretation of tonality as "a metaphor of teleological order: it represents the nature of the cosmos and the goodness of existence in the world, all resolved into a unity," while "atonality denies the goodness inherent in tonal order" (Timms 17). Leonard Bernstein took an essentialist approach when he stated that it was even difficult for Arnold Schoenberg to "maintain his atonality, because of the innate tonal drive we all share universally" (273). For decades, composer Fred Lerdahl has used empirical psychology to argue that the human brain requires music that is organized according to certain principles or compositional constraints in order for cognition to function properly—constraints

---

[7] Joseph N. Straus made a data-driven case against the ostensible hegemony of atonality in the academy in "The Myth of Serial 'Tyranny'" (301–343). Anne C. Shreffler countered that statistics cannot measure prestige or perception, and argued that if he had combined atonal and serial styles in a single category, as listeners are apt to do, the results would have been different (30–39).

[8] Björn Heile observes something similar about the period in which postmodern music appeared to supplant modernist music. "It is hard to dispel the suspicion that for many musicologists the attraction of postmodernism lay primarily in its seeming to offer an intellectual cover for anti-modernist sentiment: all of a sudden the familiar, basically conservative, resentment against modernism sounded fashionable, up to date and even ideologically progressive." Heile, "Introduction" (1–12; here, 1).

[9] See Ronald Radano and Tejumola Olaniyan, eds., *Audible Empire: Music, Global Politics, Critique* and especially the chapter by Kofi Agawu, "Tonality as a Colonizing Force in Africa" (334–355).

[10] See also C. J. Stevens, "Music Perception and Cognition: A Review of Recent Cross-Cultural Research" (653–667).

that essentially boil down to tonality and metric regularity with little regard for acculturation, learning, exposure, or openness (Lerdahl, "Cognitive Constraints").[11] In the realm of aesthetics, the philosopher Diana Raffman recently made the assertion that "a composer cannot intend to communicate pitch-related musical meaning by writing twelve-tone music. . . . To that extent, twelve-tone music is fraudulent, and so not art" (86).[12]

Those of us with an affinity for post-tonal music may be the minority, but we do exist. My personal, non-scientific observation is that we do not suffer ill effects from prolonged and repeated engagement with post-tonal music, whether in the form of musicking or humanistic study, but actually find such engagement pleasurable in a variety of ways (of more below). The existence of this subset of the population challenges the arguments articulated above that post-tonal music is a threat to goodness, contradicts an innate human tonal drive, is incomprehensible, and fraudulent. Whether an affinity for post-tonal music is due to training, acculturation, exposure, inherent preference, openness, or other factors is the question. Quite apart from my own curiosity, however, it behooves us as music educators to consider how post-tonal music might contribute to human flourishing.[13]

Music Cognition and Post-Tonal Music

"Music cognition" does not have an entry in the *Grove Dictionary of Music and Musicians*. Instead, it receives extensive coverage in the 2013 entry for "music psychology," which Harold Fiske and Jack Heller define as "a subdivision within *music education* that focuses on the perceptual, cognitive, and affective nature of musical learning, and research-based pedagogy concerning music listening, performance, and creativity [emphasis added]."[14] They assert that the biggest challenge in the area of cognition research generally is the design of external measures that adequately reflect what is happening in the brain, and they identify three promising lines of inquiry. These are the relationship between music and language (psycholinguistics);

---

[11] For a critique of Lerdahl's work see John Croft, "Musical Memory."

[12] For a rejoinder, see Walter Horn, "Tonality, Musical Form, and Aesthetic Value" (201–235).

[13] It is noteworthy, though beyond the scope of this chapter, that post-tonal music is often employed in movie soundtracks, where a much larger swath of the population seems to not only tolerate but enjoy it.

[14] https://doi-org.proxy.library.vanderbilt.edu/10.1093/gmo/9781561592630.article.A2267271 consulted July 6, 2019.

"neurophysiological examinations of brain activity that takes place during music listening"; and a comparative approach between musical cultures, which acknowledges the Western tonal bias to which I referred above, but does not distinguish between tonal and post-tonal musics within Western repertoires. *The Routledge Companion to Music Cognition* also situates its subject in psychology ("addresses fundamental questions about the nature of music from a psychological perspective"); but, unlike Fiske and Heller, it makes no mention of the discipline of music education. Instead, it emphasizes its most scientific credentials, encouraging "readers to understand connections between the laboratory and the everyday in their musical lives." The index contains no entries for "atonality," "post-tonal," or "nontonal," and the entry for "dissonance" directs the reader to "see [the entry for] consonance and dissonance," suggesting that dissonance exists only as an aberration to consonance and is simply awaiting resolution.

To this non-expert seeking to understand the human experience of post-tonal music, it appears that nearly all the empirical research in music cognition is based on hearing and playing tonal music (and this was confirmed by Mencke et al.). I knew based on participant-observer experience that many listeners experience hearing and playing post-tonal music very differently from tonal music, so I did not think it reasonable to extrapolate from the findings of tonally based research to answer post-tonal questions. The assumption that music should be consonant, and harmonically and melodically intelligible upon first hearing, is common among casual listeners and trained musicians alike. The expectation is that music should be predictable within certain parameters and conform to the rules of tonality. These conventions apply equally to common-practice art music and to most folk and popular music in the West, which means that even casual listeners who have grown up in Western cultures know them. Even if they lack the formal training to articulate these expectations, listeners are acculturated to them, can anticipate and recognize the patterns, and experience a degree of satisfaction when the music behaves as predicted. The power, prevalence, and signification of these expectations is not to be underestimated, yet awareness of this bias does not seem to inform all music cognition scholarship.[15]

My search for data-driven scholarship on post-tonal music in the area of music cognition unearthed numerous studies on the perception of consonance and dissonance (I also searched using the term "atonal music," since

---

[15] See, for example, Stouten, Gilissen, Camps, and Tuteleers (189–195).

that is more common). Such studies focus on isolated sonorities, such as individual chords with no musical context, rather than large-scale non-tonal musical passages. To this outsider, it appears that this is what the available tools do well, and research questions are formulated accordingly. The event-related potential (ERP) model, measured through electroencephalography (EEG), is well suited to this kind of research. Another widely used method is single-unit recording, which measures electro-physiological responses in single neurons. Musicologist Roni Y. Granot's review of *The Cognitive Neuroscience of Music* summarizes a study using the latter (albeit applied to cats rather than humans):

> Part III, "The Neurons of Music," consists of three chapters dealing with relatively low-level processing. M. Tramo, P. Cariani, B. Delgutte and L. Braida (ch. 9), tackle the age-old question of consonance versus dissonance. They suggest that consonance is more than a lack of disturbing rough sensation (as ascribed to dissonance). Using single cell recordings (in cats) they provide evidence that consonant intervals create a clear representation, not only of the fundamentals and all or most partials underlying the interval, but also of implied harmonically related pitches akin to Rameau's *bass fondamentale*, which could possibly serve as a basis for Western harmony. In contrast, dissonant intervals create irregular distributions of firing patterns that contain unclear information regarding the constituent components of the interval, with no clear representation of related bass notes. This difference between dissonant and consonant intervals is proposed as a complementary explanation to the traditional roughness based accounts of dissonance. (Granot 453–461)

Elsewhere, Gavin M. Bidelman and Ananthanarayan Krishnan measured frequency-following responses (FFRs) in human non-musicians using "nine musical intervals that varied in their degree of consonance and dissonance." Their experiments indicated that "brainstem neural mechanisms mediating pitch processing show preferential encoding of consonant musical relationships and, furthermore, preserve the hierarchical pitch relationships found in music, even for individuals without formal musical training." They infer from these findings that "basic pitch relationships governing music may be rooted in low-level sensory processing and that an encoding scheme that favors consonant pitch relationships may be one reason why such intervals are preferred behaviorally" (13165–13171).

These studies seem to support the conventional wisdom that Western tonal music is the natural and inevitable world order, but the research is based on neural responses to hearing discrete simultaneities without any musical context. These are not studies of responses to *music*. The results are interesting in their own right, but they do not get any closer to discovering why some people like post-tonal music and what happens in our bodies and minds when we engage with it, either by listening or by other means, or to testing my hypothesis that post-tonal music can contribute to human flourishing.

A third example is the work of Nicola Dibben, a scholar of music and psychology, who ran two experiments using atonal music. She wanted to determine "whether listeners hear atonal music in terms of structural stability at all" and "which factors contribute to the creation of this stability" (269). The first experiment used mm. 1–4 of Schoenberg's Six Piano Pieces Opus 19 no. 3, and the second used a chord sequence derived from the first movement of Anton von Webern's Cantata no. 1 Opus 29. The musical materials were then fragmented, and subjects heard the excerpts in Musical Instrument Digital Interface (MIDI) format to prevent them from using performers' choices to interpret structure. She based her work on the generative theory of tonal music (GTTM), put forth by composer Fred Lerdahl and linguist Ray Jackendoff. GTTM presents "a formal description of the musical intuitions of a listener who is experienced in a musical idiom" based on the premise that trained listeners understand tonal music according to four hierarchical systems: grouping, meter, time-span reduction, and prolongational reduction (awareness of patterns of tension and relaxation) (1). The trained listener is key, because that training alters brain function. Alluri et al. have shown that, in a naturalistic listening situation, "musicians automatically engage neural networks that are action-based while non-musicians use those that are perception-based to process an incoming auditory stream" (2955).

Dibben determined that experienced "listeners do infer the relative structural importance of events" (Alluri et al. 292). I was intrigued but ultimately found the experiments unsatisfying for my purposes for two reasons. First, the musical excerpts were fragmented and performed on a MIDI rather than the instruments for which the music was originally scored. Second, measuring responses to atonal music using a structural listening model designed for and based on tonal music strikes me as problematic. As Rose Subotnik and others have observed, that is not the only way to listen, and wielding structural listening as the universal "yardstick of aesthetic (and moral) value" for all musics and listeners deprives us of the full range of musical experience and community (Dell'Antonio 1). Similarly, Brattico observes that "the predominant topics and models within cognitive neuroscience of music leave little space to aesthetic processes such as evaluative judgments, appreciation, and taste formation" (3).

Positive Studies and Post-Tonal Music

Three concepts from the positive studies literature have been particularly useful. First, I began with the conceptual model for the role the arts and humanities might play in the science of human flourishing as proposed by Tay, Pawelski, and Keith (215–225). They identify subjects of interest and then devise a model based on modes of engagement, activities of involvement, and four mechanisms that they predict will lead to positive effects: immersion, embeddedness, socialization, and reflectiveness. The mechanisms are "reactions to, or psychological experiences arising from, the modes of engagement and activities of involvement within the arts and humanities" (4). The mechanisms are also the means and conditions that facilitate collective or communal flourishing. For my purposes, as noted above, I separate the musicking (artistic) component from the humanistic enterprise. I propose three modes of engagement with non-tonal music as a humanistic undertaking—consumption, study, and critique—as well as several attendant activities of involvement: reading, listening, writing, analyzing, watching, and playing an instrument.[16] Tay, Pawelski, and Keith tend to focus on engagement with music in the forms of playing instruments and composing, and I refer to those only inasmuch as they support scholarly engagement (the humanities) in order to separate them from the domains of performance and composition (the arts).

The three modes of consumption, study, and critique are fundamental to scholarly engagement with any music. For maximum benefits with regard to post-tonal music, I expect that these modes need to be engaged repeatedly and frequently, which is to say both in brief, concentrated periods and over time, in isolation and in conjunction with one another. Consumption may

---

[16] The modes of engagement and activities of involvement are from Tay, Pawelski, and Keith (3). They attribute the modes of engagement to Dudley and Faricy (eds.), *The Humanities*. They attribute the activities of involvement to Davies, *The Philosophy of Art*; Harpham, "Finding Ourselves" (1–26); and Mathae and Birzer, *Reinvigorating the Humanities*.

take the form of listening or, when possible, score reading. There is value in undertaking them separately as well as simultaneously. An attitude of open-mindedness, an awareness of one's assumptions about tonal and post-tonal music, a willingness to stretch—these are all prerequisites that will increase the likelihood of positive outcomes; they may also be examples of flourishing outcomes.[17] This is particularly the case when it comes to listening as a mode of consumption, which is more often emotionally fraught than the other modes of study or critique. Not surprisingly, listening is the aspect of musical experience that has received the most scientific attention. The other two modes (study and critique) tend to be less emotionally fraught and are probably the means by which even those who do not initially express an aesthetic preference for non-tonal music may find pleasure in the repertoire. Study and critique are also more accessible to non-hearing persons as a mode of engagement than listening.

All these modes and activities "have different well-being effects on those participating in them" (Brattico, Bogert, and Jacobsen 3). Classically trained musicians who have mastered structural listening skills to engage with tonal music may need to learn to let go of some of those expectations (in fact, individuals with no such training may be at an advantage). Instead of thinking of non-tonal music as an obstacle, or a privation, a mindset of open-ness allows one to hear, read, analyze, write about, and play as an opportunity to prioritize other musical elements, sometimes described as surface characteristics, such as timbre, gesture, rhythm, tempo, and dynamics. Perhaps this kind of listening can be described as rhizomatic, which is to say non-hierarchical, heterogeneous, and post-structural.[18] What are the benefits of allowing oneself to prioritize listening to musical elements other than the patterns of melodic repetition and harmonic development? In addition to allowing one to attend to non-tonal music differently, the cultivation of such a skill in and of itself is a positive outcome because it has implications for listening to tonal music as well.

The model for engaging post-tonal music in Figure 3.1 is derived from that put forth in Tay, Paewlski, and Keith. I have adapted it by adding the

---

[17] Openness and stretch are akin to attitude, intentionality, affective forecasting, and focus, all of which are crucial to aesthetic experience (Brattico, Bogert, and Jacobsen 206). See also Brattico, Brattico, and Vuust 128–130.

[18] See Denise Gill, who builds on Deleuze and Guattari in her *Melancholic Modalities: Affect, Islam, and Turkish Classical Musicians* (Oxford: Oxford University Press, 2017).

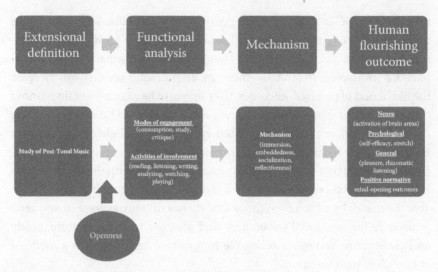

Figure 3.1. Model for Engaging Post-Tonal Music

mindset of openness as a prerequisite to modes of engagement and activities of involvement.

Second, literary scholar Rita Felski developed the concept of "positive aesthetics" as a counterbalance to critical theory's tendency to operate from a position of suspicion and negativity. Responding to Paul Ricoeur's call for a "hermeneutics of affirmation," her model champions four positive uses of literature: recognition, enchantment, knowledge, and shock (Felski 22). Put another way, these uses—which amount to rationales for the study of literature—are different experiences of pleasure, and pleasure is a contributing factor in well-being.

I recognize all four of these experiences as reasons I listen to and study music. I propose a fifth fundamental use or rationale: *stretch*, which may either stand alone or produce one of the other four. I use "stretch" to refer to the process of challenging and overcoming one's own resistance to something unfamiliar—in this case, post-tonality. It may take two forms, both of which can give pleasure. The acquisition, mastery, and deployment of knowledge and skills for engaging non-tonal music through study and critique can be a source of satisfaction and confidence (self-efficacy); and the experience of attending to non-tonal music (consumption) can result in pleasure, in the form of one or more of Felski's four foundational uses (recognition, enchantment, knowledge, and shock). It is possible to have one without the other. Competency can be its own reward, even if one never develops a preference for a post-tonal sonic aesthetic.[19] It is also possible to cultivate the ear so that listening to non-tonal music is a pleasurable experience without developing a profound technical and historical knowledge of tone rows or total serialism, and to commit deeply to the non-aural modes of engagement and activities of involvement.

Therefore, *stretch* can refer both to the process of achieving mastery and to the state of having done so, which requires willingness to exceed one's current level of skill and comfort, a prerequisite for personal growth in any domain; each can be a source of pleasure. It can also refer to the experience of challenging and overcoming one's own deeply engrained preconceptions, and to the state of having done so—in this case, preconceptions about how music should sound. Evolutionary psychologists have argued for an evolutionary function in this process, whereby the use of music for cognitive stimulation and the exploration of novel acoustic experiences are considered to be adaptive (Fitch 17–34; Snowdon, Zimmremann, and Altenmüller 17–34).

Third, as a subset of the humanities, musicologists might consider how a eudaimonic turn could benefit us generally. Not only from a crude instrumental perspective (justify our worth to the neoliberal university by adopting the language of wellness and the sciences, thereby securing our disciplinary survival and livelihood),[20] but also from an intellectual perspective (as a line of scholarly inquiry that produces new knowledge, thus contributing to human flourishing) and even a human one. What Pawelski describes as the eudaimonic turn elsewhere in the humanities is simply a movement in which "well-being is explicitly acknowledged" as a central value (Pawelski "Bringing Together," 208). With regard to post-tonal music in particular, I have tried to show that the previous two concepts from positive studies (the model for the arts and humanities in human flourishing, positive aesthetics) can be leveraged to make the case for its role in well-being.

Neuroaesthetics and Post-Tonal Music

If positive studies offers the best path toward testing the hypothesis that humanistic engagement with post-tonal music can contribute to human

---

[19] Regarding a model for cognitive mastery, see Leder and Nadal (443–464).

[20] Alejandro Madrid (Chapter 5 of this volume) discusses in greater depth than I can go into here the links between neoliberalism and positive psychology with regard to the field of music.

flourishing, neuroaesthetics may be the best hope for answering my original questions: Why do some people like post-tonal music, and what happens in the mind and body when we engage with it? Brattico describes music neuroaesthetics as "a paradigm shift from neuroimaging studies focused exclusively on music perception, cognition, and emotion to studies that consider aesthetic responses such as liking, preference, and aesthetic judgments" (1). Second, researchers have developed a technique for measuring responses to entire pieces of music rather than isolated sonorities and miniscule segments, which addresses one of my frustrations with the music cognition literature I have read (Poikonen et al. 58–73). Finally, they have already begun studying human engagement with atonal music because "there is still a need to stress the importance of an approach that treats music purely as art, by encompassing arguably the most innovative, experimental and challenging of musical styles, namely 20th–21st-century art music" (Mencke et al. 2). The refreshing innovation is that, unlike some of the research discussed above, they do not take the lack of predictability in the music or a listener's inability to discern patterns therein as problematic. Instead, they accept that it is possible for the experience of uncertainty to be a source of pleasure (Mencke et al.).

Mencke et al. provide a valuable summary of the state of empirical research in atonal music, noting that there has been little behavioral work on perceptual and cognitive processing and even less research in neuroscience (4–5). They observe that an information theoretical perspective has proved useful going all the way back to music philosopher Leonard Meyer, and ground their hypotheses about deriving pleasure from AM in that theory.[21] The key clarity and pulse clarity functions from the MIRtoolbox for Matlab allowed them to describe music with quantitative and automated methods because the MIR (Music Information Retrieval) approach has "clear quantification of features over time" (Mencke et al. 5). Parameters are established based on analysis of a corpus of 100 pieces of music (50 TM, 50 AM), and AM pieces selected that are both atonal and ametric because they exhibited a higher degree of structural complexity and density, and contrast most strongly with TM pieces.

Although we use different language to describe why and how individuals might derive pleasure from encountering post-tonal/atonal music, I was

---

[21] The current literature they use includes Pearce, *The Construction and Evaluation of Statistical Models*; and Huron, *Sweet Anticipation*.

struck by the degree of conceptual overlap. They divide their mechanisms into three categories of factors: person-related, extrinsic, and intrinsic. Among the person-related factors, they propose that individuals with a preference for AM may score high in "openness to experience, novelty-seeking, and preference for complexity," which I correlate to my prerequisite of openness (Mencke et al. 10). With regard to extrinsic factors, they posit that aesthetic framing, attention, and cognitive mastering are vital to a positive experience, and I understand the latter to be similar to my notion of competence in the model for the role of the humanities in human flourishing (Mencke et al.) Among intrinsic factors, they suggest that increased exposure (the mere exposure effect) and what I would call comfort level with unpredictability are key since tonal music is both predictable and the music most people already know. In the model above, I argued that repeated exposure would be vital to positive outcomes.

Conclusion

The research in positive studies and neuroaesthetics that is most relevant to my questions and to testing my hypothesis is still theoretical and has yet to produce all the data for which I began this quest in the first place. My hope is that, having found colleagues with overlapping interests and complementary skills, we may be able to collaborate on research that can expand the scope of investigation from hearing to other aspects of humanistic engagement with post-tonal music: reading, listening, writing about, analyzing, watching, and playing music.

Works Cited

Agawu, Kofi. "Tonality as a Colonizing Force in Africa." *Audible Empire: Music, Global Politics, Critique*, edited by Radano, Ronald, and Olaniyan, Tejumola. Durham, NC: Duke University Press, 2016, pp. 334–356.

Alluri, Vinoo, Petri Toiviainen, Iballa Burunat, Marina Kliuchko, Peter Vuust, and Elvira Brattico. "Connectivity Patterns during Music Listening: Evidence for Action-Based Processing in Musicians." *Human Brain Mapping*, vol. 38, no. 6, June 2017, pp. 2955–2970.

Ashley, Richard, and Renee Timmers, editors. *The Routledge Companion to Music Cognition*. New York: Routledge, 2017. https://www.taylorfrancis.com/books/e/9781315194738. Consulted July 18, 2019.

Babbitt, Milton. "Who Cares if You Listen?" *High Fidelity*, February 1958, pp. 38–40, 126–127.

Ball, Philip. "Schoenberg, Serialism and Cognition: Whose Fault if No One Listens?" *Interdisciplinary Science Reviews*, vol. 36, no. 1, March 2011. Available at SSRN: https://ssrn.com/abstract=1817535.

Bernstein, Leonard. *The Unanswered Question: Six Talks at Harvard*. Cambridge, MA: Harvard University Press, 1976.

Bidelman, Gavin M., and Ananthanarayan Krishnan. "Neural Correlates of Consonance, Dissonance, and the Hierarchy of Musical Pitch in the Human Brainstem." *The Journal of Neuroscience*, vol. 29, no. 42, October 21, 2009, pp. 13165–13171.

Brattico, Elvira. "The Neuroaesthetics of Music: A Research Agenda Coming of Age." *The Oxford Handbook of Music and the Brain*, edited by Michael H. Thaut and Donald A. Hodges. Oxford: Oxford University Press, 2018, pp. 364–390; DOI: 10.1093/oxfordhb/9780198804123.013.15.

Brattico, Elvira, B. Bogert, and T. Jacobsen. "Toward a Neural Chronometry for the Aesthetic Experience of Music." *Frontiers in Psychology*, vol. 4, 2013, p. 206. doi: 10.3389/fpsyg.2013.00206.

Brattico, Elvira, Pauli Brattico, and Peter Vuust. "The Forgotten Artist: Why to Consider Intentions and Interaction in a Model of Aesthetic Experience: Comment on 'Move me, Astonish Me . . . Delight My Eyes and Brain: The Vienna Integrated Model of Top-Down and Bottom-Up processes in Art Perception (VIMAP) and Corresponding Affective, Evaluative, and Neurophysiological Correlates' by Matthew Pelowski et al." *Physics of Life Reviews*, vol. 21, 2017, pp. 128–130. doi: 10.1016/j.plrev.2017.06.014.

Carterette, E. C., and R. A. Kendall. "Comparative Music Perception and Cognition." *The Psychology of Music*, 2nd ed., edited by D. Deutsch. San Diego: Academic, 1999, pp. 725–791.

Croft, John. *Musical Memory, Complexity, and Lerdahl's Cognitive Constraints*. Master of music thesis, The University of Sheffield, 1999.

Davies, Stephen. *The Philosophy of Art*. Malden, MA: Blackwell, 2006.

Dell'Antonio, Andrew. "Introduction: Beyond Structural Listening?" *Beyond Structural Listening? Postmodern Modes of Hearing*, edited by Andrew Dell'Antonio. Berkeley: University of California Press, 2004, pp. 1–12.

Dibben, Nicola. "The Perception of Structural Stability in Atonal Music: The Influence of Salience, Stability, Horizontal Motion, Pitch Commonality, and Dissonance." *Music Perception: An Interdisciplinary Journal*, vol. 16, no. 3, Spring 1999, pp. 265–294.

Dudley, Louise, and Austin Faricy, editors. *The Humanities*, 5th ed. New York: McGraw-Hill, 1973.

Etter, Brian K. *From Classicism to Modernism: Western Musical Culture and the Metaphysics of Order*. Aldershot, UK: Ashgate, 2010.

Felski, Rita. *Uses of Literature*. Malden, MA: Blackwell, 2008.

Fitch, W. Tecumseh. "The Biology and Evolution of Music: A Comparative Perspective." *Cognition*, vol. 100, 2006, pp. 173–215.

Fritz, Thomas, Sebastian Jetschke, Nathalie Gosselin, Daniela Sammler, Isabelle Peretz, Robert Turner, Angela D. Fiederici, and Stefan Koelsch. "Universal Recognition of Three Basic Emotions in Music." *Current Biology*, vol. 19, 2009, pp. 573–576.

Gill, Denise. *Melancholic Modalities: Affect, Islam, and Turkish Classical Musicians*. Oxford: Oxford University Press, 2017.

Granot, Roni Y. "Review of R. J. Zatorre and I. Peretz, eds., *The Cognitive Neuroscience of Music* (Oxford: Oxford University Press, 2003)." *Psychology of Music*, vol. 33, no. 4, 2005, pp. 453–461. [The previous edition of this text was entitled *The Biological Foundations of Music.*]

Harpham, G. G. "Finding Ourselves: The Humanities as a Discipline." *An American Literary History*, vol. 25, 2013, pp. 1–26.

Heile, Björn. "Introduction: New Music and the Modernist Legacy." *The Modernist Legacy: Essays on New Music*, edited by B. Heile. Burlington, VT: Ashgate, 2009, pp. 1–12.

Holmes, Jessica A. "Expert Listening beyond the Limits of Hearing: Music and Deafness." *Journal of the American Musicological Society*, vol. 70, no. 1, 2017, pp. 171–220.

Horn, Walter. "Tonality, Musical Form, and Aesthetic Value." *Perspectives of New Music*, vol. 53, no. 2, Summer 2015, pp. 201–235.

Huron, D. *Sweet Anticipation: Music and the Psychology of Expectation*. Cambridge, MA: MIT Press, 2006.

Kostka, Stefan. *Materials and Techniques of Post-Tonal Music*, 4th ed. London and New York: Routledge, 2016.

Leder, H., and M. Nadal. "Ten Years of a Model of Aesthetic Appreciation and Aesthetic Judgments: The Aesthetic Episode—Developments and Challenges in Empirical Aesthetics." *British Journal of Psychology*, vol. 105, no. 4, 2014, pp. 443–464.

Lerdahl, Fred. "Cognitive Constraints on Compositional Systems." *Generative Processes in Music: The Psychology of Performance, Improvisation, and Composition*, edited by J. Sloboda. Oxford: Oxford University Press, 1988, pp. 231–259.

Lerdahl, Fred, and Ray Jackendoff. *A Generative Theory of Tonal Music*. Cambridge, MA: MIT Press, 1983.

Mathae, Katherine Bailey, and Catherine Langrehr Birzer (editors). *Reinvigorating the Humanities: Enhancing Research and Education on Campus and Beyond*. Washington, DC: Association of American Universities, 2004.

Mencke, Iris, Diana Omigie, Melanie Wald-Fuhrmann, and Elvira Brattico. "Atonal Music: Can Uncertainty Lead to Pleasure?" *Frontiers in Neuroscience*, vol. 12, article 979, January 2019, pp. 1–18.

Meyer, Leonard. *Emotion and Meaning in Music*. Chicago: University of Chicago Press, 1956.

"Music Psychology." *Grove Dictionary of Music and Musicians*. 2013. https://doi-org. proxy.library.vanderbilt.edu/10.1093/gmo/9781561592630.article.A2267271. Consulted July 6, 2019.

"Neuroaesthetics." https://en.wikipedia.org/wiki/Neuroesthetics. Consulted June 12, 2019.

Pawelski, James O. "Bringing Together the Humanities and the Science of Well-Being to Advance Human Flourishing." *Well-Being and Higher Education: A Strategy for Change and the Realization of Education's Greater Purpose*, edited by Don Harward. Washington, DC: Bringing Theory into Practice, 2016, pp. 207–216.

Pawelski, James O. "What Is the Eudaimonic Turn?" *The Eudaimonic Turn: Well-Being in Literary Studies*, edited by J. O. Pawelski and D. J. Moores. Madison, NJ: Fairleigh Dickinson University Press, 2013, pp. 1–26.

Pearce, M. T. *The Construction and Evaluation of Statistical Models of Melodic Structure in Music Perception and Composition*. Doctoral dissertation, City University London, 2005.

Poikonen, Hanna, Vinoo Alluri, Elvira Brattico, Olivier Lartillot, Mari Tervaniemi, and Minna Huotilainen. "Event-Related Brain Responses While Listening to Entire Pieces of Music." *Neuroscience*, vol. 312, 2016, pp. 58–73.

Radano, Ronald, and Olaniyan, Tejumola (editors). *Audible Empire: Music, Global Politics, Critique*. Durham, NC: Duke University Press, 2016.

Raffman, Diana. "Is Twelve-Tone Music Artistically Defective?" *Midwest Studies in Philosophy*, vol. 27, no. 1, 2003, pp. 69–87.

Shreffler, Anne C. "The Myth of Empirical Historiography: A Response to Joseph N. Straus." *The Musical Quarterly*, vol. 84, no. 1, Spring 2000, pp. 30–39.

Small, Christopher. *Musicking: The Meaning of Performing and Listening*. Middletown, CT: Wesleyan University Press, 1998.

Snowdon, Charles T., Elke Zimmremann, and Eckart Altenmüller. "Music Evolution and Neuroscience." *Progress in Brain Research*, vol. 217, 2015, pp. 17–34.

Steege, Benjamin. "Helmholtz, Music Theory, and Liberal-Progressive History." *Journal of Music Theory*, vol. 54, no. 2, Fall 2010, pp. 283–310.

Stevens, C. J. "Music Perception and Cognition: A Review of Recent Cross-Cultural Research." *Topics in Cognitive Science*, vol. 4, 2012, pp. 653–667. doi: 10.1111/j.1756-8765.2012.01215.x.

Stouten, Jeroen, Sandra Gilissen, Jeroen Camps, and Chloé Tuteleers. "Music Is What Feelings Sound Like: The Role of Tonal and Atonal Music in Unethical Behavior." *Ethics & Behavior*, vol. 22, no. 3, 2012, pp. 189–195.

Straus, Joseph N. *Introduction to Post-Tonal Theory*, 4th ed. New York: W. W. Norton, 2016.

Straus, Joseph N. "The Myth of Serial 'Tyranny' in the 1950s and 1960s." *The Musical Quarterly*, vol. 83, no. 3, Autumn 1999, pp. 301–343.

Tay, Louis, James O. Pawelski, and Melissa G. Keith. "The Role of the Arts and Humanities in Human Flourishing: A Conceptual Model." *The Journal of Positive Psychology*, vol. 13, no. 3, 2018, pp. 215–255.

Timms, Andrew. "Modernism's Moment of Plenitude." *The Modernist Legacy: Essays on New Music*, edited by B. Heile. Burlington, VT: Ashgate, 2009, pp. 13–24.

Tommasini, Anthony. "Finding Still More Life in a 'Dead' Idiom: Babbitt Has Never Expected His Music to Be Popular but Contrary to Myth, He Does Care if You Listen." *New York Times*, October 6, 1996, p. H39.

4

Can "Old-Fashioned" Approaches to Listening Contribute to Human Flourishing?

Michael Beckerman

This chapter involves one actual experiment, which the reader is free to undertake along with me, and then a series of thought experiments based on it. Here is the experiment: sit down somewhere with something to read—a newspaper, your latest article, a novel, even this chapter. Now put on some music, any piece at all, and read the same passage. You do not need state of the art speakers or headphones, nor is a comfortable chair essential. After reading for a bit, shift your attention and listen carefully to any aspect of the music; it could be following an instrumental line, dissecting harmonic activity, etc.

I have done this experiment many times in many different venues with different groups. Although there is the occasional human subject who will say: "I can never read anything, even if there's a tiny bit of music in the background," this (if true) is very much an outlier response. The vast majority of people can read perfectly well with music in the background. But once the sound is foregrounded, *attended* to, it usually becomes impossible to read anything, or really to have fully conscious thoughts. In fact, one experiences a kind of temporary aphasia. To realize this is somewhat amusing, but also deeply confounding. In my own case, for example, if I am following the oboe line in the first movement of the second Brandenburg Concerto, I cannot read more than one or two words; in order to read, I have to "take my ear off" the concerto, and then, of course, I can read perfectly well.

What such a thing strongly suggests is that there are different physiological processes engaged depending on where we concentrate our mental energy, and that, to a certain extent, this involves both different parts of our brains and different ways of processing stimuli.

Michael Beckerman, *Can "Old-Fashioned" Approaches to Listening Contribute to Human Flourishing?* In: *Music and Human Flourishing*. Edited by: Anna Harwell Celenza, Oxford University Press. © Oxford University Press 2023. DOI: 10.1093/oso/9780197646748.003.0005

Some of these ideas have already been put to excellent therapeutic use. Neurologists have shown that stroke victims who, even after extensive speech therapy, cannot recover spoken fluence, can "speak" normally by conceiving of their utterances as song (and then gradually modulating that song down to something more "speech-like") (Altenmüller and Schlaug 18–20; La Gasse and Thaut 154–160). There is also a growing and extensive literature on the use of music in various ways involving dementia patients. Both of these worlds of music therapy are to a great extent based on the ideas regarding the relationship between music, certain activities, and parts of the brain. In the case of the stroke victim, the disabled speech centers can be replicated by reference to musical systems; and dementia patients can often participate fluently in musical activity even if speech and cognition seem to be impaired or even completely lacking.

In order to speculate further about how these ideas tie into the notion of human flourishing (itself not necessarily an easy concept to explain), I would like to turn to the question of obsession. "Obsession" is a word we use frequently in ways both simply descriptive and diagnostic. When we use the word to describe, say, repetition in Beethoven or Janáček, we do not usually imply a deep pathology, rather something like an analogy with "strong insistence" (Christiansen). We also tend to understand that such unlike things as worrying when your pet is missing and falling in love may involve obsession in ways that do not represent a challenge to long-term concepts of human flourishing. The word has many meanings, but I will use it in this case in the simple sense of "not being able to stop thinking about something," whatever that "something" is, in such a way that it creates active discomfort.[1] As above, one cannot say automatically whether obsession is good or bad: the deep and ongoing activities of many creative artists, extraordinary chefs, and successful football coaches can be so described. Even so, there are enormous numbers of people whose lives are affected adversely—some more mildly and some profoundly—by obsession. Most of the so-called garden variety mental disorders (known mostly as "neurasthenia" in earlier times) involve obsession, and of course, they are not experienced as garden variety in any way by their sufferers. While obsession is most obvious in so-called obsessive-compulsive disorders, incorporating the word itself into the disorder, it is equally a part of many different types of anxiety, involving such

---

[1] The latest edition of the *Diagnostic and Statistical Manual of Mental Disorders* (DSM-5) defines obsession as "Recurrent and persistent thoughts, urges, or images that are experienced, at some time during the disturbance as intrusive and inappropriate, and that cause marked anxiety and distress."

things as paranoia (someone is following me and I cannot stop thinking about it), catastrophic thinking (the little pimple on my big toe is a malignancy and I cannot stop thinking about it), agoraphobia (I will lose control outside and I cannot stop thinking about it), post-traumatic stress disorder (I cannot stop going back to certain experiences), and panic attacks.

For reasons that we still do not fully understand, something like a tape loop—a "thought loop"—takes over what might in other circumstances be a much more varied and nuanced series of thought patterns, returning the individual to a kind of perpetual discomfort which, again, may be focused on a specific idea, thing, or condition, or may be of a more general nature. Once again, despite an enormous amount of research, and claims of various kinds by medical professionals and pharmaceutical companies, we do not fully understand the biology, etiology, or cultural aspect of such disorders, but it is also likely that the various forms of depression also involve what I am referring to in terms of obsession.

My question then is quite simple: if one can almost immediately move between parts of one's brain, and between radically different capacities of cognition simply by *deciding* to listen in a certain way to a composition, and if the efficacy of using music as a therapeutic tool has been established in several areas, is it also possible that what I have termed "old-fashioned listening" can offer some kind of relief in dealing with obsessive states and therefore increase the chances of what we are calling human flourishing? And here at the outset I would like to make a distinction between this approach and two others.

The first of these involves the more general use of music to provide broad relief, as implied by such lines as the following from the writer, scholar, and concentration camp survivor H. G. Adler: "And so we began to offer our art to the wretched people, so that they could forget for a while the miserable conditions in which they found themselves" (524). Adler is, of course, speaking here about life in the Terezín (Theresiesnstadt) camp, described variously as a ghetto, a transit camp, and a concentration camp. While this is an extreme example, it is based on his sense, and ours as well, that the very presence of music in dark places can be a source of comfort and necessary distraction from negative conditions. At the same time, it should be noted that such lines as those from Shakespeare's *Richard II*, "how sour sweet music is when time is broke and no proportion kept," conjure up situations where music brings no comfort, because a particular condition is thought to be beyond redemption. This other side of Adler's positive viewpoint can also be found in certain concentration camps where it was reported that hospital patients said things like, "just let us croak in peace," when musicians came to play, or even when they could no longer recognize the thing as music at all. We might consider this the polar opposite of music and human flourishing, and this is also important to articulate, for there really are those times when music either causes pain or ceases to have any effect whatsoever on human beings.

A second idea about music's positive effects involves more general ideas around the notion of "mindfulness," suggesting that certain modes of regulated attention can be an important factor in stress reduction. (Bishop 230). The word "mindfulness" itself is broadly used to involve everything from generalized and popularized practices of meditation and concentration to far more rigorous types of mental training with the goal of reducing "cognitive vulnerability to reactive modes of mind that might otherwise heighten stress and emotional distress or that may otherwise perpetuate psychopathology" (Bishop 231). This has a robust history in psychotherapeutic circles, particularly in the past two decades. While it may be possible to describe my concerns as operating somewhat within this broad sphere of mindfulness, the specific goals and effects are somewhat different, as are the demonstrated differences in just what parts of the brain are engaged.

Before exploring the subject of listening as therapy more fully, though, it should be noted that I apply the notion of "cost-benefit" to almost all human conditions. For example, while one might be tempted to state unequivocally that a given mental disorder "works against human flourishing," that would almost certainly be an oversimplification. We note that certain conditions falling under the heading of "mental disorders" can have certain positive ramifications that may contribute to human flourishing in a variety of ways. At the very least, sufferers of anxiety and depression can, depending on circumstances, develop a kind of deep empathy for others that would not have been possible without the experience; and we know that in certain cases, dealing with a mental disorder can create a stronger and more resilient personality. To give an example of this, in a negative way, those of us who have been treated by healthcare professionals who have never themselves experienced the particular condition for which we are undergoing treatment, whether we are speaking here of a broken leg or major depression, may have noted at times the inability of the caregiver to adequately treat the patient because they have no idea what it *feels* like to experience a particular kind of pain or discomfort. So, while the vast majority of human beings would adamantly reject the idea of ever *choosing* to suffer from certain conditions, we understand that there are those who recognize the positive aspects of having experienced those conditions.

Considering a related issue, avid readers of artist biographies routinely note that certain kinds of setbacks, anxieties, depressions, and broadly speaking, anguish experienced by their subjects are invoked as a causal factor in adding dimension, depth, and variety to an artistic palette, whether we are speaking of the work of Van Gogh, the poetry of Sylvia Plath, or the music of such figures as Beethoven, Schumann, and Mahler. While it is almost impossible to argue this on a completely empirical basis, life experiences we would consider "negative" can add to the figurative and literal palettes of artists, increasing their affective range.

And yet, even as we note these exceptions, the vast majority of those suffering from such states crave relief, whether or not, in the abstract, they can imagine that the state itself has some value. There are as many ways to treat anxieties and depressions as there are gradations of such things: diet and exercise, talk therapies, traditional psychoanalysis, prescribed medications and other drugs, homeopathic remedies, cognitive therapy; and the list goes on. While some of these are free and wholesome, or at least harmless, others are either quite expensive, or, in the case of certain medications, can have harmful side effects, including everything from sexual dysfunction to dangerous dependencies. Further, although it is the goal of certain types of therapy to ease symptoms by identifying and treating so-called underlying causes, we still understand little about how traumas, for example, actually function, and still less about how to "cure" them.

For this reason, I would posit that even a temporary interruption of the tape loop of obsession can bring welcome relief, and also possibly with it, a greater chance for human flourishing. To make clear that which I have already somewhat bluntly implied: since listening to music in a particular manner "takes us out" of the parts of the brain that perform otherwise normal activities, such as reading and conscious thinking, it seems possible that this kind of active listening could play a role in disrupting obsessive thoughts.

But what exactly is this kind of listening, that I refer to as "active" or "linear"? Despite an enormous amount of work on the subject of listening, much about the process remains unknown. Yet a certain part of the education of musicians within many world music traditions involves training in a kind of self-conscious listening. These range from learning the ability to reproduce sounds from written notation to the opposite, transcribing audible sounds into notation, and bring together such things as ear training, sight singing, and various other kinds of theoretical training in such things as harmony and form. As an example of the last named, training in formal listening will usually teach the student a (hopefully) broad range of formal models and practices and give them experience in, once again *consciously* following what are sometimes described as "musical ideas." As indicated above, some of this process is self-conscious in the early stages of training. This is, of course, potentially problematic for one's long-term relationship to sound, because how can one have a deep and full engagement with music if one is consciously "ticking off" what one is hearing? The reality, though, is that just as a violinist learns "positions" on the instrument only to internalize them at a more advanced stage, these listening skills are meant to coalesce into some more natural and less self-conscious process. To conclude this description, it should be made clear that by suggesting this kind of listening as a therapeutic tool, I am not insisting in any way that it is somehow a better, or still less, *the* correct way to listen, or that, indeed, there is any correct way to listen. Rather the argument is that this particular mode of listening does engage the brain in a special way. And once again, I would like to distinguish between one notion of "deep listening" that imagines a listener constantly (and consciously) "ticking off" fully articulated technical details, and what I have in mind, which is a process whereby a listener *attends* to the music without that kind of self-conscious theoretical articulation.

If my hypothesis, then, is correct, that one can get relief by engaging in a certain type of listening, there is a certain irony involved: after all, at the present moment there are many who have argued that this notion of "linear listening" is at the very least outdated, if not symptomatic of all the things about "classical music" we might wish to leave behind, including master narratives of history, narrow notions of formal construction and traditional musical analysis, and two dangerous kinds of separation. First, some might argue that by seemingly locating our relationship to music in the brain, linear listening reinforces a brain/body dichotomy which misrepresents human experience, and second, that such hermetic listening practices, through their very abstraction, reinforce a problematic separation of such things as music and politics. More recently, then, the traditional pedagogical idea of following the abstract *argument* or story of a musical composition closely with, what I suppose we might call "one's ears and brain," has given way to notions of embodied listening (whether one can hear with one's body and what that precisely means is still not entirely clear) and further constructions of "subject position," where such things as race, identity, gender, alterity, subalternity, etc., may determine responses and should be consciously articulated. That this old-fashioned type of listening, often treated in a rather suspect way by newer approaches, could possibly bring relief to certain states of obsession, anxiety, and depression may be, at the least, counterintuitive and challenging. And of course, this type of listening, sometimes considered problematic because of its associations with elite high culture, is not so very distant from the type of concentration required to follow a scholarly article, even an article which might demonize such an approach.

At this point, though, we might ask that, if following an oboe line in a Brandenburg Concerto is somehow like reading a book, why not just read the book? The answer to this is provisional of course, but going back to our first experiment, we engage with musical sound in mental places not only untouched by words, but perhaps untouchable by them. And were we to continue our speculations further, we might posit that it is not only the idea of attending closely to something that "distracts" us, possibly ending the obsessive cycle, or even what part of the brain is involved in the process, but it is also the nature of the substance itself we are tracking.

Part of this inquiry takes us into the realm of music and emotion. For though I have suggested that following an oboe line is something like a rational activity, we still find, both in scientific and lay writing about music, the invocation of *emotion* at the core of our experience with music. We witness this in Shana Redmond's chapter (Chapter 2). And Melvin Butler (Chapter 10) references the effect as a form of transcendence. But definitions of emotion, or even a clear understanding of what the word means, are not easy to come by. In fact, such definitions are generally circular, or simply baffling: it's not clear, in the end, whether an emotion is a "thing" or a concept. One could argue that it doesn't really matter, that we all know what we mean by "emotions," and no sophisticated thinker or investigator ever expects to find a perfect definition of anything. My problem with the word "emotion," though, goes deeper, because there is an implication in most definitions that emotions are "instinctive feelings" that do not have "ideas" somehow embedded within, or that a conscious idea is entirely separate from an emotion, or even that emotions are unmediated reactions, a form of mindless play, more akin to reflexes than considered thought. Yet even if we think we endorse this position, most of us do not actually believe in such a binary view of human experience. Our mental life cannot be reduced to a *Star Trek* episode with Mr. Spock and Captain Kirk talking about emotional Earthlings and rational Klingons.

From this it may follow that the special property of music, offering as it does a powerful combination or integration of what we call the "emotional" and the "rational" (though as above, they are indeed not separate) has the capacity not only to distract us by breaking cycles of obsession, but to do so with enough challenge and complexity to help us maintain a state of engagement for a long enough period of time to disrupt these negative states and replace them with more positive ones. Once again, the "states" which music creates, or replicates, or evokes, or displays, engage the human brain in ways that are neither emotional nor intellectual alone, but in their combination of elements offer at the very least a chance of short-term change in one's sense of being. And if I am correct in these suppositions, a certain kind of close listening may make an important contribution to the flourishing of human beings who otherwise are caught in cycles of fear, anxiety, and despair.

We should also note that just as separating what are sometimes called the rational and the irrational, or the emotional and ideational/intellectual, is deeply problematic, dividing so-called mental disorders into simple levels such as "neuroses" and "psychoses," or "psychotic and non-psychotic" states has its own real dangers. With this caution in mind, though, I do understand that the idea of using concentrated listening as a therapeutic tool may not be appropriate for people suffering from certain serious disorders.

It is one thing, of course, to suggest that this entire process of aural engagement as therapy could be done at home entirely on one's own, and yet another to imagine the presence of a therapist trained in the process. So, as a conclusion, or as more tentative writers sometimes say, in lieu of a conclusion, I should at least offer a fantasy of how such guided therapy might work. As I suggested at the beginning, I am not sure that, say, using a good sound system and offering your patient a comfortable chair actually makes a difference in this procedure, but let us imagine such things anyway. A patient enters the room. The therapist asks several general questions to assess the patient's state of mind (making it clear that this is not in any way a formal psychoanalytic practice). The therapist explains to the patient (or research subject) that they will hear a piece of music, and encourages them to relax. After a few minutes, the therapist explains what "attentive listening" is, and works with the patient to focus attention on musical details, following an instrumental line, listening for specific things. The patient is then asked to articulate aspects of the experience, and on this basis, changes can be made in the instructions given and even the choice of composition. It is not out of the question that some simple pedagogies could be a part of the process. While

I have usually imagined this practice in relation to Western classical music, it is not clear that this repertoire has any claim to special status in these matters, and that the same thing could not be accomplished listening to the Grateful Dead, John Coltrane, or gamelan music. And it is also not out of the question that a skilled practitioner of this as-yet-nonexistent profession, could fine-tune, as it were, the procedure by choosing specific compositions for a given patient.

As Puck says at the conclusion of *A Midsummer Night's Dream*, it may be that this "weak and idle theme" is "no more yielding than a dream." At present there is no proof that my hypothesis that attentive listening can disrupt obsessive cycles in various mental disorders is a viable one. The kinds of disorders may be so varied, both in their type and their intensity, that such generalized speculations are useless. Or further, it may be that millions of people are already using music in this way, without any recourse to the more specialized mode of listening that I outline here. But if our simple experiment at the beginning of this chapter does carry some reality and some weight, and I believe that it does, future studies along these lines may be useful, revelatory, and a positive step in treatment for people whose lives are taken over by patterns of thought they cannot resist.

Works Cited

Adler, H. G. *Theresienstadt 1941–1945: The Face of a Coerced Community*. Cambridge: Cambridge University Press, 2017.

Altenmüller, Eckart, and Gottfried Schlaug. "Music, Brain, and Health: Exploring Biological Foundations of Music's Health Effects." *Music, Health & Wellbeing*, edited by Raymond MacDonald, Gunter Kreutz, and Laura Mitchell. Oxford: Oxford University Press, 2012, pp. 18–20.

Bishop, Scott R. "Mindfulness: A Proposed Operational Definition." *Clinical Psychology: Science and Practice*, Autumn 2004, vol. 11, no. 3, pp. 230–241.

Christiansen, Paul. "On Janáček and Obsession," *ECHO: A Music-Centered Journal*, vol. 8, no. 1, 2006. https://echo.humspace.ucla.edu/issues/on-janacek-and-obsession/

La Gasse, A. Blythe, and Michael H. Thaut. "Music and Rehabilitation: Neurological Approaches." *Music, Health & Wellbeing*, edited by Raymond MacDonald, Gunter Kreutz, and Laura Mitchell. Oxford: Oxford University Press, 2012, pp. 154–160.

PART II
CRITIQUE

5

Understanding Music Studies, Well-Being, and the Humanities in Times of Neoliberalism

Alejandro L. Madrid

I would like to start this chapter with a confession of sorts. When I was invited to participate in the Humanities and Human Flourishing Project (HHF), I was not sure I had anything to contribute to the conversation. I was suspicious of the largely optimistic rhetoric about well-being and human flourishing, because it reminded me of a series of endeavors I was exposed to back when I was a teenager, which I had always been very skeptical about. In the mid-1980s, before I decided to be a musician and many years before I even thought about becoming a musicologist, I spent a year pursuing a degree in communications at the Mexico State campus of the Instituto Tecnológico y de Estudios Superiores de Monterrey (Monterrey Institute of Technology and Higher Studies; ITESM). This is one of Mexico's most prestigious private colleges and also one with a specific history of alignment with practices and ideologies that in Mexico are perceived as "American." For example, ITESM privileged the university as a place for the production of professionals, where one acquires administrative or technological expertise in order to get a job. It is not an institution that values the humanities or encourages the development of critical thinking. Its curricular practices were supposedly based on those of U.S. colleges, and the annual tuition and fees were calculated according to the rate of the U.S. dollar. The historical moment when I attended ITESM is particularly significant: the 1980s was the decade when neoliberal policies began to be applied systematically in Mexico due to pressures from the International Monetary Fund and the World Bank (in response to the devastating economic crisis in the country in the 1970s). I studied at the Monterrey Institute when the college was immersed in the implementation of its Programa Emprendedor (Entrepreneurial Program), a project based

Alejandro L. Madrid, *Understanding Music Studies, Well-Being, and the Humanities in Times of Neoliberalism* In: *Music and Human Flourishing.* Edited by: Anna Harwell Celenza, Oxford University Press. © Oxford University Press 2023.
DOI: 10.1093/oso/9780197646748.003.0006

on the idea that it was "desirable for students to have an entrepreneurial attitude and that their goal should not be to simply occupy a position in an existing company" ("Historia del programa emprendedor," Tecnológico de Monterrey). At the time, I was not exactly sure what bothered me about this rhetoric. It was not that I disagreed with the promotion of a risk-taking mentality. Nonetheless, I felt that transferring the "self-made-man" model that was apparently successful in the United States as an instigator of productivity and wealth was myopic in a country like Mexico, characterized by huge economic gaps and privilege, where having one last name instead of another could make the difference between a life of economic success or a life of struggle.

The second reason for my hesitation to participate in the well-being project was that I felt the language around it was closer to the rhetoric and goals that characterize clinical psychology and the cognitive sciences, rather than the humanities. My negative impression of these fields was informed by my experience with music cognition at the Ohio State University (OSU) when I was a PhD student at the turn of the twenty-first century. In those years, OSU's School of Music was invested in developing a hybrid music cognition/ethnomusicology program where questions about the brain and how we process and make sense of music in biological/neurological ways intersected with ideas about how we make music meaningful within specific cultural frameworks. At the time, I was interested in generative linguistics, especially the cultural overtones in the work of Steven Pinker, and the possibilities that such a weird but potentially productive transdisciplinary move could afford the field excited me.[1] Unfortunately, the actual fruits of this academic marriage did not engage the kind of political and social questions I was interested in and that I felt were urgent to ask in order to make music studies relevant beyond the School of Music. After taking a couple of seminars within the program, I noticed that the way cognitive ethnomusicology was developing, the kinds of questions it was asking, the kinds of hypotheses it was putting forward, and the testing methods it privileged were in many ways reifying the brain; it was almost as if the brain had become the last bastion of positivism in music studies. Like Joy Calico, who discusses non-tonal music and the brain in Chapter 3 of this volume, I was concerned that biased cultural

[1] I was interested in the potential of the ideas expressed in Pinker's *The Language Instinct*, but not in the more problematic essentialist assumptions that led him to publish *The Blank Slate*. See Steven Pinker, *The Language Instinct: How the Mind Creates Language* (New York: William Morrow, 1994); and Steven Pinker, *The Blank Slate: The Modern Denial of Human Nature* (New York: Penguin, 2002).

assumptions were driving much of the research. It seemed to me that the field was obsessed with finding an unlikely "objective truth" about musical meaning. Thus, my hesitation about joining this research project was not only about the celebratory tone in the language used to discuss well-being, it was also about what I felt were the shortcomings of a field that seemed to me to be the natural outlet for these intellectual concerns.

When I realized that the connection between these three, apparently un-related moments in my life—ITESM's rhetoric about efficiency and the self-made man, the essentialist and positivist overtones of cognition as a disciplinary field I encountered at OSU, and the celebratory tone in the rhetoric about well-being—was neoliberalism, things clicked for me. I understood I had something to contribute to this conversation concerning music and human flourishing. With this I do not mean to say that HHF is a neoliberal endeavor. In fact, as James Pawelski states, this project is critical of instrumental uses of the humanities that obstruct their eudaimonic value, prizing instead their "economic value, with sales of music, art, and literature closely tracked to assess their worth as investments or as ways of making a living [or] their entertainment value [where] their absorbing content is taken up by many as a means of rest and relaxation" (Pawelski, "Bringing Together," 208). In that sense, HHF clearly resists neoliberalism's utilitarian interest in the humanities. Nevertheless, my intention here is to warn about places in which rhetoric or argumentation about the project may be in an inadvertent danger of reproducing some of the neoliberal premises it should instead forcefully oppose.

Well-Being, Capitalism, and the Nation-State in the Nineteenth Century

Our modern understanding of the humanities, human flourishing, and well-being have been inextricably connected, in a political and almost utopian way, to the birth of capitalism in the nineteenth century and the establishment of the nation-state as a viable form of organization. A unifying thread behind these ideas and these political and economic entelechies can be found in a particularly cohesive way in G. W. F. Hegel's philosophical system. For the German philosopher, the spirit (*Geist*)—rational and self-determining life—comes to its full realization with the emergence of what makes human beings human: their ability for self-recognition and an awareness of their place in the world through imagination, language, and the understanding and exercising of freedom (Hegel 25). During the nineteenth century, the Industrial Revolution and the birth of modern capitalism began to change attitudes toward work and leisure. People began to consider work as a basic human good and leisure as a path toward personal improvement—at least among the upper and middle classes, who benefited the most from the changing conditions afforded by labor mechanization. These changing attitudes saw the rise of individuals reading, playing, or listening to music, and participating in dilettante philosophical, historical, and artistic circles, as well as a new understanding of these activities not only as pastimes, but as paths into the realization of an individual's full potential. This state of well-being starkly contrasted with the alienating conditions of the working classes from whom, according to F. Engels, the Industrial Revolution had taken their "leisure for healthful work in garden or field, work which, in itself was recreation for them" (Engels 2). Clearly, the right to leisure as an essential constituent of well-being and what makes life worth living, regardless of the specific ethical systems that give value to these leisure activities, is central to discussions about the cultural consequences of the Industrial Revolution and the inception of modern capitalism.

At the same time, the crystallization of the so-called Westphalian system and the growing appeal of the nation-state as a viable form of political organization in Europe, which took place through the end of the nineteenth century, could be read in Hegelian terms as the triumph of a specifically humanistic view of history in which the state comes to replace God as the axis of political, economic, and cultural organization in human societies. If music and other humanities-related endeavors were central to leisure and ideals of human flourishing embraced by the European bourgeoisie in the nineteenth century, the scientific study of the objects that inspire these practices—*Musikwissenschaft*, history, philosophy, literary studies, etc., that is, the humanities—also became central in the validation of the imperialist, colonialist, nationalist, and often xenophobic projects that gave meaning to these new political formations. As Jonathan Coopersmith reveals in his discussion of music and human flourishing in Chapter 1 of this volume, much of the curriculum and cultural assumptions that became inherent in music conservatories grew out of this leisure culture of nineteenth-century Europe.

Of course, many of these disciplines had been around for centuries before the so-called Age of Progress. My argument is that in the development of nineteenth-century nation- and empire-building projects, these disciplines acquired a new political valence. Thus, my intention here is not to take Hegel and Engels's problematic and historically determined philosophical and economic argumentations at face value, but rather to show the important place of the humanities and of human flourishing in nineteenth-century cultural and political projects, epistemologies, and their historical critiques. As such, music practice, as well as music scholarship, have played central roles not only in defining the value and potential of the humanities as a path to human flourishing, but also in reinforcing power structures and dynamics that have systematically dehumanized entire populations.[2]

Music, Music Scholarship, Ideology, and Well-Being

Born out of idealist and romantic epistemes that privileged colonial and civilizatory beliefs regarding what the humanities should accomplish, how they should accomplish it, and who their agents could be, early musicology and music theory emphasized specific aesthetic and philosophical ideals that reflected these criteria—an emphasis on the master and his masterwork, organicism, harmonic complexity, teleology, progress, universalism, Judeo-Christian forms of spirituality, formalism, etc.—and in doing so hinted at a perceived superiority of Western European music over types of musical practice that do not privilege these values. In this context, music scholarship, like many other academic approaches to art and literature, became a propaganda machine for the values and ideologies embodied in Western European musical practice. This propagandistic understanding of the humanities lasted until the end of the twentieth century, when postcolonial and critical scholarship unveiled the performative power of many scholarly fields to reproduce power imbalances inherited from imperialism and colonialism. One could argue that in the case of music scholarship, regardless of the cultural turn in the 1980s, this has lasted well into the twenty-first century, when recent de-colonial calls have argued for the need to overhaul the music education system in response not only to less elitist approaches to musical practice, its meaning and value, but also to the systematic attack against the humanities under neoliberalism.

---

[2] For a review of the development of the "gig economy" in music in the eighteenth and nineteenth centuries and its negative repercussions on individual well-being, see Anna Celenza's Chapter 11 in this collection. A radicalization of this entrepreneurial system has led to the type of precarity neoliberalism that I discuss later in this chapter.

Some of my recent work has reflected on this critical moment in music scholarship.[3] I have argued for an approach to music studies that transcends the limited and narrow episteme that the discipline inherited from nineteenth-century humanities in an attempt to engage the kind of intellectual concerns that have moved other fields in the humanities and social sciences forward and outside of the small intellectual ghettos that nurtured them for over a century. In the case of musicology, the late nineteenth and the first half of the twentieth centuries witnessed the development of the field into an exceptionalist space that discouraged questions about musical value beyond the locus of the production of the musical text, its interpretation, or the specialized aesthetic discourses that surround it. As such, regardless of the fact that music facilitates an aesthetic and affective experience that transcends these formalistic coordinates, musicologists tended to be suspicious of the work on music produced by scholars in other humanities fields. At the end of the twentieth century, these conditions led to the somewhat absurd situation of having a number of parallel bodies of scholarly work about music informed by radically different scholarly values: musicologists centered around European/Western art music and questions about aesthetics; ethnomusicologists focusing on non-Western music traditions and questions about culture; and scholars in sociology, communications, anthropology, history, psychology, ethnic studies, performance studies, literary studies, etc., interested in popular music and everyday life. Although the work of ethnomusicologists and popular music scholars frequently intersected, musicologists largely managed to avoid their scholarly production. The elitism traditionally associated with the humanities rooted in the nineteenth-century propagandistic paradigm allowed musicologists to get away with this type of isolationism. As part of this discussion, I have argued for the need to adopt a transdisciplinary gaze. Instead of simply borrowing methods from other fields to try to answer old disciplinary questions, I would argue that it is vital to decenter our disciplinary perspective in order to be able to conceive of different questions from our objects of study. One way of doing this is by embarking on collaborative transdisciplinary projects that move music scholarship beyond the narrow confines of the discipline so that

---

[3] See Josh Kun and Alejandro L. Madrid, "Exceptional Matters, Exceptional Times: A Conversation about the Challenges of US Music Scholarship in the Age of Black Lives Matter and Trump" (pp. 239–263); Alejandro L. Madrid, "Diversity, Tokenism, Non-Canonical Musics, and the Crisis of the Humanities in U.S. Academia" (pp. 124–129); "American Music in Times of Postnationality" (pp. 699–703); and "Palabras inaugurales del Premio de Musicología Casa de las Américas" (pp. 46–48).

it can better contribute to broad intellectual conversations concerning contemporary humanities and social sciences (including their relevance in our current world). The value of such collaborative endeavors is made clear by Nancy Yunhwa Rao's Chapter 8 in this volume. As she demonstrates, teaming up with scholars whose disciplinary training is different allows scholars to see different things when approaching music or musical practices. These types of collaborative projects are probably the easiest way to provide unique spaces to challenge the shortcomings of our disciplinary training. Nevertheless, one must also try to develop individual research projects with the goal of estranging our academic gazes. It is more difficult to escape the boundaries of the disciplinary formations we have been trained in by ourselves, but one way of doing it is by privileging modes of relating to our objects of study that defy the norms of our academic fields. Concentrating on these experiences may provide ways not only to make unfamiliar our objects of study, but also to estrange our own gaze on them by placing value on ways of aesthetic enjoyment often considered beyond the realm of "objective" academic inquiry. I have proposed that focusing on the affective and emotional experiences that give meaning to musicking and that address questions of well-being at the center of the search for the significance of music as a human experience should be a fundamental aspect of contemporary music scholarship if it is to establish dialogues with other fields in the humanities and social sciences. In fact, this is a premise that resonates deeply with the overall goals of the HHF project.

The Humanities, Music Scholarship, and Neoliberalism

My ideas concerning the intellectual goals of music scholarship resonate with James Pawelski's call for an alliance between the humanities and the science of well-being that would eventually "help the humanities connect with the larger interest of society [and make this] scholarship more informed and more relevant to contemporary debates" (Pawelski, "Bringing Together," 209, 213). Pawelski suggests a eudaimonic turn in the humanities that would place human flourishing at the center of scholarly inquiry. Pawelski's concern is with the crisis of the humanities in academia and their inability "to reactivate links between their practice and the larger interest of a society based on individual freedom and self realization," which he believes to be the cause of declining enrollments and generalized misinformation as to these fields' contribution to contemporary society (Geoffrey Galt Harpham, quoted in Pawelski, "Bringing Together," 208). In making his argument, Pawelski suggests that the eudaimonic turn would also provide a way to "connect powerfully with administrators, funding organizations, government agencies, and the general public" (Pawelski, "Bringing Together," 209). It may not be possible to measure the humanities according to the type of quantitative evaluative methods and efficiency models that the neoliberal turn has made pervasive among administrative units in higher education, bureaucratic agencies, and policymaking bodies. Nevertheless, Pawelski, Louis Tay, and Melissa Keith indicate that recent studies have found "a robust connection between the arts and humanities and human flourishing" and suggest the adoption of a conceptual model for the study of these connections based on the ways in which humans engage with them (Tay, Pawelski, and Keith 1–2). The results are measured in terms of neurological, physiological, and psychological reactions; psychological competencies; subjective, psychological, and physical well-being effects; and positive normative outcomes (ethical, moral, and civic) (Tay, Pawelski, and Keith 5–6). Evidently, this line of argumentation is a direct response to the quantitative models that the neoliberal turn privileges; and although these scholars mean well when seeking to engage the quantitative momentum, I believe that, in the end, the tricky neoliberal overtones in this line of reasoning work against the well-being project they try to advance.

Neoliberalism, as an ideology and an economic tendency, is based on a premise of liberalization that, like the modern humanities, has its origin in the political, social, and epistemological processes that characterized nineteenth-century European culture. Neoliberalism's emphasis on laissez-faire economic liberalism and creatively entrepreneurial free market capitalism has had important repercussions on the understanding of human beings as free-willed individuals and consumers. As Javier León points out, "this new rising economic order was celebrated for allowing individuals to exercise their individual freedom through a rapidly growing array of economic opportunities and consumer choices made available by the rapidly diversifying markets" (131). This celebratory tendency also informs some of the most original and innovative early scholarship on globalization. In *Consumers and Citizens* (2001 [1995]), Néstor García Canclini proposes that, despite the repercussions of neoliberal globalization on traditional rights such as the welfare state, the new cultural dynamics it triggers present individuals with new possibilities to articulate concerns with citizenship based on consumption (45–46). There seems to be a potential correlation between neoliberalism's concerns with economic growth, human freedom, and the potential of citizen's participation through individual agency and consumption, and well-being. Nevertheless, one must always be careful not to uncritically commend the apparent positive repercussions of these kinds of epistemological tectonic moves within the power dynamics that such moves generate economically and politically, and their impact on ideas about race, class, and ethnicity in everyday human relations.

Regardless of the optimistic messages that politicians, economy theorists, and private entrepreneurs delivered at the outset of the implementation of neoliberal policies worldwide in the 1970s and 1980s, the fact is that neoliberalism has generated more inequality and economic gaps between classes than ever before in the history of humanity. One of the contradictions at the core of neoliberalism is that, in order to generate wealth, it promotes the corrosion of the social fabric and collective well-being with the intention to create conditions of economic and social insecurity that foment individual cut-throat competition. Here, the rhetoric about individual freedom and self-realization translates into an every-man-for-himself kind of attitude. Thus, as a system, neoliberalism blossoms because it is able to produce and maintain an underprivileged class, a massively global reserve of individuals willing to work for less than minimum wages in less than human conditions. Therefore, regardless of the optimistic utopian ideas about citizenship through consumption that fueled the imagination of those who embraced the ideology in the 1970s and 1980s, the fact is that the nature of neoliberalism is highly anti-human, as it thrives in human precarity and conflict.[4] These kinds of uncertain conditions and the sense of insecurity and anxiety they generate on individuals have a hugely negative impact on their well-being.[5]

In this scenario, I argue that playing into the data-driven strategy to validate the humanities means reproducing the neoliberal value system and giving up on alternative notions of well-being. The managerial model that neoliberal administrators have slowly forced upon the university system worldwide questions the value of the humanities in utilitarian terms. Reacting to these dynamics, Stanley Fish declared in a rather provocative way that the

---

[4] For more about precarity at the core of neoliberalism, see Alex Foti, *General Theory of the Precariat: Great Recession, Revolution, Reaction* (33–38).

[5] See David Neilson, "Class, Precarity, and Anxiety under Neoliberal Global Capitalism: From Denial to Resistance" (184–201); and Marc Pilkington, "Well-Being, Happiness and the Structural Crisis of Neoliberalism: An Interdisciplinary Analysis through the Lenses of Emotions" (265–280).

humanities had no value. As I have suggested elsewhere, I have always taken this statement as a refusal to engage the managerial model to evaluate the humanities and to evade falling into the trap of utilitarianism in order to validate them (Madrid, "Diversity, Tokenism, Non-Canonical Musics," 129). I propose that, instead of retreating and giving up, this is a moment to counterattack, to be bold about letting everyone know our beliefs in the centrality of the humanities to mediate human civilization and keep under control the neoliberal methods, models, and policies that have already proved to be devastating throughout the world.

Music, Music Scholarship, and Alternatives to Neoliberal Well-Being

The fight against neoliberalism is a fight for well-being and an attempt to support true human flourishing beyond an emphasis on individual achievement and happiness through competition.[6] Thus, rather than reinforcing the type of individualism that Geoffrey Galt Harpham has invoked in his call to make the humanities more relevant, I propose that the humanities' engagement with notions of well-being moves away from these values in order to generate a project that supports alternative notions of well-being rooted in collective flourishing as the basis of human flourishing. James Pawelski notes that the notion of human flourishing is a botanical metaphor that can be used to describe "both individual plants and entire ecosystems" (Pawelski, "The Positive Humanities," 2022). I believe that in order to avoid the perilous alienation of individuals at the core of neoliberalism, one must pay particular attention to the ecosystems alluded to in this metaphor, as no individual can flourish if not in tandem with their ecosystem. In pedagogical music approaches such as the Suzuki method, there is an emphasis on the continuous participation of the community in order to provide a productive environment for children's learning. Parents are called to participate actively in the training of their kids, which often results in the education of the parents themselves. Children play along with their peers in collective weekly lessons, and their first performances in public are not individual showcases, but rather collaborative moments of sharing music with their classmates

---

[6] For a critique of these neoliberal values in the pursue of well-being, see Richard Layard, *Happiness: Lessons from a New Science* (163).

and parents. This environment generates a collective well-being that in turn provides the opportunity for individuals to flourish. It is all about sharing music; it is not about competition. It is about being and flourishing with others. This it-takes-a-village-to-raise-a-musical-child metaphor is probably one of the most powerful descriptions of individual well-being through collective well-being.[7]

Instead of calling for a type of music scholarship that renews, even if inadvertently, the values and ideologies that gave meaning and political valence to the humanities in the nineteenth century—as it does when music programs continue to require undergraduate students to take music history and theory sequences that focus on Western European classical music and canons—I suggest a type of music scholarship that dwells on what happens when music happens (Blau, "More than 'Just' Music"). We should focus on how our listening helps us emotionally co-produce the meaning of any musical experience. This is especially important because the values that attempt to set music and music competence aside in an almost exceptionalist way often reproduce ideas behind oppressing structures in society. An approach centered on the emotional agency of individuals would engage larger intellectual questions in the humanities and social sciences while also articulating issues of well-being central to our affective life with and through music. It is in the production of citizens committed to the public good that the humanities can find an index of their measurability. I am optimistic that in rejecting to engage transdisciplinarity for the sake of measurable neoliberal outcomes, this type of music scholarship can also open the door to identify paths to well-being and flourishing alternative to those traditionally articulated in clinical psychology. Thus, recognizing ideas about well-being coming from environmental science and environmental humanities, decolonial studies, sociology of emotions, or ecomusicology should be a must for this kind of transdisciplinary music scholarship. Focusing on the connections between music, music-making, and listening with the natural world, intimacy, community activism, spirituality, urbanism, and everyday life could help us understand human well-being more holistically, beyond mere physiological parameters, and thus in a manner more in tune with collective well-being, individual emotional development, and human flourishing.

---

[7] Melvin Butler's Chapter 10 in this collection, which touches on free improvisation in music as a way to pursue collective expression, resonates with my emphasis on collective well-being as the foundation of any individual flourishing.

Some of the ideas I have exposed here have serious implications on how we understand society and social relations at large and may be considered utopian, idealistic, or unrealistic. I would argue not only against such easy conceptualizations, but also about the need to avoid giving in to the type of bleak cynicism that reifies postmodern futility in relation to the political in its misconstrued "relativistic drive to abandon ideas about truth and social progress" (Bewes 31). Before outlining how music scholarship and well-being could intersect, I would like to map out three current interconnected intellectual and social battlegrounds. These areas are: the struggle against the perceived crisis of the U.S. higher education system; the challenge that inequality and the reproduction of privilege pose on late-capitalist societies; and the re-evaluation of identity politics as a tool for social progress.

The so-called crisis of the humanities in the United States has become a problem precisely because the university as an institution has uncritically embraced the values of neoliberalism and unintentionally neglected the foundational liberal-arts ideals it should stand for.[8] Thus, the need to reconceptualize what higher education means and should mean in contemporary society, without conceding to the monetary value system that sees it as a means to getting a job, would encounter an ally in an alternative, more collective-oriented notion of well-being that has as one of its aims the education of citizens for a more just, fair, and democratic society. This is the kind of society that would enable human flourishing on an individual level.

Under neoliberal capitalism, the source of oppression for one specific social group may also be the source of wealth and well-being for another. Yet again, talking about well-being in this unequal social and economic scenario is a delusion. A system in which a large percentage of its members have to experience hostile conditions detrimental to achieving human flourishing, in order for a small fragment of that society to experience conditions conducive to well-being, is a system destined to collapse. It will eventually, but unmistakably, lead to a generalized proliferation of the economic and social conditions that would prevent human flourishing. Promoting a communitarian vision of well-being is the only possible way out of a situation that offers no opportunity or reward in the long run.

[8] Wendy Heller's discussion of the development of the changing role of music performance at Princeton University's Department of Music in this collection (Chapter 7) sheds light on certain aspects of the cultural and economic dynamics I analyze here.

So, is it possible to even speak of well-being in societies as polarized as those in the era of late capitalism? The resurgence of authoritarianism and the social polarization currently taking place in contemporary Western societies at large, from the United States to the United Kingdom and Italy, and from Poland to Brazil and Mexico, make one feel pessimistic. The fragmentation of these societies that class- and race-based marginalization promote can only further damage the communitarian social fabric and the ability to create conditions for lasting well-being. In some of my recent work I have argued for critical sameness as a move against identity politics in an attempt to pursue inclusion and the recognition of common foes among individuals on opposing poles of the political spectrum who may not realize their shared experiences of exploitation and who may only experience limited conditions for human flourishing (Madrid, "Listening," 225–227). I would argue that such a blatantly political intellectual project is one that would encourage well-being in its promotion of equality and rejection of exceptionalism.

The three battlegrounds that I have outlined here have something in common: they all signal the ways in which an uncritical embrace of neoliberal values has corroded the link between the humanities and liberal arts as conducive to creating the conditions for well-being and human flourishing in society at large. There are signs that administrators at top R-1 colleges in the United States have finally decided to tackle this problem. Take, for example, Gretchen Ritter's 2017 address to Cornell University's faculty in the College of Arts and Sciences to use the liberal arts "to liberate the mind—to make the familiar unfamiliar; to open us to new ways of understanding the world; so that the world ahead is not simply a place you travel through but a place you discover or a place that you help to create" (Ritter, "Dean Ritter Addresses the State of the College," n.p.). This is an open call to reclaim the proactive role of the humanities as the critical apparatus of society. To me this is undoubtedly and ultimately a project about well-being and human flourishing. The fact that music scholarship occupies itself with a manifestation that people relate to mostly in a deeply emotional and affective manner could make it a central intellectual endeavor in this project. But that would only happen as long as music scholars understand the need to reorient the field beyond the myopic ways of neoliberal ideals and decidedly abandon the largely propagandistic traditions that originated it in the nineteenth century.

Musical Well-Being: Concluding Thoughts

In this chapter I have offered an alternative to notions of well-being centered around neoliberal rhetoric. In doing this, I share the concern of many of this volume's contributors about figuring out how to go about a type of music scholarship that promotes well-being and what kind of well-being that may be. My concern with ideas of well-being that articulate neoliberalism comes from the understanding that as an economic and administrative model, neo-liberalism thrives in human precarity and conflict, notions that are radically opposed to well-being. I propose an approach to musical well-being that emphasizes collective well-being as the foundation for individual well-being. This approach calls for a rejection of the propagandistic colonialist, imperialist, and white supremacist musical institutions and exceptionalist epistemes that have dominated the humanities, including music scholarship, since the nineteenth century. Questioning these institutions in an attempt to pursue intellectual and academic projects that prioritize the affective and emotional connections that make music meaningful to listeners will enable us to engage with the human flourishing and well-being potential of musicking.

Works Cited

Bewes, Timothy. *Cynicism and Postmodernity*. London: Verso, 1997.

Blau, Jnan. "More than 'Just' Music: Four Performance Topoi, the Phish Phenomenon, and the Power of Music in/and Performance." *Trans. Revista Transcultural de Música*, vol. 13, 2009. https://www.sibetrans.com/trans/articulo/44/more-than-just-music-four-performative-topoi-the-phish-phenomenon-and-the-power-of-music-in-and-performance. Accessed January 16, 2019).

Canclini, Néstor García. *Consumers and Citizens: Globalization and Multicultural Conflicts*, translated by George Yúdice. Minneapolis: University of Minnesota Press, 2001.

Engels, Frederick. *The Condition of the Working-Class in England in 1844*, translated by Florence Kelley Wischnewetzky. London: Swan Sonnenschein, 1892.

Fish, Stanley. "Will the Humanities Save Us?" *New York Times*, January 6, 2008. https://archive.nytimes.com/opinionator.blogs.nytimes.com/2008/01/06/will-the-humanities-save-us/.

Foti, Alex. *General Theory of the Precariat: Great Recession, Revolution, Reaction*. Amsterdam: Institute of Network Cultures, 2017.

Hegel, G. W. F. *The Philosophy of History*, translated by J. Sibtree. Mineola: Dover, 1956.

"Historia del programa emprendedor." Tecnológico de Monterrey. https://tec.mx/es/emprendimiento. Accessed July 21, 2019.

Kun, Josh, and Alejandro L. Madrid. "Exceptional Matters, Exceptional Times: A Conversation about the Challenges of U.S. Music Scholarship in the Age of Black Lives Matter and Trump." *Sounding Together: Collaborative Perspectives on U.S. Music in the 21st Century*, edited by Charles Hiroshi Garrett and Carol J. Oja. Ann Arbor: University of Michigan Press, 2021, pp. 239–263.

Layard, Richard. *Happiness: Lessons from a New Science*. New York: Penguin, 2005.

León, Javier F. "Introduction: Music, Music Making, and Neoliberalism." *Culture, Theory and Critique*, vol. 55, no. 2, 2014, pp. 129–137.

Madrid, Alejandro L. "American Music in Times of Postnationality." *Journal of the American Musicological Society*, vol. 63, no. 3, 2011, pp. 699–703.

Madrid, Alejandro L. "Diversity, Tokenism, Non-Canonical Musics, and the Crisis of the Humanities in U.S. Academia." *Journal of Music History Pedagogy*, vol. 7, no. 2, 2017, pp. 124–129.

Madrid, Alejandro L. "Listening from 'The Other Side': Music, Border Studies, and the Limits of Identity Politics." *Decentering the Nation: Music, Mexicanidad, and Globalization*, edited by Jesús Ramos-Kittrell. Lanham, MD: Lexington Books, 2020, pp. 211–230.

Madrid, Alejandro L. "Palabras inaugurales del Premio de Musicología Casa de las Américas." *Boletín Música*, vol. 31, 2012, pp. 46–49.

Neilson, David. "Class, Precarity, and Anxiety under Neoliberal Global Capitalism: From Denial to Resistance." *Theory and Psychology*, vol. 25, no. 2, 2015, pp. 184–201.

Pawelski, James O. "Bringing Together the Humanities and the Science of Well-Being to Advance Human Flourishing." *Well-Being and Higher Education: A Strategy for Change and the Realization of Education's Greater Purposes*, edited by Donald W. Harward. Washington, DC: Bringing Theory to Practice, 2016, pp. 207–216.

Pawelski, James O. "The Positive Humanities: Culture and Human Flourishing." *The Oxford Handbook of the Positive Humanities*, edited by Louis Tay and James O. Pawelski. New York: Oxford University Press, 2022, pp. 17–42.

Pilkington, Marc. "Well-Being, Happiness and the Structural Crisis of Neoliberalism: An Interdisciplinary Analysis through the Lenses of Emotions." *Mind & Society*, vol. 15, no. 2, 2016, pp. 265–280.

Pinker, Steven. *The Blank Slate: The Modern Denial of Human Nature*. New York: Penguin, 2002.

Pinker, Steven. *The Language Instinct: How the Mind Creates Language*. New York: William Morrow, 1994.

Ritter, Gretchen. "Dean Ritter Addresses the State of the College." The College of Arts and Sciences. Cornell University. https://as.cornell.edu/news/dean-ritter-addresses-state-college. Accessed July 23, 2019.

Tay, Louis, James O. Pawelski, and Melissa G. Keith. "The Role of the Arts and Humanities in Human Flourishing: A Conceptual Model." *The Journal of Positive Psychology* vol. 13, no. 3, 2018, 1–2.

6

The Music Scholar as a Type
of Non-Musician

Todd Decker

In 1988, sociologists Jon Frederickson and James F. Rooney published an article
with the provocative title "The Free-Lance Musician as a Type of Non-Person."
Frederickson and Rooney use the experiences of classically trained musicians
who play for pay in pick-up groups (mostly pit orchestras) to propose a contemporary variety of non-personhood. At once highly trained and low status,
such "free-lance" professionals are "expected to use [their] skills according to
the dictates" of others and with no artistic investment in a stable ensemble.
Such musical work for pay, the authors suggest, violates "the artistic ideal of
music as a unique personal expression." Freelance musicians become a specific
type of "non-person" in the public display of their musical skills and expressivity in contexts where "they are defined as people who are not really present"
(Frederickson Rooney 221–239). These contexts, and the experiences such
musicians have there, offend a particularly musical "ideal of personhood"—
defined by Frederickson and Rooney in strongly positive terms as grounded in
deeply personal and socially acknowledged creative activity. Clearly, this type
of non-personhood implies a situation where the possibilities for human flourishing inherent in the identity of musician are suppressed.

The present chapter—with a title that riffs on Frederickson and Mooney—
similarly concerns a specific group of musicians. I posit an analogous, if differently nuanced, situation experienced by music scholars: loss of the status
of musician in the shift from the applied pursuit of music (making and performing musical sound) to the academic study of music as a humanities discipline (writing and speaking about musical sound). I define music scholars
and musicians in strictly limited terms for this discussion. Music scholars
are individuals pursuing or holding a PhD in music theory or historical
musicology and working in the Anglophone academy or in so-called alt-ac

Todd Decker, *The Music Scholar as a Type of Non-Musician* In: *Music and Human Flourishing*.
Edited by: Anna Harwell Celenza, Oxford University Press. © Oxford University Press 2023.
DOI: 10.1093/oso/9780197646748.003.0007

positions. (Some ethnomusicologists may find their experience reflected here as well.) The identity *musician* operative in this chapter is founded on the training and experience as a maker of musical sounds gained by most such music scholars while they are children, youths, and young adults in various institutionalized, mostly notated Western musics (classical music primarily, but also jazz and musical theater learned in private and group contexts). Such training virtually always forms the foundation for a career as an elite performing professional musician in these musical styles. Most all music scholars forge a musician identity in childhood and youth in the pursuit of music as a nonverbal practice of bodily discipline, public accomplishment, and personal expression. This frequently foundational identity as a skilled and trained yet still amateur (pre-professional) musician, usually supported financially by parents and schools, is set aside when an individual makes career-defining choices to pursue a post-graduate research degree in music studies, the requisite educational path toward becoming a music scholar—a professional identity located primarily within the academy. In this transition, the music scholar—already an experienced musician, often with the performance-centered bachelor or even master of music degree in hand—becomes a specific type of non-musician: a musician who knows how to make music at a high level but who is not required to do so, even as music forms the focus of their (now professional) work as a scholar. And while the transition to this type of non-musician is likely felt most keenly by music scholars who are new to the academy (graduate students and early career professors), the tensions created by this loss might easily endure across an academic career, and even affect the structure and hierarchy in a university's Department of Music, as described in the following chapter by Wendy Heller.

I strive below to consider in general terms the inherent tension between the identities of musician and music scholar so defined, particularly as related to embodied experience and creative action (what each identity makes and does). Individual readers with personal connections to my topic will no doubt resist some of my admittedly schematic, narrowly defined descriptions of what musicians and music scholars do and make. I hope such readers will also find points of resonance with my characterizations of these two identities.

In running counterpoint to these generalizations, I offer an account of my own journey from musician to music scholar. My path from one identity to the other—and my efforts to hold on to my musician self—necessarily undergirds my interest in this topic and my writing of this chapter. The stakes in the transition I discuss here are too personal to go without some disclosure on my part. And so, rather than keep this exercise safely in the abstract, I reveal below formative experiences that inform my perspective. Such disclosure is uncomfortable for my music scholar self. I write in personal terms here in response to early readers of this chapter, among them several of my graduate students, as well as colleagues represented in this volume. I thank these readers for their generous input and hope this contribution—personal as it now is—might help others think through the experience of becoming and being a music scholar.

And so, this chapter alternates between a theoretical construction of a generalized music scholar as a type of non-musician and my own lived experience of this identity (paragraphs in italics). My intended audience includes the broader humanities academy but, given my topic and my story, this chapter relates most directly to other music scholars. I especially hope to provide young musicians considering the profession of music scholar or already embarked on graduate education in music studies with a sense of the trade-offs inherent in a choice that many, including myself, have made before them. I offer no solutions, since, as considered below, the identities of musician and music scholar are fundamentally at odds: musicians make musical sound, while music scholars make sentences about musical sound; musicians practice and rehearse to remain in condition for performance, while music scholars prioritize the production of well-made arguments for publication and oral presentation. The lived, day-to-day differences between these types of doing and making cut to the core of the status of the music scholar as a type of non-musician.

Becoming a musician when young carries self-evident value in contemporary Western middle-class culture and among aspiring social classes worldwide. The cultivation of an accomplished and trained musician identity develops mind and body in tandem and opens a path of positive and progressively challenging individual growth and social engagement. Making music builds self-esteem in the mastering of a skill and self-confidence in performing such mastery for others. The moment of performance offers proof of self-discipline and courage in the projection of a sounding public self. Young people often devote themselves to the years-long personal and interpersonal project of becoming a musician with tremendous commitment. The pleasure that musical performance provides to peers and elders alike—returned to the musician in the sound of applause—only adds to the attractions of music as a serious pursuit for young people during primary and secondary education and the collegiate years. For many, being a musician—walking through the world as the girl toting a cello case—defines the social and personal, public and private self.

I was eager and asked repeatedly to begin piano lessons in second grade and, once I got started at the instrument, progressed quickly. I also sang in church (sometimes solo) and in children's choirs. Beginning in early middle school, I sang and danced on stage at a semi-professional dinner theater in Fresno, California, where I grew up. In short, I can scarcely remember a time when I was not considered by those who knew me (or recognized me from the theater) as a musician or performer. Making music in front of an audience was a de-fining aspect of who I was and, crucially, who I had chosen to be.

After three years at the theater (giving six performances weekly), I quit to focus on classical piano. At the end of high school, I gave a solo recital that in-cluded Gershwin's Rhapsody in Blue *and classical "hits" by Bach, Debussy, Liszt, and Chopin. In college, I eventually abandoned plans to pursue a career as a concert pianist, switched to harpsichord as my primary instrument, and turned toward accompanying—in part because I fell for a singer who remains my partner in life and music over three decades later. Just after marrying during our senior year of college, we moved to Berkeley, California, so I could pursue a master's degree in harpsichord performance at the San Francisco Conservatory of Music.*

The above rather sanguine portrait demands leavening with the acknowl-edgment that becoming and being a musician in one's formative years can also cause physical, personal, and social distress. Performance anxiety or in-jury, destructive relationships with teachers, and failure to succeed to one's hopes in the highly competitive realm of music potentially turn the musi-cian identity into a source of lasting pain, frustration, and disappointment—despite the hard work and devotion invested in one's art.

After completing my harpsichord master's degree—a not entirely positive experience that left me, at times, expressively paralyzed at the instrument—I gigged around the San Francisco Bay Area's early music scene, taught piano lessons to make money (I hated it and was bad at it), and began to study organ in an attempt to add mastery of this keyboard to my musician toolkit. After about six months spent practicing organ for hours daily with ferocious intensity on learning the pedals, I began to experience sharp pains in my left arm and shoulder. This persistent physical discomfort, more than anything else, led me to abandon the keyboard and all plans to be a musician. I obtained a teaching credential and taught high school history for eight years. The choice made sense, as my bachelor's degree combined music and intellectual history. I had always been just as much a reader as a musician.

Music as a pursuit seems to preselect some individuals, marking them as destined to become musicians. Birth into a so-called musical family might make the acquisition of a musician identity part of becoming a full member of one's family group, with all the lifelong implications this suggests. Obvious talent or interest in music often manifests early, even unbidden, and can be taken as a kind of preordained calling. In such cases, music-making as a mode of self-expression can seem innate or natural—despite the considerable investment of time and discipline behind any musician identity.

My love of classical music had no precedent in my family, for whom piano lessons served as preparation to contribute to the musical life of our church (which I did before leaving home and later during about a decade spent in part-time Lutheran church music jobs). My interest in the Broadway musical theater stepped well beyond any expected family history. And so, my devotion to performance proved a mystery to all, but my apparent success spoke for a kind of fatedness. Being a musician and singer was, again, simply who I was and who I had made myself to be.

If music scholars mostly begin as young trained musicians in the Western tradition, then the lack of racial, ethnic, and class diversity in music scholarship is predictable. Rigorous training as a young classical or jazz musician in the United States is increasingly an upper-middle-class privilege, often instrumentalized to enhance the all-important college application. The decline or disappearance of music education programs outside of wealthy public or private schools makes it unlikely that young musicians (potential music scholars) will be nurtured in homes without the resources or time to invest in the long project of making a musician.

My class background did not prepare me to enter the ranks of professional musicians (or the academy, for that matter). Still, my parents could afford music lessons and understood some value in them—even if not the classical music values I learned and wholeheartedly embraced from my music teachers. In very different ways, the two piano teachers I studied with in succession through the end of high school ushered me into the world of classical and theater music and helped me make it my own. These two extraordinary individuals, it is no exaggeration to say, gave me the space and encouragement to become the person I chose to be: someone defined by musical skills, interests, and expressive capacities, which were displayed in performance.

The utility of cultivating the above musician identity is, however, limited to childhood and youth: the professional identity of musician remains a genuinely risky choice.[1] And so, an individual's effort to sustain a deeply cultivated musician identity—forged in youth and unconnected to making a living—faces serious practical questions at the inevitable moment when their adult future beckons. For the population of musicians considered here, the years spent as an undergraduate are often when such questions arise and when the decision to become a music scholar is made.

At age thirty-four, I decided to pursue a doctor of musical arts degree in harpsichord performance. My partner and I agreed to uproot our young family in the hopes of my eventually obtaining a university teaching position (and also so my partner could get a master's in voice—which she did). My performance pain had abated—it was never an issue with harpsichord playing—and we took the opportunity to change our lives and turn back toward our common identities as classical musicians.

In a musicology seminar during my first semester, my professor asked if I might like to switch to the musicology PhD program and offered to support my application. My immediate yes to this invitation marks the moment I decided to be a music scholar. (I had, by this time, assessed the dismal academic job market enough to know there were vastly more opportunities for musicologists than for harpsichordists.) And yet, even after switching from a performance to a research doctorate, I continued to study harpsichord with the master teacher I had moved across the country to work with—against the advice of one of my ethnomusicology professors, who told me: "You'll have to stop playing so you'll have time to read and write." I resisted mightily giving up my musician identity and even played a challenging solo harpsichord recital, the thirty Essercizi *sonatas of Domenico Scarlatti, while still completing my doctoral coursework. At the time, my research focused on connections between eighteenth-century keyboard music and opera. Shortly after the concert, and just before beginning work on my dissertation, I became an Americanist who works on the Broadway musical, Hollywood film music and musicals, and popular music broadly speaking. The rootedness of almost all my scholarly interests in my life as a musician should, by this point, speak for itself.*

Most applicants for graduate degrees in music scholarship have a ready answer to the question, "What's your instrument?" For years and years before

---

[1] Amateur musicians abound, of course, and will always outnumber the by comparison small group of individuals who can say, truthfully, that they make their living only by making music.

they consider careers writing and talking about music in the academy, these prospective scholars have devoted themselves to the practice and performance of music, sometimes beginning on an instrument before their conscious memory kicks in—in such cases, to themselves they can claim to have *always* been musicians. Finding one's instrument or, for a singer, discovering one's voice, can carry the life-changing force of finding a life partner—and grow into a relationship that is just as emotional, intellectual, and physical.

When I introduce myself as a music historian to someone not familiar with the academy, I often get the query "What's your instrument?" This predictable question reflects the inherent disconnect in the notion of a professional who is engaged with music (a music scholar) but does not make musical sound (a musician). Responding to the question necessitates a very short, spoken version of this chapter. I usually say I play keyboards—piano and harpsichord ("I actually have a master's in that," I'll sometimes add)—but that I am, by trade, a historian whose primary task is writing. In these exchanges, when I articulate who I am as an educated professional, I relegate huge tracts of my life to a tag line: just as my academic accomplishments are reduced to a sentence—"He has published four books and numerous articles"—when my (very short) performer biography appears in the program for a concert. When I perform now, sometimes with professional musicians, the years I spent becoming a music scholar are less than worthless: they become, in fact, a liability (time not spent staying in shape as a player).

The physical aspect is key, for the musician's life is irreducibly physical. Making music is an act of the body in real time. Solitary practice and rehearsal with others both involve disciplining the body (in tandem with the instrument, which for singers *is* the body) to *do* something—to *make* sound—at the exact necessary moment in a manner both technically and expressively right. Trained musicians relentlessly maintain their physical ability to perform: practice and rehearsal keeps the body in shape to make music. Lacking such repetitive work, proficiency fades—for some instruments and for virtuoso repertories at an alarmingly rapid rate. Music scholars at the start of their studies often feel their musician bodies slipping away: calluses disappear, embouchures fade. The authentic test of practice and rehearsal comes in the moment of performance. The act of performance entails physical, mental, and expressive risk—a leap, often taken with other musicians toward the making of a gift for an audience. The musician's active, sound-making body serves as the foundation for the rich personal and social experience that is music.

While doing my master's at the San Francisco Conservatory of Music, I learned and performed on multiple occasions Elliott Carter's Sonata for Flute, Oboe, Cello, and Harpsichord (1956). This experience, shared with three student colleagues, remains in my memory as an especially challenging example of the physical, mental, and expressive risks of being a musician. The Carter Sonata was—for all of us, if I remember rightly—the first modernist chamber work we had played. Simply putting it together was a considerable challenge, and we performed it to an enthusiastic reception in the chamber music small ensembles class. We were sufficiently impressive to be asked to play the Sonata on the Conservatory's summer festival, Chamber Music West, which otherwise only featured top-level professionals from around the nation. This invitation thrilled all four of us: here was (some) proof we were real musicians ready to appear beside the best. The summer concert necessitated preparation that felt both familiar and, given the ticket-buying audience we faced, new. Being graduate students together—each of us relying on scholarships, grants, and loans to live (briefly) the life of a musician—we had the time to prepare, to be in top shape, to stay in peak condition. And we were accustomed to playing in public for discriminating and critical audiences (our teachers and peers), perhaps the greatest benefit of the conservatory and school of music setting.

Leap forward twenty-five years. Having been granted tenure in my current position, I was ready, after seven years of virtually no public playing, to perform again. My partner and I started doing programs of classic American popular songs—Gershwin, Porter, Berlin, etc.—with some (hopefully witty) commentary from a historical perspective by me. After about four years of such programs, I wanted both a greater challenge and to return to the harpsichord. So, I arranged a program of Bach and Handel sonatas for myself and a St. Louis–based professional violinist on a free weeknight chamber music series my department ran in an intimate venue. I knew the violinist as my son's advanced violin teacher, but his primary work is playing first violin with a professional string quartet that records and tours internationally. He is, as the cliché goes, a consummate musician—someone who lives and breathes music making. He is also a professional musician—he (literally) makes his living by making music. Preparing a program of Handel continuo sonatas and the Bach F Minor Violin and Obbligato Harpsichord Sonata with him brought home to me the risks of musical performance. I could play the notes—yes—but not from the position of someone who had spent time every day for decades playing my instrument. No amount of practice time ever felt like enough, and the stakes of appearing with a real musician—I was also performing for him, after all—complicated the mental task. This, in turn, could compromise the physical task. The concert went well, and we even repeated it at a local restaurant venue some months later. Working with a professional of this caliber revealed to me the distance between my technical grasp of the program at hand and the sustained discipline of being connected to one's instrument that was evident in rehearsing and performing with a real musician. Reviving my musician identity in this way cut into my time as a scholar—a luxury I only allowed myself after tenure—and revealed to me as an adult just how much space music performance takes up in the brain and emotions.

I had a similar experience a few years later accompanying my partner at the piano in a recital of sixteen songs by Claude Debussy. Beyond the enormous amount of practice time required, a moment arrived in the preparation when I realized that my brain, my body, and my sheer nerve to claim I could do justice to this music was being stretched far beyond normal limits in my adult life. This was music I had only previously attempted to perform when I was a student— when I was a full-time musician. The recital became a very public exercise in embodied risk that reminded me of what I was once capable of when I defined myself by the musician identity I had set aside in the choice to be a scholar.

The act of preparing and playing all these concerts was irreducibly physical— therein lies much of the pleasure in mastery and expression as a musician.

By contrast, the scholar's body is normatively still (seated or standing with book or computer) and often sounds only in the act of speaking (addressing a class or conference). Writing, the central task of the humanities scholar, is a marginally physical act. The work of writing—putting language into meaningful order for a given purpose—happens without the expressive prosthetic of an instrument (the scholar speaks with their own voice rather than "through" something), entails very little bodily engagement (beyond pen to paper or fingers to keys) and, for the most part in the humanities, is done alone (response to comments from others the only somewhat social aspect). Behind the scholar's writing labor sits the even less physically engaged tasks of reading and thinking. The gift writers give (the finished book, article, blog post, or seminar paper) lives not in any real-time confrontation with an audience, but on the page or screen and, within the community of scholars, exists for resistant readers to critique. The music scholar's spoken work of teaching—whether delivering a lecture or facilitating a discussion— bears little resemblance to music-making. The constructed nature of the classroom "performance" and the imperative to deliver assessable information about (rather than experience of) music to the student "audience" offer inherently non-musical challenges. The music scholar's largely inactive and silent body plays almost no role in the overwhelmingly verbal discourse that is humanities scholarship. In sum, music scholars exchange the often-exhilarating physical activity of making musical sound for the desk-, book-, screen- and lectern-bound stillness of scholarship: in this exchange, music scholars lose the deeply embodied intellectual, expressive, and social challenge that is being a musician. The social challenge seems an especially significant point of contrast: the musician's audience, seeking musical pleasure in a moment of face-to-face encounter, is replaced by the music scholar's exchange of words in a conversation designed to be contentious. Scholarly and classroom talk (typically) resists; audiences (ideally) reach toward the musician, eager to be pleased and moved.

My scholarship is a seated endeavor. I wrote portions of my combat movie music and sound book at a standing desk, but much (almost all) of the time I am seated, physically still, often in a fixed position (holding a book, hands on a computer keyboard or mouse; postures that can cause damage even as they involve almost no large motions). The day after submitting my first book manuscript for production, I joined a gym. Since then, I have spent a part of each day either swimming, running, or doing resistance training. Ironically, in retrospect, after about six months of weight training, all my residual performance-related arm and shoulder pain disappeared. I might have still been a musician today if I had picked up weights when my pain started. My almost daily hour at the gym provides necessary and welcome release from all screens, books, and papers. I even avoid listening to work-related music while working out: although that can be difficult too for a popular music scholar.

Music, despite sentimental claims, is not a universal language. Far from it. Different musical traditions do, however, deliver meaning in something like the manner of a language—if only in the way music unfolds in time and makes a kind of syntactical sense. Trained musicians learn to "speak" the language of a given musical practice, a language made of musical sounds. The imperative for music scholars to produce words—more precisely, to speak or write coherent sentences—about musical sound thus proves a fundamental difference between the tasks set for music scholars and musicians. Music scholars secure their status as scholars by making sentences about musical sound. The music scholar's often high-level ability to make musical sound—their remaining musician identity—lies, in the end, outside or to the far edge of the discourse of scholarship, which is conducted in sentences. Some music scholars, of course, do make musical sound as part of their scholarly practice or while teaching, and certain areas of music scholarship, particularly ethnomusicology, are especially welcome to music-making scholars. But the profession of music scholarship as structured in the academy—as defined, for example, in job listings—generally maintains a bright line between musicians and music scholars: the former make musical sounds; the latter make sentences about musical sound.

Once starting my current position as an assistant professor, I largely stopped performing (and practicing and mostly playing) until I earned tenure. This strategic decision reflected what I perceived as the stakes for me in a tenure-track job—a job for which I am extremely grateful. When I started performing again, I realized anew and again how limiting words about music are beside music "spoken" fluently and idiomatically in performance. Musical expression, in my experience shaped by traditions that privilege close fidelity to rather prescriptive texts and defined stylistic codes, has a grandeur, freedom, and emotional vulnerability that is foreign to scholarly writing. The feelings and ideas expressed in the music I perform far outshine in their immediacy and vibrancy the ideas and concepts about music I allow—can allow? will permit?—into my scholarship. Now, not all ideas are ripe for musical expression, and often music scholarship works to explain the (sometimes pernicious) impact of musical performance on listeners—I think of the repertory of Black music for white people, like the song "Ol' Man River," that sits in the center of much of my scholarly interests. But the expressive rewards of articulating my ideas as a scholar carry almost none of the intensity of performing the music of others and making sounds for others (and myself in the act of performing) to hear. In-the-moment, in-the-musical-act fidelity to the musical text in performance remains for me a deeply integrated combination of mind, body, and emotions that writing or speaking about music just doesn't match.

Musicians, of course, do speak words about music—but typically only as a means to the end that is producing musical sound. Such talk resounds in the hierarchal encounters between teacher and student, conductor and ensemble, and coach and chamber group or combo. The sentences defining such relationships usually fall into one of two categories: (1) boringly technical ("That note you are playing is sharp") and (2) extravagantly idiosyncratic, replete with descriptive, exploratory, metaphorical, hermetic, and vague directives and sentiments. Little of this practical realm of discourse about making musical sound ends up being relevant for music scholars—unless their topic is how musicians talk about music-making.

Words spoken or written in response to music just made play a crucial role in the formation of a musician. My teachers and coaches mostly talked about how I played: they didn't demonstrate for me to copy, but used words to clarify or critique or try to get me to hear something or do something. Such words helped me learn how to play correctly in both technical and stylistic terms. Mentoring young music scholars entails similar words of critique. The scholarly mentor's primary task is to respond in words to words about music. When doing so, I— like, I bet, most of my colleagues—borrow principles from my mentors. One line I regularly borrow is this: "There are no ideas without sentences." In other words, until you start writing sentences, you don't know what you know or think. This scholarly imperative puts language about music to a completely different use than the words spoken during a music lesson or coaching. And so, musicians turned music scholars must learn to use language about music in a whole new way, a way that revolves around the making of sentences, not sound.

Musicians, as defined here, "speak" in musical sound within a given practice: for example, an orchestral musician faithfully plays the music on the stand in front of her. Reproducing a musical practice is the musician's creative goal, especially when young. In this sense, musical traditions construed as historical agents "speak" through the real-time actions of musicians who serve as vessels of the tradition. This is particularly the case for young adult musicians who are just achieving the physical, technical, and expressive mastery that allows them to play *real* music like a *real* musician. The ontological shift from becoming to being a musician—felt internally but crucially validated by one's audience—has profound implications for an individual's self-worth. The ability to "speak" a musical tradition through a chosen instrument in a way that sounds right is a precious personal achievement that, by its very nature, sounds forth into the world and bonds the individual musician to that tradition in a tight embrace. In such sounding, individuals announce, without saying a word but in a "language" with great expressive power, that they *are*—at last and now—a musician.

What would it take for me to perform the Essercizi sonatas of Scarlatti now? In retrospect, I see the concert I gave midway through my doctoral studies as a hinge moment. I was writing about the Essercizi at the time. (My first published article concerns the set. A subsequent book chapter offers a reading of the sonatas built directly on my experience learning to play them.) But was it necessary to perform them—to make a public claim on the Essercizi as music I can make and not just talk about? Necessary or not, I had the chops and was in shape and of a mind to pull it off after several years of serious practicing and regular performing. Returning to the physical and the mental discipline that goes with it, the time it would take to prepare the Essercizi *for public sharing, is probably the real impediment to my playing that recital again now.*

As a young musician, I held the perhaps romantic notion that despite my technical abilities, there were pieces I should not yet play, works that demanded a kind of maturity that only came with age: the late sonatas of Beethoven, perhaps, or Bach's Goldberg Variations *or* Art of the Fugue. *The last of these I learned on my own just after finishing my master's in harpsichord in an attempt to take the instrument back, to make it mine again. I never played the set in public and I feel the lack of not having done so. While my notion of pieces with an age limit reflects a parochial, even mystical musical education (not uncommon perhaps for young musicians who adopt Western classical music as part of their identity), the upshot has been that having reached middle age, I do not have time to learn these pieces. Indeed, if this chapter has an overarching theme, it is that being a music scholar irretrievably takes away the time it takes to be a musician (at least in certain musical disciplines and at certain levels of mastery). My longing to play these pieces now easily maps onto a longing for the life of play I enjoyed as a (student) musician.*

Music scholars, by contrast, must say something in sentences about music. The utility of this fundamentally non-musical task remains ever open to question: Why does anything need to be said about music at all? Why not just listen or play? Must the concert hall be a classroom, and who invited the professor? Young musicians—perhaps sitting in a required music history class instead of where they would rather be, in the practice room—are often the ones asking such questions. Young music scholars—often in these same classrooms—do not ask these questions and here, perhaps, lies the moment of truth for nascent scholars. Music lives its unique life in a place where a particularly intense form of human experience comes in the wordless, sound-making actions of human bodies. Scholarship is nothing if not the exchange of words—mostly in some form of print. Music, as a type of largely wordless sound, eludes the very discursive space within which scholarship lives.

I often sing and play in the classroom. It surprises students—always a good strategy—and stakes my claim to being a musician and not just a music scholar: again, the layperson's expectation that someone engaged professionally with music (a music teacher, sort of) will be able to make music applies. On very few occasions I have played and/or sung during a scholarly talk or teaching demonstration. I choose such moments carefully. When on the job market, I strategically used performance to demonstrate my musicianship, to

make a tacit but sounding point about my latent musician identity. These days,
a clear scholarly point must be in the making for me to consider demonstrating
at the piano or singing during a talk for colleagues. (I recall a senior colleague
doing so brilliantly, boldly, and entirely to a scholarly point at a talk a few years
ago: she even hit a high C.) But it would be foolish to let the odd chance to do live
musical examples guide my scholarly path. In recent years, my interests have
moved away from topics that are likely candidates for performance—perhaps
a symptom of a widening divide between my identities as musician and music
scholar.

Beyond making sentences about music, music scholars work under the
imperative to create permanent new knowledge—the fundamental task of all
research scholars in the academy. Existing scholarly discourse about music
profoundly shapes the scholar's efforts. Music scholars, like all academics,
are not at liberty to claim whatever they want about a given topic, but instead join a conversation already in progress. And unlike music critics—a
precarious words-about-music profession open to the traffic in opinion—
music scholars bear a heavy obligation to disciplinary rules of evidence, however construed but usually rather narrowly set by the historic insecurities of
the music disciplines and their compensatory conceits of scientific rigor—
hence the pseudo-scientific moniker *musicologist*. Music scholars step into
a long-running discussion about music, a crowded and unequal dialogue
encompassing all published scholarly work as well as sentences spoken aloud
by others in classrooms, colloquiums, and conferences. Once joining this discussion, music scholars are expected, in some measure, to transform or advance the conversation. In this, the music scholar as a type of non-musician
must display a sort of creativity not demanded by the identity of musician: for while the musician as vessel recreates in real time the musical tradition within which they work, the music scholar advances and transforms the
substance of the inquiry that is humanities scholarship, a discourse that can,
potentially, go almost anywhere. In this, music scholars bear a burden and
enjoy a freedom that musicians do not.[2]

Music scholars write and speak within a small community of other writers
and speakers. The topics and terms open for discussion are limited but open to
change (however glacial it can seem at times). Several of my areas of interest—
the American musical stage and screen—are comparatively recent additions to

---

[2] Here, the difference between classical and jazz musicians proves significant: at the highest levels,
the latter are expected to push musical sound into new realms of meaning.

the scholarly conversation. Indeed, I considered pursuing a PhD in musicology in the early 1990s but saw no place for myself in the field (within my limited understanding of it at that moment). The work of innovative scholars since then—proponents of the "new musicology" and those who expanded popular music studies to embrace Broadway and Hollywood—opened room for me to build a scholarly profile on topics such as race and the stage and screen musical. Still, what I can say on my chosen topics is limited by the discourse of the field, the codes and canons of academic publishing, and my graduate training. My early years as a music scholar were spent learning these limits—being "disciplined" into music scholarship, as one of my music theory professors might have said with a twinkle in his eye. This process had little to nothing in common with learning to play or perform musical sounds—and yet the central topic was, still, music.

And getting the music—however we might define that vague word—into my scholarship has been a challenge. Doing so has felt like the genuine test of my musicologist identity: my (residual) musician identity should, in some (hopefully noticeable) way, inform my scholarship on music and distinguish my work from scholars who write about music but who are not themselves trained musicians. I recognize that I burden my advisees with this notion as well. For some music scholars, this is not an issue. Their writing reaches out only to other music specialists—often by requiring the reader to also read music. For popular music scholars like me, however, it is imperative to write as a music scholar in a way that both speaks broadly and gives evidence for the musician latent in the writer.

Further advice from my mentor, passed on from his mentor: a music scholar should show in their work that they are (1) a good musician, (2) a good writer, and (3) not a pedant. The first of these is the real challenge, I think. Demonstrating that I am a good musician in my scholarly work might recover something of my first musical identity—actually being a musician. Perhaps this entire chapter is a latent reaction to my absorption (and adoption) of these three imperatives as central to what it means to be a music scholar.

It takes a decade or so of hard work in the medium of sentences to become a humanities scholar. Young musicians who take this path have likely already traveled a decade or more on the very different path toward becoming a musician, a path of hard bodily work done in the medium of musical sound. I have suggested some binary differences between these two paths above. One final difference warrants attention. Music offers an

experience of time intensified by sound that makes meaning without recourse to words. However, the intensified time of music always ends—
when musical sound falls silent and the quotidian sounds of daily human
life, including words, return. Musicians work in an ephemeral medium.
Their bodily labor leaves no trace but in memory—although the musician's
body might carry physical evidence of regular music-making (such as long
fingernails on a guitarist's right hand).[3] Music scholars, by contrast, ideally work in published words that remain on the shelf or the web. The text-
making labor of music scholarship creates a monument to conversation
among interested individuals who have committed to a shared, contentious, hopeful, and impossible project: the making of scholarly sentences
about musical sound. While this conversation cannot replace the rich life
of making music that likely led most music scholars to pursue music in the
first place, the consolations of scholarship include a kind of permanent creativity that eludes both musicians as music-makers and musical sound as
a realm of human meaning. Sentences, rendered in print, remain in a way
musical sound does not.

*When I was young, making music and becoming a musician proved to be
one way—at times the most important way—that I shaped myself into who
I wanted to be. Surely such self-fashioning cuts to the heart of human flourishing, and doing such work by way of musical performance powerfully
implicates the private self in the public sphere. The choice to become a music
scholar, and the demands of adulthood, have cut into, at times eliminated entirely, my time making music. And yet, I remained (and remain) a musician,
even as my music scholar identity has also made me a type of non-musician. I
have tried in this chapter to chart the tensions between my two music-related
identities. Fitting my musician identity into my life as a music scholar remains
a challenge at or near the core of my efforts to live a full and flourishing life.
Indeed, every time I commit to a challenging concert program, I am reminded
again of the deep human pleasures that I have only ever known in the making
of music—pleasures always at their best when done in the company of others.
And always, after the concert's been given, the tension between my younger*

---

[3] Recordings—"pictures" of musical sound captured by microphones (the sonic equivalents of
cameras)—by their nature collapse to nothing the actual space defining sounds made in real time.
Highly edited recordings present untrustworthy testaments to the relationship between musicians
and bodily labor foregrounded here.

musician and older music scholar selves endures. I doubt I am alone in this struggle.

Works Cited

Frederickson, Jon, and James F. Rooney. "The Free-Lance Musician as a Type of Non-Person: An Extension of the Concept of Personhood." *The Sociological Quarterly*, vol. 29, no. 2, Summer 1988, pp. 221–239.

7

They Say, "Music Should Be Seen but Not Heard"

Performance and Flourishing in the Liberal Arts University

Wendy Heller

The transition from high school to college is both an exciting and stressful experience for many students. While most college students encounter some anxieties upon leaving home—be it the strain of dormitory life, the absence of family, or the lack of the structured schedule of high school—those pressures may be particularly intense for students at elite liberal arts universities, where peer competition is especially intense. In some instances, this may be the first time that students receive a grade lower than an A or encounter classmates who are equally gifted academically. For most, the search for a sense of belonging can cause anxiety.

College is also a time when students reassess their interests and priorities, particularly with regard to the extracurricular activities—such as music—that were essential to their college applications. It is not uncommon for high-achieving students to be equally accomplished as musicians, and there is some evidence that musical studies help students academically (Guhn, Emerson, and Gouzouasis 308–328). Thus, there are numerous academically-gifted students who have devoted many years to developing their skills as performers by taking private lessons, playing in orchestras, bands, jazz ensembles, singing in choirs, attending preparatory music schools on the weekends, and/or going to music camps and summer festivals. Some are sufficiently accomplished to have considered—and rejected—the possibility of attending a music school or conservatory in favor of a liberal arts institution, at least at the undergraduate level. Others, without the aspirations or skills for a professional life in music, might simply love the experience of making music with others.

Wendy Heller, *They Say, "Music Should Be Seen but Not Heard"* In: *Music and Human Flourishing*. Edited by: Anna Harwell Celenza, Oxford University Press. © Oxford University Press 2023. DOI: 10.1093/oso/9780197646748.003.0008

What happens to these students when they go to college? Are they able to continue their musical studies, or do they feel compelled to put music on the back burner when faced with the challenges of Organic Chemistry or Economics 101? The question is particularly relevant given the structure of music departments in many liberal arts institutions, where the emphasis has long been on the academic study of music (musicology, ethnomusicology, and music theory) as opposed to music performance. In these departments, the priority given to the academic study of music often affects other areas, such as the distribution of tenure and tenure-track positions, the awarding (or withholding) of academic credit for music lessons and performance classes, or the exclusion of musical activities—such as orchestra or chorus—from a student's transcript. This devaluing of music performance in the academy has had negative consequences for human flourishing, especially among musically inclined students who may feel pressure to give up activities that they have previously enjoyed.

In Chapter 4, Michael Beckerman explores the effectiveness that attentive listening might have on alleviating the anxiety and mental distress often experienced by students in high-pressure situations. This chapter explores the ways in which music performance positively impacts the lives of students at liberal arts schools. I take as my example the Music Department at Princeton University, known for its rigorous graduate programs in musicology and composition, and one of several institutions responsible for shaping music as an academic discipline in the United States.[1] While the story that unfolds below is primarily about the emergence of a vibrant performance program in a single institution, there is a broader narrative here about attitudes toward music education and music performance in the United States, the ambiguous role of performance in a traditional university setting, and the benefits that playing and singing can have for students, regardless of their discipline or professional aspirations.

Music as Liberal Arts, Science, or Vocation

"The English Department doesn't teach typing, why should the Music Department teach piano?" This phrase, uttered several decades ago by a

---

[1] This list could include, but is not limited to, Harvard University, University of California (Berkeley), University of Chicago, University of North Carolina (Chapel Hill), Columbia University, University of California (Los Angeles).

former member of the Princeton University Music Department, reflects an attitude toward music performance that still lingers in many elite liberal arts schools. It is a sentiment that has had a lasting impact on the field of music, as seen in Todd Decker's discussion in the previous chapter. Although music students at both the undergraduate and graduate level might focus on musicology, ethnomusicology, theory, or (at some institutions) composition, performance is typically relegated to the realm of extracurricular activity, supported by part-time "performance" faculty who are excluded from the tenured ranks.

Over the past few decades this attitude has begun to change, as elite universities invest more in the arts.[2] The expansion of the programs in the creative and performing arts at Princeton under President Emerita Shirley Tilghman in 2006 sought to establish the University as a "global leader in the quality of its offerings and in their integration into a broader liberal arts education," underscoring the benefits for students: "by participating in the arts, our students develop cognitive abilities and forms of intelligence that complement training in other disciplines, and in some cases they discover talents and interests that will shape their careers and principal avocations" (https://arts.princeton.edu/arts-initiative). Tilghman justified Princeton's investment in the arts by emphasizing the ways in which these activities might contribute to students' professional success in other areas. She did not, however, explore the impact that these programs might provide for students' physical and psychological well-being. Simply put, she did not consider the ways that participating in music performance might lead to human flourishing, regardless of the benefits it might have for their professional development. Nevertheless, Tilghman's call for change marked an important turning point in the history of music on campus—a story that captures some of the fundamental tensions about the study of music at many American liberal arts universities.

Music became a formal part of the curriculum at Princeton relatively late, nearly two hundred years after the University's founding in 1746 (Girard 31–52). An initial endowment for a music professor funded a position for the University organist, but the first courses were not taught until 1934, when Roy Dickinson Welch came to Princeton as a guest lecturer from Smith

---

[2] This can be seen, for instance, in the building of new arts centers and concert halls, such as the one at the College of Holy Cross, the establishment of "Professor of the Practice" positions for musicians at Harvard, hiring of ensembles-in-residence in departments typically devoted to academics, such as the Lydian Quartet at Brandeis University, or the various ensembles at the University of Chicago.

College and stayed on to teach music courses. According to the history of the department penned by J. Merrill Knapp, the response to these initial courses was so enthusiastic that by 1937 "one tenth of the student body was taking at least one music course in their college career" (Knapp 327). Welch brought the composer Roger Sessions, a former Smith College colleague, to Princeton to develop courses in music theory; he was joined by Milton Babbitt (who was at Princeton 1938–1984), Oliver Strunk (1937–1966), Edward T. Cone (1946–1985), and Arthur Mendel (1952–1973). Initially a division under the Art History Department, Music became an independent department at Princeton in 1946.

From the outset, there were fundamental disagreements about the nature of a music education in the context of the University. For Welch, music was an extension of the liberal arts; the study of music theory was important as it served the cause of music history. This, however, did not take into consideration the needs of composers, for whom the study of music theory constituted "vocational" or "professional study" rather than cultural history (Girard 35). At the same time, American composers, such as Roger Sessions, saw the university as a potentially good environment for composers as it compensated for the fact that there is no "millennial cultural tradition" in the United States comparable to that of Europe, nor is music supported by private patronage or the government, free from commercial constraints. The university thus offered a "non-commercial, non-competitive experience" (Sessions 194–195). Nonetheless, as Sessions noted, universities were not necessarily interested in supporting this kind of creative work:

> Yes, the university is certainly glad to have composers around, and even encourage a certain amount of composition among the students. But its practice must be subordinate to the pursuit of scholarship, to the study of musical literature and history; it can be in fact a valuable adjunct to such study, which is the true purpose of the university music department. The creative aim must never be a primary one; and while naturally the development of a genuine composer is always to be welcomed, it is not the true business of the university and cannot be allowed in any respect to become a major aim of the department (196).

Sessions might well have been describing the situation at Princeton, for the tension between scholarship and composition was built into the very fabric of the Music Department. Brian Harkin, writing about Milton

Babbitt's encounters with academia, describes how this young "Schoenberg acolyte . . . stepped into a musical and political minefield" on his arrival at Princeton.

> The conflicts arose, not merely from a collision between conservative musical tastes, but more broadly from crosscurrents within a complex social and aesthetic environment involving the precarious position of music in the academy, the rise of musicology as a legitimate academic discipline, and individual power plays by some of the era's leading university musicians. (Harker 337)[3]

The friction between Roger Sessions and Oliver Strunk typifies the dilemma: Sessions felt that the composers were regarded as second-class citizens in relation to the musicologists (Harker 345). Princeton became one of the bastions of positivist musicology.[4] Thus, Princeton scholars were the leaders in the study of music from the more distant past (medieval polyphony, chant, Josquin, Bach), perhaps as a reaction against the modernism promoted by the composers (Kerman 39).

Initially, it was only possible to get a PhD in Music History at Princeton, the belief being that an "aptitude for scholarship and a capacity for independent research" were "neither appropriate or valuable" for a composer (*Princeton University Course Catalog*). Nonetheless, by 1961 Princeton became one of two universities (the other being Brandeis) to offer a PhD in composition. In so doing, Brandeis and Princeton differed from many peer institutions, who offered, and continue to offer, a DMA in composition.[5] Part of what distinguished the PhD in composition during this era was the fact that it involved a great deal of academic work, including a full dissertation.[6] The report that was authored by Mendel, Sessions, and Babbitt on the PhD in the wake of the founding of the program in 1960–1961 emphasizes a conception of the field that draws upon analogies with mathematics and the hard sciences:

---

[3] It is in this context that we should understand Milton Babbitt's infamous article "Who Cares if You Listen," *High Fidelity* (1958), one of the relatively few music articles to have its own Wikipedia entry: https://en.wikipedia.org/wiki/Who_Cares_if_You_Listen.

[4] See Kerman, *Contemplating Music*, especially chapter 2, pp. 31–59.

[5] These include Yale University, Eastman School of Music, Boston University, Cornell University, to name but a few. Harvard offers a PhD in Music.

[6] It is quite recently that composers petitioned the Graduate School to allow written dissertations that could be more modest, thus accommodating students who may be brilliant composers but less academically inclined.

Musical theory is today being transformed from a collection of dubiously derived and inaccurately stated prescriptives and imperatives into a subject that draws, as it must, upon the methods and results of the formal and empirical sciences: logic, the philosophy of science, analytical philosophy, physics, electronics, mathematics, experimental psychology, structural linguistics, and computer methods. Such investigations can be undertaken only in a university, and we wish to encourage them and see them take place at Princeton.[7]

Thus, what began as a separation between composition and musicology, where the former was a craft and the latter was part of the liberal arts, became reconciled in a somewhat frosty marriage where musicology (by means of positivism) and composition (through its relationship to mathematics and science) acquired legitimacy and seriousness of purpose.[8] The two prestigious doctoral programs were the jewels in the Music Department's crown, even as the University as a whole tended to lavish more of its attention on undergraduate education.

All of this has necessarily shaped the undergraduate music program, where the majority of students enrolled in music courses not as their primary field of study, but rather as part of a broader liberal arts education. For decades the most heavily enrolled course in the department was Music 103, an introduction to Western classical music, or what we used to refer to as "Music Appreciation." Particularly popular among seniors, the course also fulfilled some of the University's distributions requirements in "Literature and the Arts." The numbers of music majors were relatively low—typically between five and ten students. Music majors concentrate in either musicology or composition; as seniors they write a conventional thesis in history or theory or create a major composition. The old undergraduate curriculum, which has subsequently been revised, reflected something of this split, as it required systematic training in music theory in a four-semester sequence, with a more ad hoc approach to music history through electives. Implicit in these requirements was the sense that music history doesn't require rigor until graduate school, but every music major must master a given set of

---

[7] Cited in Girard, "Music as Science," 39.
[8] Mark Zuckerman notes the fact that the goal was not to turn music theory into a science, but rather the interest was in "borrowing scientific methods and standards (language precision, modeling)" with the goal of arriving, for instance, at more precise tools for describing music.

analytical and technical skills in common practice music to earn an undergraduate degree.[9]

Whither Performance?

All of this has implications for understanding the somewhat limited role of performance on campus for many years. If music composition—condemned once as a "vocational" practice—could be rehabilitated by its association with science and math, there was no such rubric for rescuing performance. According to Mark Zuckerman, who completed his PhD at Princeton in the 1970s and was on the faculty during those years, it wasn't so much that there was hostility toward performance, but rather that it was deemed to be less important (Zuckerman). Composers, he noted, already had to deal with the fact that the University felt that the music they wrote was too abstract and rarefied. Performance was, quite simply, less important because it was less serious and more practical. This was the context surrounding a faculty member's comment comparing teaching piano to teaching typing.

At the same time, there was music being performed on campus, but it was not central to the curriculum. Founded initially as the "Ladies Musical Committee" in 1894, the Princeton University Concert Committee—a town and gown collaboration—has had a long tradition of bringing superb professional musicians to campus. Their archives demonstrate the vital role that Princeton played in enlivening the musical culture on the New York–Philadelphia corridor throughout the twentieth century.

Students also participated in a number of performing groups, but their participation was extracurricular and, consequently, was not documented on a student's transcript. Some of these performing groups were organized by students and had no formal connection to the Music Department, while others, directed by faculty, were funded by the department. Like many peer institutions, Princeton has a long tradition of a student-organized a capella groups that have no official link to the Music Department but retain the enthusiastic support of alumni. The Nassoons, for instance, were founded in 1941, the Tigertones in 1946. The Princeton University Glee Club—initially

---

[9] The new undergraduate curriculum treats these areas more equally and gives students the flexibility to take courses in two areas: "Materials and Making" (theory, composition, and electronic music) and "Culture and Criticism" (ethnomusicology and musicology). See https://music.prince ton.edu/undergraduate/majoring-music.

an all-male ensemble—was founded in 1874, though it was not directed by Princeton music faculty until 1934, expanding to include women after the introduction of coeducation at Princeton in 1969. The Princeton University Orchestra was founded in 1896; however, it was composed of a group of professional musicians who came to play at Princeton, rather than students (http://orchestra.princeton.edu). No one imagined that there would be a sufficient number of students on campus to form an entire orchestra. Princeton also did not have the infrastructure to support performance adequately. Until the construction of the Woolworth Center of Musical Studies in 1963, the Music Department was housed in the basement of Clio Hall, where there are no practice or performance facilities. The original Woolworth included some practice rooms, but it was only in the mid-1980s, with the renovation of Richardson Auditorium, that the University had an acceptable concert hall, and the recital hall, Taplin Auditorium, was added only in the 1990s.[10] The renovation of Woolworth in 1997 supplied an adequate rehearsal space for choral groups and small instrumental ensembles.

Meanwhile, performance at Princeton continued to expand. The Music Department enlisted some musicians on a private-contract basis to give private lessons to students, providing subsidies for music majors and students enrolled in ensembles and some music courses. The most ardent champion of performance among the tenured professors was Peter Westergaard, theorist and composer, who chaired the department during 1974–1978 and 1983–1986.[11] For several years, Westergaard conducted the orchestra in addition to carrying his full-time teaching load, and toward the end of his first term as chair, he hired a professional conductor. In 1978 Michael Pratt joined the faculty. Pratt, who has led the orchestra for over forty years and directs the Program in Musical Performance, has been at the forefront of many of the battles over the status of performance at Princeton. Jayn Rosenfield, who began teaching flute at Princeton prior to Pratt's arrival, noted that there was "relatively little contact between the professors and us . . . we were all but invisible. . . . There was zero encouragement for recitals, ensemble formation, [or] reach-out between composition teachers/students and local players." Milton Babbitt referred to the teachers as the "underground conservatory," since they taught in the basement of Woolworth. It was during these years that Princeton University Opera Theater was established, with Pratt as the

---

[10] For the history of the hall, see https://richardson.princeton.edu.
[11] See Jamie Saxon, "Peter Westergaard."

music director and Westergaard as stage director, the latter supplying brilliant singing translations for the productions of such works as *Don Giovanni*, *Magic Flute*, and *Der Freischütz*.[12]

Despite these advances, many students expressed frustration over the role of performance at Princeton, and in 1988, the department and Dean of the College began preliminary discussions about establishing a performance program. Lynn Haggard, a member of the class of 1990, wrote an impassioned letter in February 1989 to Margaret Bent, then the chair of the Music Department, advocating for a greater role in performance at Princeton.

> We are not looking for an exclusive chance to perform. What we seek . . . is the opportunity to learn about and understand music in the most *comprehensive*, intensive, and immediate way possible—which for us includes working with our instruments at least part of the time. How much clearer a concept can become when we also experience it under our fingers (with apologies to voice students).

Haggard continued by explaining the important role of music performance to their education:

> Many of us chose Princeton over a conservatory, because we highly valued the benefits of a superior liberal arts education. This, however, did not mean that our interest in cultivating musical understanding and skills lessened . . . many of us wanted to develop simultaneously both an area of study and our musical education, and this is one of the few places where it seemed possible to experience "the best of both worlds." (communication to Margarent Bent)

One year later, the Music Department received a student petition, which was subsequently published in the *Daily Princetonian*. Shortly thereafter (fall 1991), the Program in Musical Performance was established with Michael Pratt as director, thus allowing students to "minor" in music performance. Paul Lansky, who was chair of the Music Department when the program was established, noted the following:

[12] See Pratt, "Peter Westergaard and Music Performance."

While there was no resistance to the establishment of the performance certificate program in the mid '90s, the historical attitudes towards performance as a less-than-respectable academic activity are deep and ingrained. It took some discussion, mainly with deans, to set up a respectable set of requirements, but once we did it was clear sailing. . . . It's ironic that the attitude towards performance as an athletic activity persists in an academic institution. But I think things have improved a lot in recent years. (email correspondence)

The result is a thriving program that admits some thirty juniors in both classical and jazz by audition; they are required to perform a senior recital, take credit-bearing performance classes (chamber music, opera, jazz ensembles), a year of music theory and some music electives, participate in non-credit ensembles, and take lessons on their major instrument or voice, one year of which must be taken for academic credit (https://music.prince ton.edu/undergraduate/certificate-programs).

The most significant change both in infrastructure and University-wide attitudes toward performance was initiated in 2006 by Princeton president Shirley Tilghman, who, as noted above, launched an "Arts Initiative," leading to the construction of the Lewis Arts Complex, which included a building each for music, dance, and theater (https://arts.princeton.edu). The Effron Music Building, devoted primarily to rehearsal and practicing, includes some twenty practice or teaching studios, jazz practice rooms, a studio for the Princeton Laptop Orchestra, and a rehearsal room large enough for the orchestra and large jazz ensembles.

Thus, nearly thirty years after students demanded more performance opportunities, it has become—along with musicology and composition—one of the three central activities of the Music Department. The number of classes that one can take for credit involving music performance has more than doubled; music majors and certificate students now take lessons for academic credit. In 2009, Princeton began a partnership with the Royal College of Music in London that allows our most serious music students an opportunity to spend fall semester of their junior year studying voice, instrument, or composition intensively in London.[13]

There has also been tremendous improvement and expansion within the conventional performance organizations (there are now two full

[13] https://music.princeton.edu/study-abroad.

orchestras, four choruses, and multiple jazz ensembles), and we have added new high-profile choral and jazz directors (Gabriel Crouch and Rudresh Mahanthappa); the department has added a number of additional faculty-led ensembles (African Music and Dance Ensemble, Princeton University Laptop Orchestra, Early Music Princeton, Steel-Drum Ensemble, and Percussion Ensemble), some of which provide opportunities for students without any prior musical training. The legacy of the attitude toward performance centrally, however, is apparent in the fact that participation in these ensembles is not noted on a student's transcript, and that the performance faculty, including the full-time conductors, are excluded from tenure-line positions.[14] Nonetheless, the current faculty in the Music Department spends a substantial portion of its endowed funds on performance; moreover, they want the students in their classrooms to be deeply immersed in performance, even if it means the department has less money to spend on other things, including research. The quality and quantity of the performance opportunities has meant that Princeton has been increasingly attracting students who are playing and singing at an extremely high level, many of whom could have attended schools such as Juilliard. Attitudes toward performance have changed drastically; now music is both seen and heard on campus.

Performance and Psychological Well-Being at Princeton

Tilghman's Arts Initiative emphasized the educational benefits for students, but did not dwell on the potential benefits that participation in the arts might have on the quality of students' lives. Adam Croom's study of the positive impact of music practice and participation points to a number of ways in which music performance supports psychological well-being, exploring music through the PERMA framework: positive emotion, engagement, relationships, meaning, and accomplishment (Croom 44–64). The benefits of the PERMA framework are also further explored by Jonathan Coopersmith in Chapter 1 of the present volume. Anecdotal evidence from students involved in performance at Princeton supports Croom's and Coopersmith's research and suggests that music performance is a key way for students in all disciplines to reduce their stress and add layers of meaning to their

---

[14] A faculty vote in April 2020 created new ranks among the lecturers that now allows for promotions for our best artists to "Professor of the Practice."

college experience. For example, students in the orchestra report that they are often reluctant to go to rehearsal because they feel pressure to complete assignments or work on their theses; but once they arrive at rehearsal, they lose themselves in the music (engagement), their mood improves as a result of playing works that they enjoy (positive emotions), they benefit from the comradeship of working together (relationships), and they come away from performances feeling exhilarated (accomplishment).

Testimony from both present and former students overwhelmingly points to the psychological benefits of participating in music performance at Princeton. This is particularly true for students who do not aspire to be professional musicians. Jennifer Rexford, who is currently the Gordon Y. S. Wu Professor in Engineering at Princeton, and received her BSE in electrical engineering at Princeton in 1991, spoke about the benefits of participating in music during her time as an undergraduate:

> Playing in my college jazz ensemble was a great stress reliever. During my freshman year, I was concerned that rehearsals were the night before my weekly physics quiz, but I soon came to realize that was a blessing in disguise. Playing my trombone was the perfect way to blow my stress away (literally!). The early years of majoring in engineering come with a heavy course load of highly structured classes, on top of (at least for me) a dose of imposter syndrome, and playing jazz every week was a great catharsis. (email communication)

Reilly Bova (class of 2020), a software engineer at Microsoft who played percussion in the Princeton University Orchestra and studied conducting with Michael Pratt, describes his time in the orchestra as "the absolute highlight of my Princeton education!"

> The academic demands that elite universities place on students are unsustainable without opportunities to step back from the endless churn of work and take a break. Orchestra rehearsals not only regularly provide such an opportunity, but also serve as a critical outlet for creativity and passion away from the wider climate of academic "over-standardization." I know that when I look back on my college years in twenty-year's time, I won't think about my classes or my research or my assignments; I will think about my rehearsals, concerts, and international tours with PUO. (email communication)

Ryan Melosini (class of 2019), who spent over twenty hours a week as the first-string goalkeeper for the Varsity Water Polo team, found that his involvement in music helped him find "true balance" in his life, and improved his performance in the pool and in school.

> Some might say that adding more activities onto your schedule ends up leaving you less time, which seems, at face value, to be true. I have found, however, that filling up your day with things you love doing makes you much more productive and much less prone to wasting time, which has allowed me to make the most of my Princeton experience. Whether it be attending Glee Club rehearsal every Monday, Wednesday and Friday or having my weekly lesson with my voice teacher, singing and music have been a way for me to release stress and tension while also developing strong relationships with the people I sing with. My favorite memories at Princeton are all music-related, and, not surprisingly, my best friends are all people I have met through music. Even though I officially did come to Princeton to play water polo as a recruited athlete, music is what made me "stay" at Princeton. (email communication)

Caroline Jones, class of 2018, a longtime participant in Princeton choirs went on to become a graduate student in the Woodrow Wilson School, also emphasizes participating in ensembles as a "valuable source of community," noting the "opportunities for leadership and learning," and—like most of her colleagues—the "welcome escape from academic stressors." Of particular note, she also draws a link between high stress and isolation:

> Music ensembles are certainly not unique in their community building function, but it's a particularly important one in an environment where stress discourages interaction. The choirs at Princeton were all small enough that I could get to know everyone in them, and they fostered some important friendships with people I may have never otherwise met. (email communication)

Caroline describes music as "an important part of her "self-care" at Princeton:

> It's so easy to treat music as a "time luxury" when there aren't enough hours in the day, but those of us who make the commitment to show up on a regular basis treat it much more as a necessity. Making music is part of taking

care of myself while under stress—it gives my brain a chance to work in a totally different way, gives me a sense of belonging to something and the chance to be part of a communal effort greater than myself, exposes me daily to beauty, helps ground me, and brings me joy. Singing in choirs is one of the only things I do for myself and myself only. In the high stress environment of an elite college, those of us who show up to an ensemble and commit to it are there because we need it, because it adds something to our lives that we can't get anywhere else.

Philosophy major James Brown Kinsella (class of 2019) breaks it down more systematically.

There are five reasons why music is an important counterpoint to my academic life: (1) rehearsals and performances are beautiful and engrossing as well as intellectually engaging; (2) the steady weekly schedule of rehearsals and semesterly schedule of concerts helps organize my days and marks the passage of my academic career; (3) apart from auditions, music-making in not an assessed activity. This freedom enables me to improve my technique, cultivate my musicality, and explore a particular piece of music, all for their own sake; (4) the feedback of music-making is immediate and specific, which contrasts well with the rather solitary actions of reading, writing, and studying that require much work over a long time, only after the fact yield feedback, and often give only general comments; (5) my musical community brings me together with people of diverse interests and backgrounds who all share a passion for music, and it's really special to learn from their perspectives and to have this bond together. (email communication)

For Caroline Zhao, also class of 2019, it was important to have music integrated into her life on campus, rather than something she pursued on her own:

As a high school student, almost all of my classical music endeavors took place off of campus. Coming to Princeton, music has become an integral part of my campus life, which has inevitably impacted my academic and social experiences, alike. Despite the fact that I will not be pursuing music as a career (at least directly post-graduation), I feel so grateful to have had the opportunity to take academic and performance classes offered by the Music Department. These experiences have not only developed my understanding of the history and analysis of music, but I have also grown as an artist through working with world-class conductors, directors, and teachers. Involvement with singing groups outside of an academic setting has also been the extra-curricular that I have spent the most time doing during the past four years. (email communication)

Ruth Ochs, who directs the Princeton University Sinfonia, is particularly sensitive to the importance of balancing performance with academics: a full-time lecturer, Ochs built Sinfonia from a group of some twenty string players who were not quite ready to play in the Princeton University Orchestra, to a full orchestra of over sixty performers who perform major repertory. Ochs has worked tirelessly to provide performance opportunities for students who are on the "non-professional track." Students in Sinfonia rehearse fewer hours a week than their counterparts in the Princeton University Orchestra. They "play for pure love of the art form, and they still work hard and improve as musicians" (email communication). There is no sacrifice of musical quality, Ochs notes, since the students are so highly motivated:

They enter a rehearsal with a precious measure of eagerness because they want to sharpen the emotional alertness that symphonic music so often asks them to do. Without a sense of competition, students motivate each other, cheering their peers through solos and challenges. While they never truly stop thinking about their projects, problem sets, and papers when they play, after rehearsal I hear them return to assignments and academic discussion with lively spirit. I cannot measure the value of the time we spend together, but I can say that my students leave rehearsal fortified with human sensibility and mentally recharged. (email comunication)

The pressure may be greater for students in Princeton University Orchestra, which maintains a more intensive rehearsal schedule and concert schedule, but it is clear that for many of these students the challenge of playing some of the most difficult orchestral works in the repertory provides them with an enormous sense of satisfaction. Jack Hill, who teaches double bass at Princeton and has been a "ringer" in the orchestra for over two decades, underscores the "sense of community" in the orchestra and "the accomplishment that they feel playing major works at such a high level. You finish a concert," he notes, "and you look around and you see kids smiling like they'd had a great time" (private conversation).

The experience may be complex for students who are contemplating careers as professional musicians or who feel pressure to play at a professional level. They seem to report the same benefits as their colleagues, but they also note that this creates yet another arena in which they feel they must excel. One student, whose parents are both professional musicians, noted that she felt a lot of pressure when she first came to Princeton and realized that her cello playing wasn't at as high a level as she had previously thought. An important part of her experience at Princeton was coming to terms with her level of playing, accepting the fact that she wouldn't necessarily be the best player in the orchestra, which—not surprisingly—actually helped her playing improve. By senior year, she had become more comfortable with her playing and thus enjoyed it more. Music provided a lesson for her in how to manage the pressure of performing, a lesson that she could transfer into other arenas.

Gloria Yin (class of 2019), who majored in math and received certificates in piano performance and computer science, is a gifted conductor as well as pianist. Director of several student-organized groups, Gloria often felt stressed by the responsibilities that leadership necessarily entails, but also derived a great deal of pleasure from these activities. She remembers all of it—including the stress—"fondly" as it "pushed her as a musician and a person." She notes that she "did it all because I was passionate about it." Although the time demands added to the academic stress, these activities also gave her "an outlet to use a different part of my brain" and "do something I really love." She concludes: ". . . music-making at Princeton might have contributed to stress, but I don't see that as a bad thing, and it was certainly fulfilling and contributed greatly to my sense of well-being!" (email correspondence).

Violinist Janice Cheon (class of 2020), who majored in German and received certificates in both modern and baroque violin, notes the extent to which music has helped "shape" her "academic path."

My motivation for learning German blossomed into my current major and an interdisciplinary interest in German and Austrian literature, art, and philosophy. Growing up listening to Bach's passions and cantatas was my first exposure to the German language. Although I was able to study and understand the textures of Bach's polyphony through theory courses, I desired to understand what was being sung. My eagerness to understand the stories that were intermingled with the music I had played and loved inspired me to begin German as a Princeton freshman. After spending a year in language courses and a summer abroad in Germany to improve my fluency, I began to expand my exploration of German culture to encompass literature, visual art, and aesthetics. Being able to take lessons and participate in festivals in historic music centers like Salzburg and Leipzig solidified my original reason for learning German, too. Returning to Princeton, I decided to major in German and pursue a certificate in music performance to keep both of my passions alive. (email correspondence)

For her the stress was more physical than psychological, as she reports being diagnosed with tendinitis as a first-year student, noting as well the extent to which learning baroque violin required her to rethink her technique and helped her deal with injuries. This points to another unexpected benefit of studying music in a liberal arts context. In general, students have less time to practice than their conservatory counterparts and may thus be somewhat less prone to injury, though it will always be an occupational hazard for musicians.

Lou Chen (class of 2019), who majored in music and received a certificate in conducting, found his sense of well-being not only through making music himself, but by providing performance opportunities for less fortunate students. During his first year at Princeton, Lou founded the Trenton Youth Orchestra, which not only gives Trenton high school students a chance to play in orchestra, but also enlists other Princeton undergraduate musicians who volunteer to teach private lessons or lead sectional rehearsals.

If we accept that there are incalculable benefits to music performance (which there are), isn't the natural next step to share these benefits with as many youths as possible? There are so many children for whom there exists a yawning gap between their love of music and their ability to afford the requisite resources: instruments, concert tickets, and most important of all, lessons. Princeton students, who represent some of the most accomplished young musicians in the country, are perfectly poised to fill this gap—and through programs like the Trenton Youth Orchestra, they're doing just that. By leading sectionals or teaching private lessons, my student volunteers are deriving new value from their musical talent, which is no longer simply a pathway to personal growth but also an instrument of social change. And for my Trenton students, the opportunity to constantly interact with such phenomenal musicians—playing alongside them, watching them in concert, learning from them—gives them the technical skills to match their musical passion, encourages them to expect more from themselves as musicians, and makes a strong argument for why music should always be an integral part of their lives. (email correspondence)

Through his work with Trenton Youth Symphony, Lou discovered his professional path: our Provost was sufficiently impressed with his work that they created a position for him at the University—as the Program Manager Trenton Arts @ Princeton, which—in addition to the orchestra—now includes dance, theater, and a chorale. Princeton is now exploring ways to integrate a service component into its music curriculum.

Liberal Arts Students as Professional Musicians

There seems little question that students in a liberal arts environment benefit from the opportunity to perform in pre-professional and amateur contexts. But what happens after college? I think it is fair to imagine that the lives of those students who go on to careers in other fields were enriched by their musical experiences. But one might also wonder whether or not a liberal arts education helps professional musicians flourish? With the expansion of the performance programs in the past few decades, an increasing number of Princeton students have gone on to have successful professional careers. Might these students have benefited from choosing a liberal arts school over a conservatory for their post-secondary school education? Students in conservatories and schools of music receive more intensive training, have more time to practice, and have far fewer distractions. They certainly do not play a concert with the orchestra after spending three hours in a chemistry lab, as is frequently the case for Princeton students. But might there nonetheless be an advantage to the liberal arts education for professional musicians?

Preliminary anecdotal evidence suggests that some of the most gifted students place deep value on their liberal arts background. Countertenor Anthony Roth Costanzo (class of 2004), who played the title role in Philip Glass's *Akhnaten* in the Metropolitan Opera's 2019–2020 and 2021–2022 seasons, sees his "formative experience studying at Princeton" as critical to his success. Costanzo speaks of the "insular" approach for people within the music industry, which may sustain "wonderful traditions" but can also "neglect the crucial need to develop new audiences, and connect to a wider public more generally." Costanzo continues:

Part of the narrow focus I often encounter can be traced to education. At a conservatory, the bulk of the students' time is centered around learning their craft, and while this is important, it doesn't spark their imagination the way a liberal arts education can. At Princeton, I was able to get a real sense of the historical context for all the music I was singing, as well as the theoretical underpinning, and most importantly, the way it connected to other disciplines. I would come to a rehearsal fresh from an ethics class, or a psychology class, and thus be able to incorporate what I had learned in other departments into my work in music. Similarly, the discipline and meticulous approach to performance that I learned in the music department created a different context and approach with which to engage with other subjects. The more performance I participated in at the university, the more I was able to develop a sense of community there, which in turn made discussions with fellow students and with faculty more fulfilling. Performance helped me to forge connections between departments, resulting in my senior thesis show, which had the support of eleven different departments. A lot of my work as a professional springs from that fundamental connection between thought and performance that was cemented at Princeton. (email communication)

Aryeh Nussbaum Cohen (class of 2015), another Princeton countertenor to win the Metropolitan Opera Auditions, also sees his liberal arts education as essential for his success as a singer. For Cohen, it is all about connecting emotionally with an audience and "having enough knowledge about the world to sing about." This, in his view, is more important than the "laser-focus" education at a conservatory, despite the "technique-specific skills" that students gain there. But he ascribes another benefit of a broader educational experience:

I believe that the social connections with non-artists that a liberal arts education provides are a great aid in my happiness in the world. The simple fact that most of my closest friends are not artists helps me flourish by keeping everything in perspective, and by keeping my eyes constantly open to a world beyond the arts. (email communication)

Conclusion

This brief overview of music at a liberal arts institution underscores the ways in which music performance helps students live happier, more fulfilled lives as college students. Through music, they are better able to withstand the pressures that are integral to life at an elite institution. While the details and specific cast of characters at Princeton may differ from those of other universities, this story is by no means unique, for it exposes some of the underlying controversies in the study of music in American colleges and universities that developed as musicologists, theorists, and composers attempted to establish a tradition for the serious study of music in a country where attitudes toward art music have always been ambivalent.[15] What this story suggests is that scholars and administrators might do well to relinquish the conventional habits and biases of academic life in favor of a more collaborative approach to the study of music. As Pratt explains:

> Being in a performing ensemble is more than a palliative for stress (as positive as that is). Performing music by J. S. Bach or Gustav Mahler or Charlie Parker is to develop the most intimate relationship—emotionally, spiritually—with masterpieces in an art form whose first impact is on the body, the heart, the spine. And the same experience is possible outside of the Western canon, or with new music. The intellectual rigors of a university are crucial in developing the character and minds of our students, and we need that process more than ever today. But enriching one's emotional sensitivity is not a class goal in Organic Chemistry. Experiencing music kinesthetically through rehearsal and performance feeds directly into this fundamental, universal need—to *feel* something deeply with one's whole being, and to open one's inner doors to the possibility of emotional transformation. (email correspondence)

Perhaps more than any other discipline in the humanities, music requires—ideally—the use of the mind, body, and emotions in perfect balance. We may never fully succeed in helping our students achieve this balance, but if we do, they will surely flourish.

Works Cited

Arts Initiative: Lewis Center for the Arts. Princeton University. https://arts.princeton.edu/arts-initiative. Accessed January 7, 2019.

---

[15] See, for instance, Horowitz, *Classical Music in America*; also reviews of several relevant books in Kowalski, "Why We Refuse to Listen?" (160–218).

Babbitt, Milton. "Who Cares if You Listen." *High Fidelity*, 1958. https://en.wikipedia.org/wiki/Who_Cares_if_You_Listen.

Bova, Reilly. Email communication, August 29, 2019.

"Certificate Programs." Princeton Department of Music. https://music.princeton.edu/certificate-music-performance. Accessed September 29, 2019.

Chen, Lou. Email correspondence, October 7, 2019.

Cheon, Janice. Email correspondence, September 15, 2019.

Cohen, Aryeh Nussbaum. Email communication, September 2, 2019.

Costanzo, Anthony Roth. Email communication, August 19, 2019.

Croom, Adam M. "Music Practice and Participation for Psychological Well-Being: A Review of How Music Influences Positive Emotion, Engagement, Relationships, Meaning, and Accomplishment." *Musica Scientiae*, vol. 19, 2015, pp. 44–64.

Girard, Aaron. "Music as a (Science) as a Liberal Art at Princeton." *Zeitschrift der Gesellschaft für Musiktheorie*. Special Issue, 2010, pp. 31–52.

Guhn, Martin, Scott. D. Emerson, and Peter Gouzouasis. "A Population-Level Analysis of Associations between School Music Participation and Academic Achievement." *Journal of Educational Psychology*, vol. 112, no 2, pp. 308–328. http://dx.doi.org/10.1037/edu0000376. Accessed May 7, 2020.

Haggard, Lynne. Communication to Margaret Bent, February 10, 1989. Princeton Music Department files.

Harker, Brian. "Milton Babbitt Encounters Academia (and Vice Versa)." *American Music*, vol. 26, 2008, 337.

Hill, Jack. Private conversation, October 12, 2019.

Horowitz, Joseph. *Classical Music in America: A History*. New York: W. W. Norton, 2007.

Jones, Caroline. Email communication, February 4, 2019.

Kerman, Joseph. *Contemplating Music: Challenges to Musicology*. Cambridge, MA: Harvard University Press, 1985.

Kinsella, James Brown. Email communication, January 29, 2019.

Knapp, Merrill. "Music, Department of." *A Princeton Companion*, edited by Alexander Leitch. Princeton: Princeton University Press, 1978, pp. 326–328.

Kowalski, Michael. "Why We Refuse to Listen?" *Perspectives of New Music*, vol. 44, 2006, pp. 160–218.

Lewis Center for the Arts. Princeton University. https://arts.princeton.edu. Accessed February 9, 2019.

Lansky, Paul. Email correspondence, February 3, 2019.

"Majoring in Music." Princeton Department of Music. https://music.princeton.edu/undergraduates/majoring-music. Accessed February 4, 2020.

Melosini, Ryan. Email communication, January 27, 2019.

Ochs, Ruth. Email communication, October 5, 2019.

"Princeton University Orchestra." Princeton Department of Music. http://orchestra.princeton.edu. Accessed February 9, 2019.

Pratt, Michael. Email correspondence, October 14, 2019.

Pratt, Michael. "Peter Westergaard and Music Performance at Princeton." Princeton University Orchestra webpage, August 21 2019, https://orchestra.princeton.edu/conductors-blog/peter-westergaard-and-music-performance-at-princeton/.

Princeton University Concert Committee. https://concerts.princeton.edu/staff/.

Princeton University Course Catalog, 1961.

Rexford, Jennifer. Email communication, September 22, 2019.

Rosenfeld, Jayn. Email correspondence, September 19, 2019.

Saxon, Jamie. "Peter Westergaard, Music Scholar and 'Composer of Formidable Skill' Dies at 88." https://www.princeton.edu/news/2019/07/02/peter-westergaard-music-scho lar-and-composer-formidable-skill-dies-88. Accessed October 12, 2019.

Sessions, Roger. *Roger Sessions on Music: Collected Essays*, edited by Edward T. Cone. Princeton, NJ: Princeton University Press, 2016.

"Study Abroad." Princeton Department of Music. https://music.princeton.edu/prospect ive-students/study-abroad.

"Welcome to Richardson Auditorium." Princeton University. https://richardson.prince ton.edu. Accessed February 9, 2019.

Yin, Gloria. Email correspondence, September 10, 2019.

Zhao, Caroline. Email communication, January 27. 2019.

Zuckerman, Mark. Email communication, February 3, 2019.

PART III
COMMUNICATION

8

Interdisciplinary and Intercultural Artistic Collaboration

Nancy Yunhwa Rao

New creativity is sparked when people collaborate in the arts, and music, by its very nature, is an art form that often exists in conjunction with others. For musicians especially, the path to human flourishing can be attained through artistic collaboration, be it with visual artists, composers, dancers, dramaturges, actors, or even other musicians. At their best, such collaborations, and the new creativity they foster, put their contributors in an exalted mood and a feeling of betterment and fulfillment. This chapter examines two types of collaborations that can lead to human flourishing in the performing and visual arts: interdisciplinary and intercultural. I will begin by exploring notions of interdisciplinarity and interculturality, then examine the common characteristics of such projects in the visual and performing arts. After conceptual and theoretical exploration, I will present two case studies that demonstrate the potential of interdisciplinary and intercultural collaborations and their effect on human flourishing.

Interdisciplinarity

Interdisciplinary collaboration in performing and visual arts is unique, quite different from that of other fields. As interdisciplinary scholars have noted, in the fields of social science or science research, interdisciplinary collaborations inevitably face complexity in terms of agendas, such as different types of research processes at all levels, definition of research subjects and problems, shaping of problems from disciplinary perspectives, interests of different stakeholders, research positions, or even policies, accountabilities, expectations of outcomes, and solutions to problems (Bendix, Bizer, and Noyes). For these fields, the notion of discipline is generally the commitment to the rigor

Nancy Yunhwa Rao, *Interdisciplinary and Intercultural Artistic Collaboration* In: *Music and Human Flourishing*. Edited by: Anna Harwell Celenza, Oxford University Press. © Oxford University Press 2023.
DOI: 10.1093/oso/9780197646748.003.0009

of disciplinary methodology, concept, and training. However, such disciplinary rigor is challenged by the very notion of interdisciplinary collaboration where disciplinary boundaries are threatened, and conflicts arise. Clashes are common among participants. There is generally an anxiety for the erosion of disciplinary rigor by boundary transgression.

The situation is quite different with interdisciplinary collaboration in the arts (performing and visual). The artistic creation is generally the objective, for example, a piece of joint production/art/performance, a radical juxtaposition and experimentation, a multimedia or intermedia performance, or a process of creative artistic production as inquiry and practice. The artistic project is enriched through creative collaborative work, through precisely the process of incorporating different artistic approaches and crossing disciplinary boundaries. Significantly, interdisciplinary creativity in the arts leads to greater aesthetic innovation. In particular, with interdisciplinary collaboration in the arts, one is often inspired to be dislodged from the formal rituals of a particular discipline and removed from the usual process toward "predetermined" and predictable goals. Instead of disciplinary rigor, such a collaboration requires that the participants take part in the creative work of unfamiliar arts, slowing down the process and letting interdisciplinary types of creativity and innovation emerge and lead the way. The process creates an alternative to what would have been had the boundaries of the same discipline been observed. Such an interdisciplinary collaboration requires constructive mutual listening between teams drawn together from different artistic disciplines and traditions, and brings the diversity of necessary skills and perspectives upon which the newly creative work will depend. To borrow terms expressed by other contributors to this volume, interdisciplinarity in the arts is a process of "stretch" and "play."

Scholars of interdisciplinarity have studied extensively different approaches to interdisciplinary collaborations. Julie Thompson Klein offers a taxonomy of interdisciplinarity with well over a dozen varieties. These varieties range from bridging to restructuring. The trends of interdisciplinarity also go from systematic integration of knowledge and fostering new, transgressive theoretical paradigms to reorganizing the structure of knowledge to encompass the parts of material fields that disciplines handle separately, as well as trans-sector transdisciplinary problem-solving (Klein 15–30). As for interdisciplinarity in arts, however, it has yet to receive its fair share of attention within academic scholarship on interdisciplinary studies, despite its significance. In a short article, performance art scholar Tanya Augsburg reflects on the scarcity of scholarship in interdisciplinary arts and identifies five categories: (1) the unified fusion of arts, as in Wagner's Gesamtkunstwerk; (2) historical legacy of avant-garde with radical juxtapositions; (3) post–World War II arts experimentation; (4) interaction between arts and science/technology in digital arts; and (5) the performance artistic project as research, inquiry, and practice. Augsburg also offers a brief review of current academic programs offering the study of interdisciplinary arts, which are surprisingly few (132–140).

In relation to music research, Georgina Born has identified three modes of interdisciplinary practice: (1) integrative-synthesis mode, (2) subordination-service mode, and (3) agonistic-antagonistic mode (205–243). The integrative-synthesis mode is the integration of knowledge and practices from different "antecedent disciplines" in a relatively symmetrical manner. Multiple criteria would come in to create a synthesis in such work. In the subordination-service mode, different disciplines would be brought together to supplement a primary discipline. The result of this arrangement is the stability of the primary discipline and the lack of fundamental change to its epistemic basis. In the agonistic-antagonistic mode, existing forms of disciplinary knowledge would be challenged and critiqued by the interdisciplinary practice to transcend the "antecedent disciplines." This mode of practice therefore has the potential to create the most radical changes or innovative approaches. Since a collaborative creative process more likely navigates among the three different modes of practices, rather than adhering to one exclusively, it would be important to consider the three practices as fluid and dynamic, bending to one or another mode at certain points of the collaboration process. It is also possible that some types of collaboration lean more naturally to one mode of practice than others, or that some genres of stage work invariably call for the dominance of one discipline over others. Nevertheless, the notions of these three modes of practice offer useful perspectives to consider some, if not all, of the key characteristics of interdisciplinarity in the performing and visual arts.

Interculturality/Inter-Asia

Since the mid-twentieth century, the convergence of plurality of cultures in contemporary society has prompted scholars, educators, policymakers, business consultants, etc., to adopt terms such as *cross-cultural*, *transcultural*, *multicultural*, and *cosmopolitan* to address the increasingly prominent trend and phenomenon of interdisciplinarity. Over time, however, many have become dissatisfied with how these terms tend to reify and preserve cultural identities on the one hand, and to imply an innocuous coexistence on the other. In the past two decades of changing lexicon, the term *interculturality* has emerged. Unlike the earlier terms, the notion of interculturality acknowledges the ways in which "cultures are endlessly evolving in a society, with the potential to be exchanged and modified" (Aman 23). In my exploration of artistic interdisciplinary collaboration, which focuses on the interaction and engagement between people, I adopt the notion of interculturality to examine the interaction between people of ethnically and culturally diverse societies. Intercultural collaboration provides an opportunity, artistic vision, or simply physical space for artists of diverse cultural background to interact and learn from one another, thereby mutually enriching and transforming each other's artistic practice while creating new practice. To collaborate on an artistic intercultural project requires from participants active, sensitive, and respectful listening skills to hear the diverse voices and aesthetic notions. Intercultural collaboration invites extensive learning of each other's artistic practice and acknowledges polycentric perspectives and modes of communication.

Current usage of the term *interculturality* also refers to interaction between diverse constellations "that are defined in terms not only of culture but also in terms of ethnicity, language, religious denomination, and/or nationality" (Dietz 1). It moves away from the static notion and representation of culture and instead toward definitions of culture as collective resources and symbolical interpretation. This notion thus underscores the fundamentally personal and interactional nature of intercultural contact, the non-static and evolving nature of cultures, and the ways in which cultures are represented and contested in the intercultural collaboration.

Further complicating the matter is another layer of complexity in intercultural collaboration, namely, the varying degree of difference/distance between participants' starting points in language and culture. From this perspective, we can consider interculturality as a "relative" phenomenon, depending on the degree of distance between the languages and cultures of participants. This is particularly useful when we address inter-Asian interculturality, since issues of similarity of culture and language are salient to participants in inter-Asian intercultural interaction and to the unfolding of that interaction. The notion of cultures, in this situation, does not work as a static frame to give shape to the collaboration, but rather is realized as the collaborative processes unfold, and is interactional and interpersonal in nature. Intercultural artistic collaborations between cultural groups that share a high degree of similarity allow their participants to reflect on their own artistic practices in unusual ways. Such opportunities offer a unique prism to view a familiar aesthetic or practice. I will return to this point later in the second case study.

The more nuanced connotations of interculturality, and the focus on the agency of participants in such interactions discussed thus far, hopefully work to dissuade readers from assigning the notion of cultural (mis)appropriation or borrowing to such collaboration. The charge of cultural (mis)appropriation or borrowing has in recent years been broadly applied to situations involving the adoption of elements of one culture by members of another culture, whereby the cultural elements are used outside of their original cultural context. Yet it is worth reiterating that culture is never static and fixed, but rather always evolving, changing, and transcending borders. Keeping cultures neatly separated from each other is no longer a feasible option or even desirable, since not only interculturality proliferates in today's societies, but also, as Edward Said notes, "The history of all cultures is the history of cultural borrowing. Cultures are not impermeable" (216). As a framework, therefore, critiques of cultural (mis)appropriation unfortunately tend to solidify the boundary between cultures, thus inadvertently perpetuating the ahistorical and static notion of culture. Rather than demystifying and revealing stereotypes, it upholds them. Fred Dervin, a scholar of multicultural education, proposed the notion of a "liquid approach" to interculturality, which is based on the idea that "knowledge, society and subjectivity are all dynamic and contextual phenomena which can be theorized in terms of dialogues between different (real and imagined) perspectives" (37–52). In this chapter, I consider the participants' serious interest in each other's cultural beliefs, values, aesthetics, and artistic practices to be an essential part of the intercultural artistic collaboration, which provides the basis for innovative and creative projects that contribute to mutual flourishing of different cultural groups.

Key Characteristics

With the drive toward creativity and innovation, interdisciplinary and intercultural collaborations in the performing and visual arts inspire unique creative practices. Both contribute significantly to the fulfillment of individuals within the context of a larger community. These collaborations share certain key characteristics. These characteristics are specific, though not necessarily unique, to artistic collaboration. I identify them here because these characteristics seem essential to the sense of fulfillment and conviviality that such artistic collaborations offer.

1. The skills that contribute to the collaborative artistic production are distributed, immanent in the network of collaboration, rather than being parsed out in individual ways. In other words, collaborators endeavor to communicate with others throughout the process. Creating arts with other art forms in mind—constantly—is a significant feature of such collaboration. There may or may not be a symmetrical relation or hierarchical relationship between the disciplines or cultures.

2. The sparks resulting from the artistic collaboration cannot be planned or predetermined, so one must be flexible and opportunistic. Collaboration does not follow a certain hierarchy within one's own discipline, but rather is shaped by the immediate context of artistic encounters. This allows for greater exploration of aesthetic possibilities. By contesting the existing rules (methods or aesthetic concepts) within an "antecedent discipline," such a collaboration transcends boundaries of various sorts.

3. The deep engagement with the complexity of a different perspective in arts through the collaborative process often means the learning or mastery of another art form, which invariably offers valuable dispositions. Because performing/visual arts are often intricately linked, such crossing of boundary into the unfamiliar yet not altogether different art form provides new perspectives on one's own discipline.

4. Such a collaborative project requires individuals to put aside their own objectives and history, and instead place their talents in service of the collective artistic collaboration, learning to be attuned to one another. The collaboration is heterogeneous in its forms and orientations. Being attuned to one another provides a momentum of collective creativity and allows individual insights and ideas to be molded into the interdisciplinary art project.

5. Most artistic projects cannot avoid dealing with the dimensions of arts in another discipline, which they normally address only in implicit ways. Examples abound, such as music alluding to image, dance making bodily gestures in conjunction with sonic elements, drama being punctuated or reinforced by rhythmic bodily gestures, etc. The often implicit approaches include allusion, metaphor, backdrop, underlying sonic or visual images, bodily expression, etc. Significantly, then,

the interdisciplinary collaboration unveils the implicitly addressed artistic dimensions, making them fully explored and examined. Through this process, the artistic project becomes jointly produced and leaves fewer artistic dimensions only implicitly or imaginarily addressed.

6. The interdisciplinary and intercultural collaborative process underscores the importance of what could be called "singing your song in a foreign land." The process not only shores up the differences between cultures, but also forces its constituents to articulate and communicate with their collaborators in different and often innovative ways. In so doing, the constituent participants are able to better visualize their own art and practice of art in a different light. Collaboration produces a kind of introspection that is otherwise unattainable.

7. More drastic compromises or negotiation becomes necessary. "Everyday categories are dissolved or inverted; normative procedures are denaturalized, becoming visible and open to challenge. . . . Both creativity and destruction may be unleashed." Also, "multiple human agencies interacting in the social world place radical limits on predictability and the broader stability of the [. . .] project." (Bendix et al. 37). As participants strive to map more closely, the landscape continues to shift under their gaze. Thus, even the most discipline-centered participants pay more holistic attention to the project, and their strengths in creativity and knowledge are supplemented by the expertise of others in the network of collaboration.

These characteristics are important to productive interdisciplinary and intercultural collaboration in artistic creation. Although some might seem challenging to achieve, they create significant momentum of changes at the same time. These are key characteristics that, if encouraged throughout the collaborative process, could create a promising field to enhance personal and collective betterment. One could also learn a great deal from collaboration with these key characteristics in terms of creating a better community. These creative collaborations promote human flourishing, bring a heightened sense of respect for different artistic perspectives, and foster meaningful interpersonal connection within the artistic community.

Trust, Suspicion, and Stereotypes

Trust is a positive outcome from the artistic collaboration across disciplines and cultures. Artistic collaboration requires that the participants build trust and respect suspicion. It is important to take risks and experimental approaches that threaten one's own identity and doctrines, while challenging that of others. Yet it is precisely in such a situation, when everyone's artistic identity is challenged, and the hierarchy and boundaries of disciplines are rearranged, that it is important to build trust among the participants who are creative individuals and most likely have become accustomed to their own creative ways. In other words, efforts need to be made to establish mutual trust in order to ensure free cognitive resources for thinking creatively and innovatively. Collaborators need to learn to cultivate trust, because anxiety is distracting and is not conducive to artistic collaborative creation.

Furthermore, building trust means creating stable expectations among participants, and free cognitive space is thus available to work on the important aspect of the interdisciplinary collaboration. The ability to create such an environment is recognized by all, and it is not only beneficial to the project and outcome, but also to the well-being and flourishing of the individuals. In performing and visual arts collaborations, building such trust could spike new creativity both within the interdisciplinary environment and the antecedent disciplinary pursuit. In particular, the benefit could be long term, and it could create a habit of trusting in interpersonal relations. These are opportunities for personal growth in artistic vision, self-image, and personal fulfillment.

The trust-building created in such a collaborative situation ranges from the minimal, which is simply the promise of responsible engagement with and contribution to the project, or the trust of other colleagues' competence to contribute, all the way to what could be described as the thicker trust, one that involves an internalized sense of trust, such that the collaborators could work on the assumption that their counterparts' full efforts would be put toward executing the art project together, rather than benefit one's own agenda, and that they would each make efforts to grasp what the other has to offer. The sense of working for the collective creative project anchors their collaboration and has the potential to lift one out of the more negative aspects associated with the artistic creation, such as self-doubt, insecurity, isolation, etc.

Just as important, however, are the ways that trust built among the collaborators provides the opportunity to learn beyond labels and to become more attuned to others in different disciplines. When a group of interdisciplinary collaborators come together, it is easy to rely on "labels" or "types" to assess new/unfamiliar collaborators and what they represent. And due to a lack of understanding, such labels could be easily reduced to stereotypes. The process of collaboration allows participants to move beyond stereotypes and pay closer attention to their similarities as well as their differences. In particular, collaboration encourages participants to find ways of complementing each other in the collective project. This is especially important because stereotypes often work to perpetuate existing inequalities by reducing the opportunity and input of ethnic minorities. Stereotypes also accord more weight to the words and ideas of the dominant population, therefore deepening the gulf between the two. Such processes become the mechanism of exclusion. Conversely, the building of trust allows one to go beyond the stereotype, dismantling its disruptive power, learning beyond the "labels,"

Two Case Studies

The two case studies presented below inspired me to delve deeper into the nature of interdisciplinary and intercultural collaboration in the arts and its larger benefit to human flourishing. They involve very different circumstances. Thinking about them beyond their immediate scope opened my eyes to the uniqueness of such collaborations, which in turn has informed my observations throughout this chapter. The first case involves my year-long effort (2017–2018) to create a course on interdisciplinary collaboration within the Mason Gross School of the Arts at Rutgers University, in New Brunswick, New Jersey. The school is composed of four departments (Music, Dance, Theater, Arts & Design) and the Filmmaking Center. The aim of this course is to establish effective ways to inspire interdisciplinary collaboration and sustain them for students of all levels. From its inception, the notion of creating such a program or course in our school was met with great enthusiasm, both from the students and from the faculty. Prior to this course, many undergraduate students had already taken the initiative to embark on a few interdisciplinary collaborative projects, but without any infrastructure support or institutional backing. The case study examines this unique type of interdisciplinary collaboration and its relation to artistic fulfillment.

The second case study describes the inter-Asia intercultural collaboration of a Korean traditional ensemble, Contemporary Music Ensemble of Korea (CMEK), and Chinese American composer Chou Wen-chung on the work *Eternal Pine*. It was a prominent collaboration between a Korean *chong-ak* traditional ensemble and a composer of Chinese heritage who, though

spending most of his life in the United States, has a long-established reputation associated with the Chinese literati (*wenren*) tradition. Chou first
emerged in the mid-twentieth-century American music scene as a protégé
of Edgard Varèse, and has since served as composition professor and as a
dean at Columbia University. He also founded The Center for U.S.-China
Arts Exchange, which promotes creativity and mutual understanding of the
arts of the two countries. Since its inception in 1978, the center has been
carrying out projects in a wide range of arts fields, including arts education, music, literature, theater, dance, painting, and sculpture. For nearly
half a century, Chou has been a tireless proponent of the concept of cultural merger in contemporary music. Yet, he never penned a composition
for Asian musical instruments in his sixty-year composition career until
this collaboration with CMEK that led to *Eternal Pine*. The unique case of
Chou reveals the power of intercultural and inter-Asia artistic collaboration. I would argue that such collaborations have the power to liberate the
creative self and enable individuals in their artistic pursuits. Both cases provide a window on how collaboration in the arts, which requires deep engagement and learning about another art form, offers opportunities for an
extraordinary sense of fulfillment, excitement, and impetus, that are otherwise unattainable.

Mason Gross Interdisciplinary Seminar

Mason Gross School of the Arts is the flagship public arts conservatory of
Rutgers University. Its four departments (Music, Dance, Theater, Art &
Design) and Filmmaking Center have thrived in the past decade. Its mission
is "to nurture creative talent and instill the insights and skills that future generations of arts professionals need to contribute to the creative and scholarly
world."[1] The school's student body includes 815 undergraduate students and
329 graduate students, and it has 260 faculty members. The school offers BA,
BM, BFA, MFA, AD, DMA, and PhD degrees. As a whole, Mason Gross is a
community of artists—dancers, filmmakers, musicians, theater artists, and
visual artists and designers—who study, teach, create, perform, and exhibit.

---

[1] These figures are from fall 2017, as presented in Mason Gross website in 2019, accessed October
4, 2022. https://www.artandeducation.net/directory/79377/mason-gross-school-of-the-arts-at-rutg
ers-university.

Given the vibrant community, it is quite curious, then, that the school has not instituted formal courses or regular opportunities for collaboration across the five disciplinary areas. The reasons are complicated, but no doubt are related to the rigorous training within each discipline of the art conservatory that requires such full devotion of the students and faculty to their own departments. While interdisciplinary collaboration is desirable in principle, and is sought after on the university campus at large, it has failed to accrue momentum with the Mason Gross community, a disappointment both to the administration and to the faculty and students. Given the immense resources and talents within the innovative artistic community, the need to create an interdisciplinary program is obvious to everyone.

Interdisciplinary collaboration is a complex endeavor, however. Mere juxtaposition of different disciplines or having different disciplines converge on the same field creates pseudo-interdisciplinarity, because such juxtaposition lacks interaction, integration, and linking. Thus an infrastructure is needed to ensure the explicit focusing and blending of disciplines to yield a true creative environment. In other words, the development of a successful infrastructure is crucial to ensure higher levels of interaction and interface. A certain degree of transfer of content from one discipline to another discipline is necessary. The ultimate goal is for the integration of all participants' approaches to the greatest degree (Klein 15–30).

While this interdisciplinary curriculum is in the process of being developed, it is clear that the main task will be to create an infrastructure that could reinforce the above key characteristics and materialize them through course designs, platforms, modes of participation, etc., in order to yield the true benefit of such collaboration. And in this process, the larger community of Mason Gross could become a true artistic community, where creativity could be sparked through interactive collaboration across different disciplines.

In the benchmark research, however, the finding is somewhat surprising. Mason Gross is not alone in its lacking of curricular support for interdisciplinary courses. While there are many schools of the arts, either as a part of larger universities, or as independent institutions, few offer courses that encourage interdisciplinary collaboration and/or educate and guide their students in interdisciplinary pursuits. On college campuses, collaborations across different disciplines in performing arts remain largely an extracurricular initiative, or a special event created for the purpose of programming. An important exception is the Creative-Innovation CoLaB program at the Trinity Laban Conservatory in London. On the school website, the program states its goal:

For two weeks each year, CoLab provides a place to take risks, be crea-tive and experiment within a rich and supportive environment. Over 900 students from across the Faculties of Dance and Music come together to create, develop and rehearse projects without the distraction of any other learning activities or performances.[2]

During these two weeks every year, students are guided by expert mentors to build artistic relationships with other artists/performers across genres, disciplines, generations, and cultures to create innovative projects and perform. Students learn to not only cross disciplines to work with others, but also reach across cultural, national, and generational divides, to col-laborate with creatives from Taiwan, Hong Kong, California, and other organizations in the community. In the process, these collaborative groups work together to redefine fundamental issues such as memory, movement, play, journey, vocabulary, etc. The opportunity inspires students to develop new genres, to take artistic risks, to embrace the unexpected, to build mutual understanding, to achieve common goals, and to make something together. As an educational model, the Creative-Innovation CoLaB is extremely successful and has inspired students to develop their own immersive projects of interdisciplinary collaboration. The conservatory's vision and its infrastructure contribute significantly to its astounding success.

Unlike Trinity Laban Conservatory, however, Mason Gross, as a part of a state university, does not have the flexibility to carve out two weeks in the university's academic calendar to devote fully to interdisciplinary collabo-ration, nor does it have a similar budget for interdisciplinary production. Yet the need for such an educational opportunity is no less urgent. After considering various curricular constraints, budgetary limits, and other stakeholders, I have determined that the elective seminar format is most practical and fulfills the educational purpose. Based on this format, a course proposal *Mason Gross Interdisciplinary Seminar* was submitted and approved by the school's curriculum committee, and is moving into the phase of imple-mentation. Figures 8.1–8.3 reproduce the mission, goals, and design of the Mason Gross Interdisciplinary Seminar.

It is hoped that the seminar will be implemented as a school-wide elec-tive seminar, and funding can be secured to provide incentives and to

---

[2] See https://www.youtube.com/watch?v=viqRxAVmY2Q, visited October 4, 2022.

Why Interdisciplinary Collaboration?

◆ Create intellectual, creative, and social bonds among participants from different artistic expertise, aspirations, and pursuits

◆ Students work closely with faculty in an interdisciplinary and collaborative setting

◆ Complement the core curriculum in own disciplines

◆ Develop skills and visions for arts of the future

Figure 8.1. Mission of interdisciplinary seminar.

Collaboration in Performing and Visual Arts

Goals of the Initiative

◆ Create high visibility

◆ Foster distinctive culture

◆ Make it an integral part of MGSA experience

◆ Diversify modes of learning

Figure 8.2. Goals of interdisciplinary seminar.

Course Name and Design

◆ **Mason Gross Interdisciplinary Seminar**

– Interdisciplinary Collaboration

– 10-week · 80-min · 1 credit · pass/fail · elective

– 2nd- to 4th-year students

– Not counted toward teaching load

– Research stipend for faculty (comparable to Byrne Seminar)

– Administered by Associate Dean of Academic Affairs

– MSGA Seminar Committee (oversight)

Figure 8.3. Design of interdisciplinary seminar.

compensate those faculty who participate by offering thematic topics and serving as mentors to students.

Eternal Pine

Composer Chou Wen-chung's work, *Eternal Pine*, was commissioned by the Contemporary Music Ensemble of Korea (CMEK). It was written for Korean traditional instruments: the *gayageum* (zither) and an ensemble of *daegeum* (flute), *piri* (double-reed instrument), *shaengwhang* (mouth organ), and *changgu* (drum). Chou composed the work upon the invitation of a *gayageum* master Yi Jiyoung. The work was dedicated to the musicologist Dr. Lee Hye-ku on the occasion of his 100th birthday in 2008.

In 2007, *gayageum* master Yi Jiyoung sought to hold a concert of contemporary *gayageum* composition, and through a friend's introduction, she got to know Chou's work and contacted him. Yi Jiyoung is a professor of Gayageum Performance in the Department of Korean Music in the College of Music at Seoul National University. She has performed internationally and has recorded over forty albums, four of which were solo. She was the first PhD in *gayageum* performance in Korean music history. In addition to traditional music, Yi Jiyoung is also a pioneer in the field of contemporary music for *gayageum*. In 2012 she published a highly acclaimed book, *Contemporary Gayageum Notation for Performers and Composers*. In nearly 400 pages, the book provides detailed discussion and illustrations of special techniques and features essential for composing modern pieces for *gayageum*, in addition to an introduction on the instrument's history and most popular genres and forms. Her desire for the book is "to both competently and artistically represent the beauty of the gayageum in writing," and "to help elucidate the world of gayageum performance technique" (Yi 7).

Chou Wen-chung, raised in a traditional Chinese intellectual family, fostered the temperament of the *wen ren* (the Confucian artist-scholar-gentleman) and yet was also well educated in readings of Western civilization. His career in the United States demonstrates that he became fluent and excelled in both artistic worlds. His compositions, *The Willows Are New* (1957) and *Yuko* (1956), were both famously based on music of *qin* (Chinese zither), but performed on Western instruments, piano for the former, and piano, violin, percussion, and five wind instruments for the latter. In these compositions, he used a variety of sonorities, careful octave doubling of a single tone in the melodic flow, and frequent shifts of melodic registral ranges to achieve an intricate texture and the modulation of lines that reflect Chinese aesthetics. His use of extended timbral effects on the Western instruments evokes the serene beauty of *guqin* (Chinese zither) and draws from a melody taken from tablature notation composed by Song-dynasty *guqin* master Mao Minzhong (毛敏仲). Chou also learned the classic divination text *I-Ching* and used its sixty-four hexagrams to create variable modes for his composition. The variable mode principle enables the music to transform itself and to "adapt itself from one tonal format to another, such as pentatonic or chromatic" (Wen-chung iv). His efforts since the 1950s have paralleled endeavors by other prominent composers such as John Cage, Henry Cowell, Colin McPhee, Hary Partch, and Isang Yun.[3] Yet, unlike Stockhausen's *Telemusik* (1966) or Philip Glass's collaboration with Ravi Shankar, Chou never included non-Western instruments in his compositions. This is all the more curious, considering that he has long expressed strongly his view of "cultural confluence" in which he made explicit that Asian culture could offer much for the enrichment of musical experience of Western audiences, strongly advocating for synthesizing the musical cultures at the conceptual level (Chou Wen-chung, "Asian and Western Music: Influence or Confluence?" 60–66; "Toward a Re-Merger in Music").

As noted earlier, the composition of *Eternal Pine* in 2008 marked Chou's first composition with traditional East Asian musical instrumentation. During the process of composition, Chou was invited to combine Korean traditional instruments with instruments of Western classical music, which he declined, insisting on the Korean ensemble alone. *Eternal Pine* was composed in the spirit of *chong ak*, traditional Korean music. The composer writes:

I was attracted to the idea of composing for Korean instruments as I have long admired the expressivity of the *gayageum*, as well as the

---

[3] Studies of Chou Wen-chung's work and comparison with his contemporaries could be found in many scholarly works. Peter Chang, *Chou Wen-chung: The Life and Work of a Contemporary Chinese-Born American Composer* (Oxford: The Scarecrow Press, 2006); Eric Chiu Kong Lai, *The Music of Chou Wen-chung* (Aldershot, UK: Ashgate, 2009); *Polycultural Synthesis in the Music of Chou Wen-chung*, edited by Mary I. Arlin and Mark A. Radice Arlin (New York: Routledge, 2018).

other instruments in the ensemble. But composing for instruments of such historical heritage in the spirit of their aesthetics was a challenge as well. As a composer, I am deeply committed to the heritage of East Asian music. In composing *Eternal Pine*, I was inspired by the traditional dedication to idealism in East Asia, as exemplified by my two colleagues. Thus, the title's reference to pine is a symbol of longevity and the eternity of nature in East Asian cultures. "Meditation on Eternity," the first movement, is a reflection on the eternity of heaven and earth, the fundamental aesthetic principle of East Asia, as expressed in the Chinese terms *tian di ren*—heaven, earth and humanity—suggesting human expression within the timelessness of the universe and the constraints on earth. The subsequent movements, "Lofty Peaks" and "Profound Gorges," allude to the depths of those two axes. In this work, I tried to adhere to the spirit of the cultural heritage and technical traditions of Korean music with the intention of continuing the heritage rather than merely adapting gestures from its music or infusing it with modern practice.[4]

A celebrated author of cultural merger, Chou Wen-chung took the opportunity to contemplate the commonality in aesthetics of Chinese and Korean cultures and found revelation in his own longtime pursuit.

Two characteristics of great significance demonstrate Chou's unique expressivity in this composition, connecting to his intense interaction with Korean musical tradition. The first concerns instrumentation and performing technique. While it is an ensemble of traditional Korean instruments, Chou chose the modern sixteen-string *gayageum*, devised an idiosyncratic whole-tone tuning (beginning with E-flat) for the instrument, and adopted techniques mimicking Chinese zither playing. His combination of *gayageum* with *daegeum*, *piri*, and *changgu* is common for a traditional Korean ensemble, all of which, though originating in China, have a clearly established Korean identity. More unusual is Chou's inclusion of a rare instrument, the *shaengwhang* (mouth organ, now also tuned to E-flat). *Shaengwhang* is derived from, and remains quite similar to, the Chinese instrument *sheng*, a mouth-blown free reed instrument consisting

[4] Chou Wen-chung official webpage, accessed August 15, 2019. https://chouwenchung.org/comp osition/eternal-pine/.

of vertical pipes. This choice reflects his segue into a pan-Asian sonority. The instrument's unique shape and sonority are noted in a poem by a poet of late Tang dynasty:

> Short and long bamboo pipes as if a phoenix
> has spread its wings,
> The notes of the *shaengwhang* (*sheng*), returning to
> the moonlit pavilion,
> Are more melancholy
> than the cries of a dragon.
>
> —Luo Ye, "In Praise of Sheng"

筠管參差排鳳翅，月堂淒切勝龍吟 。

—唐·羅鄴 《題笙》

The verses and visual imagery express aptly the powerful sonority of *shaengwhang*, the timbre of which has tremendously expressive effects on *Eternal Pine*. Working with the instruments and players, and with the unique palette of Korean and Chinese sounds, Chou creates the magnificent melding of timbre and resonance that shape the work's distinctive sound world. The astounding result is summed up by the theorist Yayoi Uno Everett: "Chou manages to infuse stately elegance and ritualistic qualities through showcasing the distinctive colors of the instruments."[5]

The second element is Korean traditional rhythm. Rhythm is one of the most important characteristics of traditional Korean music. As musicologist Lee Byungwon has noted: "Most of the rhythms of Korean traditional music are based on triple time or groups of three beats. The characteristic detail of Korean triple time is that the third beat is either articulated or accented, drawing more attention than the first beat" (Lee 62). *Gayageum* master Hwang Byung-ki also identifies *jangdan* (lit., "long-short") as basic to traditional Korean music (Hwang 813–816). *Jangdan* encompasses a variety of rhythmic cycles, each characterized by their particular rhythmic patterns and tempo, whose usage is shared among various traditional music genres.

---

[5] Yayoi Uno Everett, "Chou Wen-chung: Eternal Pine," CD liner note for Chou Wen-chung, *Eternal Pine*, Contemporary Music Ensemble of Korea; Boston Musica Viva; Yi Ji-young and Kim Woong-sik; Taipei Chinese Orchestra (New York: New World Records 8077–2, 2015).

In *Eternal Pine*, Chou adopted the *jangdan* tradition, creating the triple time rhythmic pattern and cycle akin to the Korean music. Yet in an ingenious way, he achieves a result of a flowing rhythm more akin to Chinese aesthetics. After all, a strong rhythmic profile is never a central characteristic of Chinese literati music. Figure 8.4 produces the first page of the score. Note that the drum (*changgu*) begins with a traditional Korean rhythmic pattern. In a three-beat metrical design, 9/4, the tension accrues with the strong accent on the third beat of measure 3.[6]

Collaborating with performers of Korean traditional music inspired Chou's creative work with Asian instruments to achieve his aesthetic goal, the unlocking of a new world of timbre and practice. Chou noted that "composing *Eternal Pine* was a great learning process for me."[7] He made clear what he found inspiring in Korean traditional music: "Chong ak is dedicated to the expression of human emotion inspired and symbolized by natural phenomena but projected with serenity and dignity. It evokes imageries that have inspired East Asian minds for centuries" (Chou, *Ode to Eternal Pine*, [iv]).

I think the inter-Asian connection is a key factor to the extraordinary success of this intercultural collaboration. In this engagement of interculturality, the close connection between the Chinese *wen ren* aesthetic tradition and Korean court and traditional music made possible the profound connection and mutual learning. Korean music became a prism through which Chou contemplated the *wen ren* tradition of Chinese society. Chou spent a long time learning the Korean musical tradition and characteristics of these traditional instruments, whereas the *gayageum* master also spent time learning the abstruse meaning and Chinese aesthetic that Chou uncovered in Korean instruments and that imbued this work. In other words, it is both the similarity and difference between the two Asian traditions that helped Chou unlock the key to expressing his Chinese aesthetic ideas with Asian instruments and take Yi Jiyong into a different realm of Asian sonic imagination. The intercultural interdisciplinary collaboration made possible a creative project that could not happen within its antecedent discipline alone. In particular, the Chinese-Korean inter-Asian connection made possible what otherwise had not

---

[6] For detailed discussion about the work, see Rao, "Inner," 31–42.
[7] Quoted in Radice 65–66.

to Dr. Lee Hye-ku

ETERNAL PINE

蒼松　늘 푸른 소나무

I. Prelude – Exploring the modes

调意　조의 뜻

周文中

Chou Wen-chung

Grave

Daegeum

Piri

Saenghwang

Gayageum

Changgu

hard yarn mallet

soft yarn mallet or felt timpani stick

poch.
poco

Gayageum:

* grace notes are played by bouncing the stick
** *chong ak*: traditional fingering
*** the notated pitch is the actual pitch

Copyright © 2008 by Chou Wen-chung (BMI)
All Rights Reserved.
Alle Rechte verbeholten.

Figure 8.4. Chen Weh-chung, *Eternal Pine.*
Courtesy of Paul Sacher Foundation, Basel, Chou Wen-chung Collection.

been attainable for Chou: expressing Chinese aesthetics and sensibility through Asian musical instruments.

The power of the intercultural and interdisciplinary collaboration for artistic fulfillment is immense. As testimony to the power of this unlocking, Chou continued to produce works in his pine series: he composed another version for solo *gayageum* and *changgu*, two versions for different Chinese instrument ensembles, as well as a version for Western ensemble. The inter-Asia collaboration of Chou and CMEK proved to be a creative process of remarkable enlightenment and creative flourishing for Chou Wenchung. It was also fulfilling for his collaborator, Ji Yiyoung, who revealed at an interview that *Eternal Pine* was unlike other contemporary *gayageum* compositions:

> It is not especially virtuosic or technically difficult. But it requires a tuning system that is quite unusual for *gayageum*, and also playing techniques common to the Chinese version of zither, *guzheng*, but unusual from *gayageum*. Yet these were not difficult to me, since I am very used to modern *gayageum* composition. . . . In fact, it was the philosophical and abstract sensibility, and profound spiritual depth of the composition, that was difficult to master. (personal interview with Yi Jiyoung, Seoul, Korea, July 2018)

It took Ji Yiyoung nearly ten years, well beyond her premier of the work in 2008, to gain the kind of understanding of its meaning and to feel genuinely content with her own mastery of the profound depth of *Eternal Pine*.

Conclusion

By sharing these two case studies and exploring larger underlying issues, I hope to have shown the significance and importance of interdisciplinary and intercultural collaboration in arts, both in terms of shaping innovative and imaginative artistic creation, and in terms of fostering human flourishing. I consider interdisciplinary and intercultural collaborations one of the most important endeavors in arts and arts education. Unfortunately, even though interdisciplinary and intercultural collaboration in the arts have become increasingly commonplace, current curriculum design has not yet caught up with the task of better preparing future generations of artists for it. It is critical for arts students to have the curricular support both for learning to understand the concept of worldview in the arts and how it is derived from individuals' perspectives, and for learning how to integrate different disciplinary and cultural approaches in order to transcend boundaries of various sorts through collaboration. And the extraordinary work of composer Chou Wen-chung and *gayageum* master Yi Jiyoung's intercultural collaboration serves as a powerful reminder of how interactive collaboration helps individuals achieve long-term, even lifelong, creative goals.

In his survey of the global history of happiness, Darrin M. McMahon noted that it is the belief of Chinese Dao philosophers that "[g]enuine happiness required devotion to the Dao or Way, the true order and harmony of the universe that transcended the self." While the description of the wisdom tradition is attributed to the Axial age, spanning roughly the first millennium BCE, it nevertheless provides spiritual values upon which humanity continues to draw. The key characteristics of interdisciplinary and intercultural collaboration in the visual and performing arts discussed above show that this type of devotion to the creative collaboration of artistic projects is essential to happiness and human flourishing. McMahon continues: "Regardless of the word used to describe it, however, the insight that human flourishing demanded the development of human excellence—the cultivation of particular strengths of character and mind—was [a] common assumption of Axial understanding of happiness" (McMahon 5).

This set of values is particularly acute for a creative project that typically aims for and is devoted to developing human excellence. Interdisciplinary and/or intercultural collaborations contribute to the well-being of the individual and the collective community. True happiness in this regard involves going "beyond" one's own creative training and methods, being actively engaged in and interacting with another type of creative discipline, and cultivating new perspectives that shed light on one's own creativity and performance. Needless to say, successful collaboration of this type relies heavily on trust and respect, and when those are present, the community flourishes as a whole. It is my hope that by identifying the important characteristics that lead to interdisciplinary and intercultural collaboration, I have been able to contribute to the understanding and development of such projects and their ability to enhance and encourage human flourishing.

Works Cited

Aman, Robert. *Impossible Interculturality?: Education and the Colonial Difference in a Multicultural World*. PhD dissertation, Department of Behavioural Sciences and Learning, Education and Adult Learning. Linköping University, 2014, 23.

Arlin, Mary I., and Mark A. Radice, editors. *Polycultural Synthesis in the Music of Chou Wen-chung*. Abingdon, UK: Routledge, 2018.

Augsburg, Tanya. "Interdisciplinary Arts." *Oxford Handbook of Interdisciplinarity*, 2nd edition, edited by Robert Frodeman. Oxford: Oxford University Press, 2017, pp. 132–140.

Bendix, Regina, Kilian Bizer, and Dorothy Noyes. *Sustaining Interdisciplinary Collaboration: A Guide for the Academy*. Urbana: University of Illinois Press, 2017.

Born, Georgina. "For a Related Musicology: Music and Interdisciplinarity, Beyond the Practice Turn." *Journal of the Royal Musical Association*, vol. 132, no. 2, 2010, pp. 205–243.

Chang, Peter. *Chou Wen-chung: The Life and Work of a Contemporary Chinese-Born American Composer*. The Scarecrow Press, 2006.

Chou Wen-chung. "Asian and Western Music: Influence or Confluence?" *Asian Culture Quarterly*, Winter 1977, pp. 60–66.

Chou Wen-chung. *Ode to Eternal Pine*. New York: C. F. Peters, 2009.

Chou Wen-chung. Official webpage. https://chouwenchung.org/composition/eternal-pine/. Accessed August 15, 2019.

Chou Wen-chung. "Toward a Re-Merger in Music." *Contemporary Composers on Contemporary Music*, edited by Elliot Schwartz and Barney Childs. New York: Da Capo Press, 1987, pp. 308–315.

Dervin, Fred. "A Plea for Change in Research on Intercultural Discourses: A 'Liquid' Approach to the Study of the Acculturation of Chinese Students." *Journal of Multicultural Discourses*, vol. 6, no. 1, 2011, pp. 37–52.

Dietz, Gunther. "Interculturality." *The International Encyclopedia of Anthropology*, edited by Hilary Callan (chief editor). https://doi.org/10.1002/9781118924396.wbiea1629. Accessed October 4, 2022.

Everett, Yayoi Uno. "Chou Wen-chung: Eternal Pine." CD liner note for Chou Wen-chung, *Eternal Pine*, Contemporary Music Ensemble of Korea; Boston Musica Viva; Yi Ji-young and Kim Woong-sik; Taipei Chinese Orchestra (New York: New World Records 8077-2, 2015).

Hwang, Byung-ki. "Philosophy and Aesthetics in Korea." *Garland Encyclopedia of World Music, East Asia: China, Japan, and Korea*, edited by Robert Provine, Yoshihiko Tokumaru, and J. Lawrence Witzleben. New York: Routledge, 2002, pp. 813–816.

Klein, Julie Thompson. "A Taxonomy of Interdisciplinarity." *The Oxford Handbook of Interdisciplinarity*, edited by Robert Frodeman, J. T. Klein, and C. Mitcham. Oxford: Oxford University Press, 2010, pp. 15–30.

Lai, Eric Chiu Kong. *The Music of Chou Wen-chung*. Aldershot, UK: Ashgate, 2009.

Lee, Byongwon. *Style and Esthetics in Korean Traditional Music*. Seoul: National Center for Korean Traditional Performing Arts, 1997, 62.

McMahon, Darrin M. "From the Paleolithic to the Present: Three Revolutions in the Global History of Happiness." *Handbook of Well-Being*, edited by Ed Diener, Shigehiro Oishi, and Louis Tay. Salt Lake City: DEF Publishers, 2018, pp. 1–10. DOI:nobascholar.com.

Radice, Mark A. "A Biographical Essay." *Polycultural Synthesis in the Music of Chou Wen-chung*, edited by Mary I. Arlin and Mark A. Radice. Abingdon, UK: Routledge, 2018, pp. 65–66.

Rao, Nancy Yunhwa. "Inner Liason and Dialogue in Asia: Chou Wen-chung and Korean Gayageum" (亞洲內部連結與對話：周文中與伽倻琴). *The Art of Music: Journal of the Shanghai Conservatory of Music*, vol. 156, 2019, pp. 31–42.

Rao, Nancy Yunhwa. Personal interview with Yi Jiyoung, Seoul, Korea, July 2018.

Said, Edward. *Culture and Imperialism*. New York: Vintage, 1994, 216.

Yi, Jiyoung. *Contemporary Gayageum Notation for Performers and Composers*. Seoul: National Seoul University, 2012, 7.

9

Rethinking Women's Music-Making through the Lens of Human Flourishing

Annegret Fauser

In Michelle Obama's memoir, *Becoming*, a section of her childhood recollections is dedicated to her piano lessons. Discovering the piano as an instrument, she writes, "felt natural, like something I was meant to do" (9). She casts her lessons with her great-aunt, Robbie Shields, as a laboratory of personal and musical formation, a subjective space carved out through music (12). For Obama, the piano also becomes a lens through which to understand economic and racial boundaries: the piano of her childhood is a battered upright in her great-aunt's studio. The unexpected encounter with a perfect baby grand at her first student recital turns into a disconcerting life lesson of difference, yet one that helps navigate later challenges (15-16). Studying at Princeton, for instance, "was like stepping onstage at your first piano recital and realizing that you'd never played anything but an instrument with broken keys. Your world shifts, but you're asked to adjust and overcome, to play your music the same as everyone else" (75). Eventually, the instrument fades from her story, but the piano lessons and her musical childhood experiences continue to serve as metaphors in telling her life.

Obama's memoir exemplifies how music-making—as feminist musicological inquiry has shown over the past decades—could function as a uniquely empowering activity for women young and old in Western culture, even in an environment in which other restrictions curtailed their flourishing along boundaries of gender, class, and race. Yet although musicological research has revealed the positive aspects of women's musicking, scholarly discourse and analyses often emphasize the restrictions and oppression that made individual women's achievements even more exceptional.[1] Rather than framing female musicking as eudaimonic, feminist analysis often understands

---

[1] On gender and exceptionality in Western history, see Sheriff (pp. 1–2).

Annegret Fauser, *Rethinking Women's Music-Making through the Lens of Human Flourishing* In: *Music and Human Flourishing*. Edited by: Anna Harwell Celenza, Oxford University Press. © Oxford University Press 2023.
DOI: 10.1093/oso/9780197646748.003.0010

women's music as a seismograph sonically registering, and responding to, oppression. My own research is part of that collective of writings, whether reflecting on women's self-representation in the world of music, analyzing their works and performances, or engaging with the representation of women musicians in the work of men.[2] Especially in historical musicology, the recovery of women's musical worlds and the historiography of their exclusion have led to the perception of their personal and artistic achievement as intrinsically enmeshed with its sociopolitical fields, simultaneously enabling and bounding women's musical flourishing. At its most extreme, women's musical voices were silenced, and not only in the context of the Paulinian dictum that women be silent in church (*mulieres in ecclesiis taceant*, 1 Cor. 14:34). If individuals flourished despite oppression—serving as the exemplar of the exceptional woman—or if female-centered communities such as convents offered bounded alternative spaces that enabled women's creativity, such positivity seemed not necessarily a cause for celebration. Instead, the critical and explicit engagement with the root of exclusion and its effect on women's musicking serves as an epistemological centerpiece of feminist analysis.

In this context, focusing on the question of "what causes individuals to flourish and communities to thrive" may seem counterintuitive at first (Pawelski, "What Is the Eudaimonic Turn?" 3). Indeed, if the eudaimonic turn in the humanities emphasizes research on "the things we value in life" and "a general concern with the overall question of well-being," then how can any rethinking of women's music-making through the lens of human flourishing provide a different narrative that emphasizes the empowering, creative, joyful, and affirmative quality of female musical achievement without neglecting or denying the systemic oppression of gender inequality (Pawelski, "What Is the Eudaimonic Turn?," 16–17). Such a turn in telling women's musical lives poses a number of challenges. There is a difference between the post-traumatic growth of so privileged a male composer as Ludwig van Beethoven, as discussed by Martin E. P. Seligman and Mihaly Csikszentmihalyi, and the artistic flourishing—in the face of gender and racial oppression—of a Florence B. Price (Seligman and Csikszentmihalyi 9). The interracial composer was all too aware—in her own words—that she had "two handicaps—those of sex and race. I am a woman; and I have some Negro

---

[2] See Fauser, "Lili Boulanger's *La Princesse Maleine*;" "*La Guerre en Dentelles*;" "Creating Madame Landowska;" "Oscarine and Réginette" (pp. 68–108; 83–129; 1–23; 55–70).

blood in my veins."[3] If, according to James O. Pawelski, the eudaimonic turn in the humanities might be understood as a corrective rather than a pivot so as to create balance, then the question of "how people in various times and cultures have understood well-being" might retain its emphasis on flourishing even when acknowledging gender difference and oppression (Pawelski, "Bringing Together the Humanities and the Science of Well-Being to Advance Human Flourishing," 213). As such inquiry eschews "the shallow kind of happiness that has rightly been criticized by so many careful thinkers," perhaps a eudaimonic perspective might, indeed, lead to a more "reparative" historiography of women's musicking, highlighting a gendered specificity of resilience and growth through music without descending into the murky waters of "inspiration porn" or allowing music to remain unquestioned as an expressive instrument complicit in acts of oppression (Pawelski, "What Is the Eudaimonic Turn?," 18; Grue 838-849).[4] How, then, might we structure a narrative framework of women's flourishing that is reparative—to draw on Eve Kosofsky Sedgwick's concept—when engaging with their musical history, its traces in the archives, and its performative reconstructions (Sedgwick; Pawelski and Moores 29)?[5]

These questions resonate with recent thought on how to communicate women's musical lives. In her biography of Francesca Caccini, Suzanne Cusick first diagnoses the problem of an epic historiography that created the conditions for writing pathological history where women are a priori constituted as outsiders; moreover, given their abject position, their musical work cannot be cast as producing "transhistorical resonances." She then makes the point that to engage positively with women's music-making, it is necessary to consider them as "persons whose stories and artistic work were inevitably rooted in and shaped by historically and culturally specific, gendered, and classed experiences of the material and discursive world" (Cusick, *Francesca Caccini*, xvi-xvii). As Cusick reflects on how to go about telling such stories, she draws on Adriana Cavarero's concept of relational narratives that celebrates each individual as a unique person within a network of others,

---

[3] Florence B. Price, letter to Serge Koussevitzky. I am grateful to Douglas Shadle for sharing his document with me.

[4] Grue defines inspiration porn as "(a) an image of a person with visible signs of impairment who is (b) performing a physical activity, preferably displaying signs of physical prowess, and is (c) accompanied by a caption that directs the viewer to be inspired by the image in question" (839). The classic formulation that identifies "reparative" reading in opposition to a "paranoid" one is Eve Kosofsky Sedgwick, "Paranoid Reading" (123-151).

[5] Compare also Samuel N. Dorf's notion of a "reparative encounter with our archives" (154).

a turn that draws attention to *who* someone is—not *what* (xvii–xviii). This perspective calls for taking the historical Other seriously, for listening to their own voices instead of overwriting them with our interpretations, for approaching the Other with love—in the sense of the French philosopher Emmanuel Lévinas—where the Other retains their alterity in a relation that is thus ethical.[6] Engaging with historical female-identified musicians on their own terms, then, when thinking about the humanities and human flourishing, offers a pathway to taking seriously their joy and creativity in sound, whatever pressures and constraints they might have faced in their times. It allows us—to return to Cusick's feminist project—to make their musical and "relational world seem vivid and real, so that readers can both imagine a world very different from their own and imagine their own relationships to these ancestors whose stories they have not known before" (Cusick, *Francesca Caccini*, xvii). While simultaneously acknowledging the historical conditions of misogyny and gender-specific oppression, constructing a gynocentric counternarrative that focuses on female accomplishment, networks, and empowerment offers not only a historiographic reconfiguration of the past but also a deliberate epistemological strategy of anchoring it in the female experience of the present.

Human flourishing, as discussed by Pawelski, is a concept with a definitional spectrum that ranges from framing positivity through a range of perspectives to reflecting upon it both historically and currently, including an awareness of cultural difference in identifying what might constitute flourishing and positivity (Pawelski, "Bringing Together the Humanities"; Pawelski, "Defining the 'Positive,'" 357–365).[7] In this contribution, I will focus on three aspects from this broad spectrum that might help with thinking about women's musical histories in more eudaimonic terms. The first two—engaging with creativity, on the one hand, and musical agency, on the other—relate to writing these histories as scholars; the third addresses arts and humanities education through my almost two decades of experience teaching introductory courses on female-identified musicians in the general-education curriculum of a public university in the American South.

---

[6] This idea of "love" as mode of engagement with an Other that Lévinas proposed in 1961 has since entered scholarly discourse (prominently through the mediation of Sedgwick) as an alternative approach to scholarship. As William Cheng writes, "a reparative musicology would simultaneously restore love for people and reconstruct the opportunities for care among them" (98).

[7] See also the wide range of essays in Susan A. David, Ilona Boniwell, and Amanda Conley Ayers, *The Oxford Handbook of Happiness*.

Creativity

As I am starting this section, the first citation that comes to my mind is the twenty-year-old Clara Schumann's confession, in 1839: "I once believed that I possessed creative talent, but I have given up this idea. A woman must not desire to compose—there has been none able to do so. Should I expect to be the one?" (Reich 216). Schumann's words echo those of Fanny Hensel confessing her apprehension of her brother's judgment when she finally decided to publish her music, and Nadia Boulanger's statement that she gave up composing "because I wrote music that was not even bad, just useless."[8] Despite my self-set task for this chapter to focus on the empowering, creative, joyful, and affirmative quality of female musical achievement, my understanding of women's music history is so thoroughly "paranoid"—to evoke Sedgwick's second concept—that thinking positively as a scholar becomes itself a challenge.[9] Yet while paranoia might be a strong theory with the goal of exposing injustice, violence, and oppression, it is also "a theory of negative affects," placing "its faith in exposure" alone (Sedgwick 136–138).[10] Perhaps— and this is an aside, but an important one—bringing human flourishing into conversation with the arts and humanities then also might induce a form of the "reflectiveness" that Louis Tay, James O. Pawelski, and Melissa G. Keith have identified as a core mechanism of flourishing when it comes to confront one's scholarship with its habits and worldviews (4). Furthermore, as Marcia Citron already pointed out twenty-five years ago, with the gendered concept of genius that developed in the late eighteenth century, women were far more apt to consider themselves as inferior creators in comparison to men (44–79). How should we create a counternarrative to such a self-critical perspective?

Positive quotations by women composers about their creativity are harder to recall instantaneously, perhaps even to find. When women do address the power of music as a positive force, they often focus on music's role in their lives rather than on their creative achievements. "The practice of art is the largest part of my being," fifty-year-old Clara Schumann writes in a letter to

---

[8] Nancy Reich gives a digest of Hensel's letters to her brother, Felix Mendelssohn Bartholdy, in "The Power of Class" (28-29). Boulanger's comment about her decision to stop composing is so pervasively cited that it even made it into her obituary in the *New York Times*. See Allen Hughes, "Nadia Boulanger."

[9] Sedgwick posits queer theory, in particular, as having "a distinctive history of intimacy with the paranoid imperative" (126).

[10] Sedgwick's notion of "reparative" readings, by contrast, can be understood as being "about pleasure" and "frankly ameliorative," thus mapping better onto the notion of a eudaimonic historiography (144).

Johannes Brahms: "to me, it is the air that I breathe" (mugi.hfmt-hamburg. de/en/artikel/clara_schumann.pdf). Similarly, and at around the same age, Wanda Landowska wrote in a letter to the French musicologist Paul-Marie Masson that she rejoiced in her various enterprises as a musician, including her recently founded École de Musique Ancienne, and invited him to share her joy: "I am sure that you share my happiness, because you know to what extent I live for my music which, nowadays, is everything in my life."[11] And while in exile in the United States during World War II, Boulanger (also in her fifties at that time) wrote to the conductor Serge Koussevitzky that "for us—and perhaps for the world, salvation and truth lie in art."[12] This individual response to music as a means to personal flourishing, if not survival, might find a transhistorical echo in Hildegard von Bingen's famous statement "symphonialis est anima" (the soul is musical) that, when set in relation to her letter from 1178 to the prelates of Mainz, claims an embodiment of that musical soul that includes—implicitly—her own: "The body is truly the garment of the soul, which has a living voice; for that reason it is fitting that the body simultaneously with the soul repeatedly sing praises to God through the voice" (*Hildesgardis* 65).[13] Hildegard's gender-positive affirmations of women's creativity can be found throughout Western music history as female creators produced programmatic texts to validate their musicking, such as the oft-quoted preface of Madalena Casulana's *First Book of Madrigals* (1568), wherein she states that she wanted "to show the world, as much as I can in this profession of music, the vain error of men that they alone possess the gifts of intellect and artistry, and that such gifts are never given to women."[14] Not for nothing does this quotation form part of the Wikipedia article on the composer—it is, after all, a powerful and catchy declaration.

It is, of course, an epistemological commonplace that public utterance and personal expression—as well as historical and cultural difference—create important variations in the creation and interpretation of such quotations.

---

[11] Wanda Landowska, letter to Paul-Marie Masson: "Je suis sûre que vous partagez mon bonheur, car vous savez combien je vis pour ma musique qui, maintenant, est tout dans ma vie."

[12] Nadia Boulanger, letter to Serge Koussevitzky: "pour nous—et peut-être pour le monde, le salut, et la vérité, sont dans l'art."

[13] See Marianne Richert Pfau and Stefan Johannes Morent, *Hildegard von Bingen* (313).

[14] Madalena Casulana, dedication to Isabella de' Medici-Orsina, *Il primo libro de madrigali a quattro voci* (1568). The translation is somewhat approximate and comes from https://en.wikipe dia.org/wiki/Maddalena_Casulana [a more appropriate translation can be found in LaMay (41)]. The Italian original reads: "di mostrar anche al mondo (per quanto mi fosse concesso in questa professione della Musica) il vano errori degl'uomini, che de gli alti doni dell'intelletto tanto si credono patroni, che par loro, ch'alle Donne non possono medesimamente essere communi." See Heere-Beyer (63).

Moreover, the quotation-game does not really bring about a eudaimonic turn in the historical exploration of women's music-making. Perhaps a reparative historiography might want to take each individual and their unique creative flourishing on their own terms, following Cusick's challenge to the implied normativity of a masculinist construction of genius by focusing on a narrative of women's flourishing. Creativity, then, might mean a life lived in and through music, professionally as much as private.

Telling the creative stories of Wanda Landowska's musical life might mean foregrounding her joy in playing the music of Johann Sebastian Bach and her pleasure in Jean-Philippe Rameau, her excitement and pride at collaborating in the creation of the Pleyel harpsichord, her passion for arguing for her vision in performance through lecture recitals and publications, her excitement in creating her school and embracing her musical authority, her resilience of surviving her spouse's death (or, as she believed, murder) as well as exile and economic challenge by immersing herself in music both through performance and through scholarship.[15] Such emphasis could offer a richer perspective of what living through music might have meant for Landowska. Indeed, her comment to Masson, cited above, may have been less about resignation and more about a life well lived because it was musical.

A narrative centering on women's flourishing in and through music might also emphasize compositional affirmations of female creativity, from as early on as Hildegard's musical output, a creative venture "of extraordinary significance to her" given its close intertwining with her theological worldview, one both sonic and gynocentric (Meconi 17). The sequence, "O virga ac diadema" (part of her *Symphonia armonie celestium revelationum* from the 1150s), for example, celebrates the *forma mulieris* (form of the woman) in salvation history. Not for nothing does the sequence lead, in a soaring and melismatic passage, to the acclamation of Mary as the *salvatrix* who "offered a new light to the human race" ("que novum lumen humano generi protulisti").[16] Compositional claims to female musicality can be found throughout Western music history, often in the context of invoking the Virgin Mary. One example is Francesca Caccini's spiritual madrigal, "Maria, dolce Maria," from her *Primo libro delle musiche* (1618). As Cusick has pointed out, Caccini is

[15] Though not mentioned in Samuel Dorf's discussion of Natalie Clifford Barney, Landowska was among Barney's lesbian circle, which would open up his restorative engagement with this circle to an eudaimonic inclusion of Landowska. See Dorf (47).

[16] For a general discussion of *Symphonia armonie celestium revelationum*, see Meconi (46-50). The sequence can be found in Briscoe (18-19).

giving voice to the singer through "the increasingly ecstatic response" to the name of Christ's Virgin mother—a musical celebration of female vocality through its character as a meta-song (Cusick, "Francesca Caccini, 1587–after 1641," 49).

Both musical examples are from a privileged world, in which a divine female model could serve as an anchor for a positive configuration of feminine expression. Nonetheless, focusing historiographies of women's musical flourishing on their creations as much as on historical and personal documents might help to recast their stories in eudaimonic terms, even in moments of crisis. Florence B. Price chose to set Langston Hughes's poem "Hold Fast to Dreams" in 1945 when her own dreams of a successful career had come crashing down yet again. With her vocal emphasis on the exhortation to "hold" the "dreams," she contrasts the rich sonority of a world where dreams might still have wings to a barren life without, when the piano falls away for a moment without music. Dreams, Price's music tells us, reside where beauty and hope are laying—and to hear her struggling to return to the rich arpeggios of the opening dreamscape after its disruption not only displays sonic resilience but also ensounds the transformative impact of the loss. If we take women's musical choices seriously and open our minds to their voices lovingly (to return to Lévinas's stance), our reparative historiography can acknowledge resilience in the face of the negative and oppressive in a way that a paranoid analysis cannot ignore or silence. One might ask, as a consequence, whether eudaimonic historiography is additive, intersectional, or contrary as it responds to the weight of a pathological and paranoid understanding of gendered history.

Musical Agency

Thinking about women's musical agency, it seems to me, offers a fascinating way in which to explore flourishing in and through music. Agency, in this framework, can take on a number of forms, whether artistic choices made by a composer or the musical work of a performer. I am particularly intrigued by individuals who use their gendered position as caregivers to deploy music as a means to promote flourishing in others. It is well known in the history of music therapy that female nurses and caregivers during World War I promoted music as a means of emotional and physical healing and well-being in the face of trauma. Not only were women performers offering concerts to distract and entertain wounded soldiers in hospital wards, but they also started to develop somewhat scattered initiatives to use music more systematically as a therapy to deal with conditions then identified as shell shock and other forms of neurasthenia.[17] Individual performers such as the American Paula Lind Ayers toured European military hospitals with the YMCA; she became known as the "girl who sang away shell shock" (Reschke-Hernandez 284). Two other American women were closely involved in these early forms of music therapy: Isa Maud Ilsen, a trained nurse, and Harriet Ayer Seymour, a pianist and teacher. Ilsen considered her therapeutic work through music "almost as precise as any existing medicine or surgery" and became—after a short period in the employ of the U.S. War Department—the director of Hospital Music in Reconstruction Hospitals for the Red Cross (Davis 38). In this position, Ilsen instituted rules of conduct for the use of music in hospital settings—in particular the requirement for close communication between the music therapist and the patient's physician—that are still relevant for current practice. Her therapeutic work was strongly influenced by a third female music therapist, Eva Augusta Vescelius, whose writings were published in such well-known journals as the *Musical Quarterly* and who, in 1903, had founded the National Therapeutic Society of New York City. Indeed, one of her articles about "Music and Health" (1918) explored systematically how the vibrations of music and those of the body might become aligned through music therapy, and cautioned practitioners to be careful with their therapeutic work because ill-chosen music might act as a poison (Vescelius 388–391). While these early attempts at music therapy remained somewhat isolated, their often successful results with soldiers provided the starting point for the more systematic exploration of music therapy during World War II.[18]

In past publications, I have focused on a paranoid reading of the way these initiatives by women musicians and nurses were sidelined; the medical and military establishment of the 1940s, with its masculinist, even mechanistic, conception of physical and mental health, began to frown upon seemingly autodidactic female practitioners whose musical and therapeutic skills were acquired through keen observation and empathy with their patients. Hand in hand with its professionalization, at the end of World War II, music therapy as a discipline rejected both what was considered amateurish and what was

[17] On the historical terminology, see Jones, Fear, and Wessely (1641–1645).
[18] On music therapy in the United States during World War II, see Fauser, *Sounds of War* (127–134).

seen as focused on flourishing and well-being. Instead, the pathological turn in psychology also affected music therapy when the War Department and the Surgeon General took over (Fauser, *Sounds of War*, 130–133). Yet in the case of these early music therapists, a eudaimonic approach to their musical achievements might not only give voice to their focus on flourishing through the therapeutic uses of music that they promoted—with its emphasis on human well-being and an unabashedly holistic vision of the mind-body connection—but also offer an earlier, alternative model within the history of music therapy that fulfilled a similar function to (and were influenced by) the contemporaneous concepts of well-being, from the New Thought movement to Carl Jung.

Centering on musical activism as a historiographic lens might offer another pathway to understanding individual women's agency. Such musical activism could be put into the service of sociopolitical causes, for instance when Dame Ethel Smyth composed "The March of the Women" in 1910. Cicely Hamilton's words were added after the melody had already been written—an instance where the sonic pre-dated the verbal, and the verbal captured if not qualified the character of a tune.[19] This catchy march-song with its exhortation to "Shout, shout, up with your song!" became one of the signal tunes of suffragist musicking, not only in the United Kingdom but also in other regions of the anglophone world such as the United States. A eudaimonically focused historiography might not so much trace the march's transnational circulation, however, as focus on its entanglement with specific female agency both in its creation and in its various performances, carefully delineating a gynocentric "sonic vernacular," but one understood as generated by individual women whose distinct voices are acknowledged in their own right.[20] A focus on this interplay of the individual and the collective—for activism does insert the individual into a community either in actual or in aspirational terms—offers a holistic view of women's musicking, one in which human flourishing is simultaneously cast as musical and sociopolitical.[21] Indeed, focusing on women's individual and collective

---

[19] The composer reported the following about the creation of "The March for Women": "In those early days of my association with the W.S.P.U. occurred an event which, in her pride, the writer must recount . . . namely the formal introduction to the Suffragettes of 'The March of the Women,' to which Cicely Hamilton fitted the words after the tune had been written—not an easy undertaking." See Smyth (201).

[20] Tausig defines "sonic vernaculars" as being "composed of locally trenchant sonic and aural practices and the symbolic meanings that they transduce and mediate" (26).

[21] On community in music, see Shelemay (349–390).

agency in music through a eudaimonic lens offers a window on human flourishing that, in effect, rounds out the picture of a given society both in the past and in the present.

Female-Identified Musicians in the Curriculum

In my tellings of stories about women of the past, I have focused deliberately on narrative strategies and scholarly approaches rather than another aspect of this entangled historiographic challenge: its role in university education. Over the past two decades, I have taught a number of courses relating to women and music, both in the United Kingdom and in the United States. During that period, I have changed how I told women's stories so that—as Cusick put it so persuasively—my students might "both imagine a world very different from their own and imagine their own relationships to these ancestors whose stories they have not known before" (Cusick, *Francesca Caccini*, xvii). Few of my students specialize in music: many have played a musical instrument when growing up or are performing in the university's ensembles, whether in marching band or in our women's *a cappella* group, The Loreleis. Some are simply music lovers with no practical experience—and some need to meet a requirement with a course that fits their timetable. For most students in these classes, music serves foremost to entertain, to give pleasure, to support studying, to have fun performing as amateurs, to dance, or to worship. Yet in my "Introduction to Women and Music" they face, from the outset, a range of questions that address gender binaries, sexuality, and intersectionality, among others. And suddenly, music becomes an art that stretches their ears and understanding through listening closely to repertoire as different as Mitski's "Your Best American Girl" (2016) and Hildegard's *Kyrie*, an art no longer without sociopolitical and cultural context. Music, they discover, is an agent within human life. It can be joyously beautiful, as in Janelle Monáe's "Pynk" (2018); it can be heartbreakingly painful, as in Lili Boulanger's "Dans l'immense tristesse" (1916). My students get angry in discussion when they encounter the matter-of-course fat-shaming of female performers in the world of opera, the routine disempowerment of female-identified performers in the music business, or the dismissal of women's contributions to a genre such as American country music in the so-called Tomato-gate scandal in 2015, when radio consultant Keith Hill explained women's absence in playlists and billboards by describing them as the garnish (Smith, "#SaladGate").

Given that I do not check my paranoid academic persona at the classroom door, I was and am surprised when students send emails or write in their feedback that these encounters "empower" them. The students are quite clear: their feeling of empowerment does not come from their merely being inspired by musical ancestors overcoming obstacles; anger and engagement, they tell me, are empowering because these stories about female-identified creators and their music are situated in the world—their world and those of different cultures and times. Music, they discover, is both pleasure and a conduit into confronting social injustice and oppression, a reality they often do not associate with the medium. It can be uncomfortable and painful to listen closely to music about sexual violence—such as Tori Amos's "Me and a Gun" (1991)—and to face gender representation in recent Bro-country songs or Robin Thicke's video "Blurred Lines" (2013).

As I reflect on the humanities and human flourishing in this context, I realize that teaching the stories of women's musicking in history and across cultures allows me to contribute to the flourishing of very diverse groups of undergraduates directly—through their encounter with musics they already love or sometimes learn to love—and indirectly, when such newly discovered ancestors engender stories that enable a better and more passionate understanding of past and present life by emphasizing the uniqueness of each and every voice, whether a composer, a performer, or any participant in the worlds of music.[22] Moreover, emphasizing the uniqueness of feminine creativity within the context of an often hostile world resists the traditional master narrative that casts especially Western music history as a teleological plot of masculine genius and greatness. It is not a question of conforming to normative and troublesome notions of "greatness," but rather of celebrating accomplishment, agency, and creativity. A solely paranoid feminist historiography often reduces individual voices into a pattern of either submission or resistance, even as it centers the focus on female-identified musicians, contrary to their somewhat tokenistic presence in many a contemporary

---

[22] I am drawing on the following paragraph from Tay, Pawelski, and Keith: "This research suggests that positive absorption in the arts and humanities may enhance human flourishing directly, through positive physiological and psychological reactions and increased hedonic well-being. At other times, however, immersion in the arts and humanities may enhance human flourishing indirectly, through physiological and psychological reactions that are unpleasant in themselves but that ultimately serve to broaden experience, promote emotional breadth and depth, and increase eudaimonic well-being" (3).

American music-history textbook. Instead, a concept such as Cavarero's that foregrounds relational narratives of unique creativity and artistic resilience presents a pathway toward rejoicing in the power of music's vibrations without airbrushing away the negativity of sociocultural conditions. It was the entanglement of the paranoid and the reparative both in my teaching and in the students' responses that brought an outcome that speaks compellingly to the possibilities of the arts and humanities in the project of human flourishing.

I have sketched briefly three areas where it might be fruitful to think about how to recast the historiography and pedagogy of women's music-making through the lens of human flourishing. I found the imagining of a more reparative telling of the history of women's musicking far more difficult than I expected. Thirty years of academic activism and paranoid interpretations have carved grooves that are not easy to escape. Yet if a balanced rather than revisionist configuration of women's musical history might contribute to the project of integrating human flourishing into the humanities, I can see empowerment, in the words of my students, rather than "inspiration porn" as its result, just as Michelle Obama's piano lessons contributed to her flourishing and well-being not by ignoring inequality and oppression, but by allowing her to respond to them through the joy of music.

Works Cited

Boulanger, Nadia. Letter to Serge Koussevitzky, November 6, 1940. Library of Congress, Music Division, Serge Koussevitzky Archive, box 8.

Briscoe, James, editor. *New Historical Anthology of Music by Women*. Bloomington and Indianapolis: Indiana University Press, 2004.

Casulana, Madalena. Dedication to Isabella de' Medici-Orsina, *Il primo libro de madrigali a quattro voci*, Venice: [Girolamo Scotto], 1568.

Cheng, William. *Just Vibrations: The Purpose of Sounding Good*. Ann Arbor: University of Michigan Press, 2016.

Citron, Marica J. *Gender and the Musical Canon*. Cambridge: Cambridge University Press, 1993, pp. 44-79.

Cusick, Suzanne G. *Francesca Caccini at the Medici Court: Music and the Circulation of Power*. Chicago and London: University of Chicago Press, 2009.

Cusick, Suzanne G. "Francesca Caccini, 1587-after 1641." *New Historical Anthology*, edited by James Briscoe. Indiana University Press, 2004, pp. 48-50.

David, Susan A., Ilona Boniwell, and Amanda Conley Ayers, editors. *The Oxford Handbook of Happiness*. New York: Oxford University Press, 2013.

Davis, William B. "Keeping the Dream Alive: Profiles of Three Early Twentieth-Century Music Therapists." *Journal of Music Therapy*, vol. 30, 1993, pp. 34-45.

Dorf, Samuel N. *Performing Antiquity: Ancient Greek Music and Dance from Paris to Delphi, 1980-1930.* New York: Oxford University, 2018.

Fauser, Annegret. "Creating Madame Landowska." *Women & Music: A Journal of Gender and Culture*, vol. 10, 2006, pp. 1-23.

Fauser, Annegret. "*La Guerre en dentelles*: Women and the Prix de Rome in French Cultural Politics." *Journal of the American Musicological Society*, vol. 51, 1998, pp. 83-129.

Fauser, Annegret. "Lili Boulanger's *La Princesse Maleine*: A Composer and Her Heroine as Literary Icons." *Journal of the Royal Musical Association*, vol. 122, 1997, pp. 68-108.

Fauser, Annegret. "Oscarine and Réginette: A Comic Interlude in the French Wagner Reception." *The Politics of Musical Identity: Selected Writings*, Ashgate Contemporary Thinkers on Critical Musicology, vol. 13. Farnham, UK, and Burlington, VT: Ashgate, 2015, pp. 55-70.

Fauser, Annegret. *Sounds of War: Music in the United States during World War II.* New York: Oxford University Press, 2013.

Grue, Jan. "The Problem with Inspiration Porn: A Tentative Definition and a Provisional Critique." *Disability and Society*, vol. 31, no. 6, 2016, pp. 838-849.

Heere-Beyer, Samantha. *Claiming Voice: Madalena Casulana and the Sixteenth-Century Italian Madrigal.* MA thesis, University of Pittsburg, 2009.

Hildesgardis Bingensis Epistolarium. Edited by Lieven van Acker. Turnhout: Brepols, 1991.

Hughes, Allen. "Nadia Boulanger, Teacher of Top Composers, Dies." *New York Times*, October 23, 1979, Section A, p. 1.

Jones, Edgar, Nicola T. Fear; and Simon Wessely. "Shell Shock and Mild Traumatic Brain Injury: A Historical Review." *American Journal of Psychiatry*, vol. 164, 2007, pp. 1641-1645.

LaMay, Thomasin. "Madalena Casulana: *my body knows unheard of songs*." *Gender, Sexuality, and Early Music*, edited by Todd M. Bergerding. New York and London: Routledge, 2002, pp. 41-71.

Landowska, Wanda. Letter to Paul-Marie Masson, July 23, 1930, Paris: Bibliothèque nationale de France. F-Pn l.a. 63 (25).

Lévinas, Emmanuel. *Totality and Infinity: An Essay on Exteriority*, translated by Alphonso Lingis. Pittsburgh: Duquesne University Press, 1969.

"Maddalena Casulana." Wikipedia. https://en.wikipedia.org/wiki/Maddalena_Casulana.

Meconi, Honey. *Hildegard von Bingen.* Urbana, Chicago, and Springfield: University of Illinois Press, 2018.

Obama, Michelle. *Becoming.* New York: Crown, 2018.

Pawelski, James O. "Bringing Together the Humanities and the Science of Well-Being to Advance Human Flourishing." *Well-Being and Higher Education: A Strategy for Change and the Realization of Education's Greater Purposes*, edited by D. Harward. Washington, DC: Bringing Theory to Practice, 2016, pp. 207-216.

Pawelski, James O. "Defining the 'Positive' in Positive Psychology: Part II. A Normative Analysis." *The Journal of Positive Psychology*, vol. 11, no. 4, 2016, pp. 357-365.

Pawelski, James O., and D. J. Moores. "The Eudaimonic Turn in Literary Studies." *The Eudaimonic Turn: Well-Being in Literary Studies*, edited by James O. Pawelski and D. J. Moores. Madison, NJ: Fairleigh Dickinson University Press, 2013, pp. 26-63.

Pawelski, James O. "What Is the Eudaimonic Turn?" *The Eudaimonic Turn: Well-Being in Literary Studies*, edited by James O. Pawelski and D. J. Moores. Madison, NJ: Fairleigh Dickinson University Press, 2013, pp. 1-26.

Pfau, Marianne Richert, and Stefan Johannes Morent. *Hildegard von Bingen: Der Klang des Himmels.* Cologne, Weimar, and Vienna: Böhlau Verlah, 2005.

Price, Florence B. Letter to Serge Koussevitzky, July 5, 1943. Library of Congress, Music Division, Serge Koussevitzky Archive, box 50.

Reich, Nancy. *Clara Schumann: The Artist and the Woman*, revised edition. Ithaca, NY: Cornell University Press, 2001.

Reich, Nancy. "The Power of Class: Fanny Hensel and the Mendelssohn Family." *Women's Voices across Musical Worlds*, edited by Jane A. Bernstein. Boston: Northeastern University Press, 2004, pp. 18-35.

Reschke-Hernandez, Alaine E. "Paula Lind Ayers: 'Song-Physician' for Troops with Shell-Shock during World War I." *Journal of Music Therapy*, vol. 51, 2014, pp. 276-291.

Schumann, Clara. Letter to Johannes Brahms, October 15, 1868. Given in Janina Klassen, "Clara Schumann." Musik und Gender im Internet. https://mugi.hfmt-hamburg.de/receive/mugi_person_00000752?lang=en.

Sedgwick, Eve Kosofsky. "Paranoid Reading and Reparative Reading, or, You're So Paranoid, You Probably Think This Essay Is about You." *Touching Feeling: Affect, Pedagogy, Performativity*. Durham, NC: Duke University Press, 2003, pp. 123-151.

Seligman, Martin E. P., and Mihaly Csikszentmihalyi. "Positive Psychology: An Introduction." *American Psychologist*, vol. 55, no. 1, 2000, pp. 5-14.

Shelemay, Kay Kaufman. "Musical Communities: Rethinking the Collective in Music." *Journal of the American Musicological Society*, vol. 64, 2011, pp. 349-390.

Sheriff, Mary D. *The Exceptional Woman: Elisabeth Vigée-Lebrun and the Cultural Politics of Art*. Chicago and London: The University of Chicago Press, 1996.

Smith, Grady. "#SaladGate: Expert Draws Ire Comparing Country Music's Women to Tomatoes." *The Guardian*, May 27, 2015. https://www.theguardian.com/music/2015/may/27/saladgate-tomatoes-women-country-music?curator=MusicREDEF.

Smyth, Ethel. *Female Pipings in Eden*. Edinburgh: Peter Davies, 1933, 201. Given in Erica Fedor, *Transnational Smyth: Suffrage, Cosmopolitanism, Networks*. MA thesis, University of North Carolina at Chapel Hill, 2018, 43.

Tausig, Benjamin. "Sound and Movement: Vernaculars of Sonic Dissent." *Social Text*, vol. 36, no. 3, 2018, pp. 25-45.

Tay, Louis, James O. Pawelski, and Melissa G. Keith. "The Role of the Arts and Humanities in Human Flourishing: A Conceptual Model." *The Journal of Positive Psychology*, vol. 12, 2017, pp. 1-11.

"UNC Loreleis." http://loreleis.com/

Vescelius, Eva Augusta. "Music and Health." *Musical Quarterly*, vol. 4, 1918, pp. 376-401.

10

Playful Transcendence

Paths to Human Flourishing in Black Music Research and Performance

Melvin L. Butler

The concepts of transcendence and play have long been used to explore music's capacity to represent, shape, and structure ordinary and extraordinary human experiences. We witnessed this earlier in the volume, with Shana Redmond's chapter on the (positive) science of Black music (Chapter 2). As she revealed, the study of music as a vital aspect of both transcendence and play may provide a wellspring of experiences that reveal how these concepts interrelate and influence human flourishing in societies around the world. Conventional and academic discourses of play and transcendence, however, sometimes pit them against each other, inscribing a mutual exclusivity that I believe is problematic. In the United States, it seems we are conditioned to relegate "play" to the realm of childlike or "make-believe" activities. The notion of "transcendence," especially religious transcendence, most often calls to mind "serious" endeavors. Even when experienced as a source of personal pleasure, such endeavors are not easily associated with laughter, joking, mimicry, and other "playful" aspects of social behavior. In social and religious settings around the world, however, play and transcendence are two sides of the same coin. This chapter reflects my fascination with how play and transcendence interrelate and stimulate human flourishing within and beyond ritual contexts.

Drawing on my ethnomusicological fieldwork within African American and Caribbean Pentecostal communities, along with my work as a jazz musician, I posit "play" and "transcendence" as complementary and overlapping modalities. Music—as sound, behavior, and concept—helps to bring the connections between these two multivalent concepts into focus. The following questions guide my discussion: Under what conditions does musical and spiritual transcendence become a playful phenomenon? What can music

Melvin L. Butler, *Playful Transcendence* In: *Music and Human Flourishing*. Edited by: Anna Harwell Celenza, Oxford University Press. © Oxford University Press 2023. DOI: 10.1093/oso/9780197646748.003.0011 tell us about the human capacity to achieve transcendence through play, play through transcendence, and an experiential blurring of boundaries between the two? How might ethnomusicological research on Black music-making stimulate fresh thinking about what it means to flourish in ritual contexts? Finally, to what extent might this type of scholarly work itself constitute a form of playful transcendence? My discussion touches on multiple forms of literal and symbolic expression while navigating the contested epistemological boundaries between work and play, scholarship and performance, and ritual and everyday life.

Viewing African diasporic rituals through the lens of "playful transcendence" yields a sharper understanding of the musical tools that human beings around the world use in their efforts to flourish. In the pages that follow, I explore musically induced experiences of transcendence, religious and otherwise, and assess the ways in which the "playfulness" of these phenomena might influence human flourishing. Ethnographic vignettes, some of which describe my own wrangling with experiential and conceptual boundaries between play and transcendence, provide insight into how play and transcendence take musical form. My objective here is to connect my experiences as a musician, scholar, and religious practitioner to much broader fields of musical, social, and theological inquiry. In transcending conventional boundaries between self and other, home and field, ethnomusicologist and religious practitioner, I also embody a particular kind of play. This chapter thus exemplifies the playful transcendence it sets out to analyze. The risk of this endeavor is not lost on me. Reflexivity can fall down a slippery slope into a pool of overindulgence. But I see this exercise as a worthwhile mode of representation that points to new ways of being "scholarly" in a constantly changing academic marketplace. It is a way to transcend the limits that, as Alejandro Madrid explains in Chapter 5, have been imposed on musical scholarship since the nineteenth century. I begin unpacking the terms "transcendence" and "play" as I and other scholars have deployed them. This discussion is followed by a call for understanding the interplay of these two concepts. Through a series of cases studies, I show how transcendence and play work in tandem and contribute to human flourishing in a widening range of intellectual, social, and ritual contexts. We often speak of "playing" music. I suggest, however, that "play" may also be applied metaphorically to many other realms of activity. Likewise, "transcendence" applies to many kinds of human experiences. Taken together, these terms help to uncover some creative ways in which humans learn to thrive in dynamic social and cultural contexts. In this chapter, I strive to push us toward new ways of considering the interplay of transcendence and play in relation to musical strategies for human flourishing. To that end, let me begin by unpacking transcendence and play as multivalent and interrelated concepts. I will then turn to other types of "playful transcendence" that exemplify how scholars, musicians, and religious practitioners find ways to flourish.

Risk-Taking and Boundary Crossing

My understanding of "transcendence" has been shaped by both personal experience and ethnographic research.[1] Since childhood, I have attended Pentecostal church services in which felt manifestations of the Holy Spirit—sometimes described as a spiritual "quickening"—are commonplace. As a form of religious transcendence, these quickenings take numerous forms. For example, some believers report an overwhelming feeling of inner joy that causes them to weep. Others describe it as an electrical shock that compels their bodies to twitch or jerk from side to side. Some Pentecostals cry out with ecstatic utterances or in unknown tongues. But this type of religious transcendence can also be felt outside of a worship service, as Redmond has shown. While music may facilitate religious transcendence, it is not always vital. In fact, Pentecostals can feel quickened during moments of silent meditation, prayer, and even conversation. Describing the "holy touch" experienced by a Pentecostal believer, anthropologist Glenn Hinson writes, "No 'ritual context' induced its occurrence; no ceremonial surround of sound, motion, and sensory saturation invoked frames of expectation and enactment; no relentless rhythms drove consciousness down an alternate path" (2). How, then, are we as music scholars to deal with such phenomena that cannot be fully tracked, transcribed, or theorized with the tools of musicological analysis? And in settings where music plays a major role, what challenges await "non-musical" theologians and anthropologists seeking to grasp the meaning of transcendence? It is true that "speaking of soul, Spirit, and experience draws talk into a realm rarely explored by academic inquiry"? (Hinson 2). I submit that the difficulties academics face on this front arise, in large part, from the need to transcend disciplinary and

---

[1] Empirical studies of transcendence in music include Trost et al., "Mapping Aesthetic," 2769–2783, and Zentner, Grandjean, and Scherer, "Emotions Evoked," 494–521.

epistemological boundaries. As my colleagues and I discovered during the discussions that facilitated the creation of this volume, rising to the challenge of transcending disciplinary boundaries requires a willingness to take intellectual risks by "playing" outside of the experiential sandboxes in which we feel most at home.

Ethnomusicologists have made some notable efforts to explore transcendence as both a religious and "secular" phenomenon, and these bold forays have benefited from other academic disciplines. Judith Becker's music-centered discussion of "deep listeners" draws not only on fieldwork among religious trancers in South and Southeast Asia, but also on scientific studies of the brain. She uses the term "deep listeners" to describe individuals who are "profoundly moved, perhaps even to tears, by simply listening to a piece of music" (Becker 2). Katherine Hagedorn's 2001 study of Cuban Santería channels a range of anthropological and philosophical theories to examine the role of dramatic folkloric performances in evoking transcendent experiences. Borrowing Jean Baudrillard's notion of "simulacra," she concludes that staged representations of the "real" can be spiritually fulfilling events that induce spirit possession "even when the context and the intent of the performance . . . [are] apparently secular" (Hagedorn 117; Baudrillard 1). These insights push me toward a recognition of the power of music to engender feelings of transcendence that need not accompany adherence to any particular "faith" or religious community.

In studies of Caribbean music, transcendence has been linked to an aesthetic of "heating up," which guides performances and ritual events as diverse as Vodou ceremonies, popular dance concerts, and Carnival celebrations.[2] As I have noted elsewhere, transcendence also occurs in Pentecostal Christian worship services in Haiti (Butler, "In Zora's Footsteps," 85). Despite claims of theological and experiential distinctiveness among the country's Pentecostal Christians, the goals of "heating up" the ritual space and inviting spiritual manifestations are shared across Haiti's religious and social landscape. Gage Averill's description of "carnival exuberance" points to Haitian Creole terms that suggest both similarities (*chofe, balanse, mete men nan lè, sote*) and differences (*anraje, gwiye, souke*) between carnivalesque revelry and Pentecostal transcendence:

---

[2] See, for example, Averill, "Anraje to Angaje," and Brown, *Mama Lola*.

The peak of carnival exuberance—the ambiance of carnival in its final days on the road—is known as *koudyay* (French, *coup de jaille*, a spontaneous bursting forth). . . . Carnival and *koudyay* enthusiasm, an intersubjective peak experience, is described in terms such [as] *debòde* (overflowing, exuberant, furious), *anraje* (worked-up, turned-on, crazy, enraged), or the colorful *antyoutyout* (exuberant, excited). Carnival participants achieve these states in a progression of escalations involving music and movement. Musicians try to *chofe* (heat) the crowd with exhortations to physically respond. Revelers are encouraged to *lage ko-w!* (let go of yourself!), *mete men nan lè* (put hand in the air), *balanse* (sway), *bobinen* (spin), *souke* (shake), *vole* (fly), *gwiye* (grind the hips), and *sote* (jump). (Averill 223)

The "intersubjective peak experience" Averill describes applies to a range of popular expressions, including *rara* (processional Vodou and Carnival music). A transcendent state of *koudyay* is achieved through collective celebrations that involve dancing while singing humorous and "vulgar" songs known as *betiz*. Elizabeth McAlister has provided the only book-length study of Haitian *rara*. Her work also stands apart from others in that it takes *betiz* seriously as a unit of analysis. *Betiz* songs are a type of "popular laughter" through which participants "perform the cultural work of affirming not only the existence but also the creative life of a people in the face of insecurity and everyday violence" (60). Scorned by Haiti's elite classes, *rara* processions, along with the *betiz* featured within them, constitute a form of ritual that accomplishes several things at once. They are religious ceremonies, boisterous street parties, and mobile platforms for sociopolitical critique. *Rara* processions also show how the attainment of a transcendent state may open cultural and spiritual pathways for marginalized groups in Haiti to flourish. McAlister devotes an entire chapter to a discussion of "work" and "play" as complementary modes of expression. She notes that "while the 'tone' or 'ambiance' of Rara parading may seem secular, the festival should more properly be understood as a synthesis of Carnival behavior and religious practice. Specifically, Rara consists of an outer, secular layer of Carnival 'play' surrounding a protected, secret inner layer of religious 'work.' These two values are enacted structurally through performance codes, use of private and public space, gender relations, and social hierarchy" (McAlister 31.). This genre of Haitian popular culture is thus an apt case study for understanding religious music as both serious and fun. Even when religious belief fuels a heightening ritual atmosphere, we may understand music-making as both "playful transcendence" and "transcendent play."

In a conventional sense, the concept of play is used in reference to what André Droogers refers to as "the human capacity to deal simultaneously with two or more ways of classifying reality" (34). To play is to carve out a set of activities or adopt a stance that is separated from "real life." Put otherwise, play happens in the realm of "make-believe," wherein nothing of significance is changed in the world outside the play frame. The *doing* of play, that is, the process itself, is the primary objective. Play is similar to "ritual," although the goal of the latter is generally to effect some sort of transformation that has real-world consequences. Arnold van Gennep posits in his classic study of *rites de passage* that rituals "accompany transitions from one situation to another and from one cosmic or social world to another" (Van Gennep 13; Turner 80). But as the example of *rara* shows, it is at the crossroads of ritual and play where opportunities for human creative and spiritual flourishing emerge. This resonates with Shana Redmond's discussion of the crossroads as an intersection of performance and the unforeseen. The process of experimental, risk-taking music-making can be captivating for both musicians and audiences, perhaps because it evidences "the intrigue of the impossible— those performances within popular Black musical cultures that go off script and are rarely, perhaps never otherwise, achieved" (Redmond, Chapter 2 in this volume). My fieldwork in Haiti taught me much about the role of play in ritual and has enabled me to build on the insights gleaned from the work of Averill and McAlister. As helpful as conventional definitions of work, play, and ritual may be, however, I find it beneficial to toy with them in hopes of revealing some of the underappreciated aspects of musical playfulness.

Playful Transcendence in Haiti

The notion that Christian worshippers are uplifted and empowered through celebratory song and dance is neatly summed up in an often-quoted passage of scripture, which reads, "The joy of the Lord is my strength" (Nehemiah 8:10, King James [Authorized Version] Bible). This assertion serves as a mantra for African American Pentecostals who revel in exuberant worship. But exuberance is also a quality of both "secular" and sacred musical performances and rituals throughout the African diaspora, and my fieldwork in the Caribbean has borne this out. The ways that "heating up" happens in the settings that

I discuss are different in some ways, but quite similar in others. Musical styles emerge from very specific kinds of cultural and historical contexts, but in each situation, the melodies, harmonies, rhythms, and repertories employed are key factors in determining the extent to which practitioners are able to derive a sense of spiritual satisfaction and pleasure. Musical style, in particular, can be a source of significant controversy—particularly when a style is deemed too "worldly." Even when it is considered permissible to "have fun" in church—through "holy dancing," for example—such "fun" must not involve the "wrong kind" of dancing, the wrong kind of pleasure, or the wrong kind of transcendence. Debates over what constitutes the proper form of religious expression are deeply tied to a politics of transcendence. The most revelatory aspects of my fieldwork in the Caribbean concerned the myriad ways that the boundary-crossing tensions I experienced in the United States arise in similar but distinct ways in Haitian ritual contexts.

During one of my early fieldwork trips to Haiti, I was invited to a Pentecostal church different from any I had attended before. This was a heavenly army church—that is, a congregation that featured groups of spiritual soldiers appointed by God to wage spiritual warfare against unseen enemies. The worship service I attended was an eight-hour affair. It began around 9 a.m., and concluded late in the afternoon. Music was sung and played throughout, with short breaks taken for mini-sermons by the pastor and spoken testimonies by various congregants. I was most fascinated by the period of the service during which the "army" began to "work." They formed a circle, rotated it in a counterclockwise direction as they sang slow hymns and choruses. Gradually the tempo and volume increased, as more congregants joined in, and the atmosphere heated up. After about thirty minutes, the pastor, now in a trance-like state, motioned for the instrumentalists to stop playing. The abrupt cessation of drumming pushed the sounds of the vocal cries into the foreground of the sonic space. Many army members displayed signs of being under the Spirit's influence. Four teen girls twirled around several times, while speaking in tongues, before finally hurling themselves to the ground as though yanked by an invisible force. They also began to *tire* (i.e., "shoot")—a term referring to the "pya pya" sounds imitating gunfire (Butler, "'Nou Kwe Nan Sentespri,'" 98). This was spiritual warfare of the highest ritual significance. Unlike mere "child's play," there was something at stake here for these practitioners, who understood this ritual fighting as a way to combat forces of social misery that were negatively impacting the lives of women, men, and children in the church and its wider community.

In the midst of this heightened spiritual atmosphere, however, there also arose the sounds of laughter. It started with a few of the older women who appeared to be tickled by the move of the Spirit on the younger participants. Between chuckles, the older women offered commentary on the proceedings— a kind of parallel discussion about how dramatically and demonstratively the younger women were behaving. "The Spirit is really showing them!" I imagined them saying. How, I wondered, could they feel so free to laugh in the middle of what otherwise appeared to be "serious" ritual moment? It seemed to be the vulnerability of the normally shy girls that prompted the laughter—a recognition of the futility of human efforts to fend off manifestations of the Holy Spirit or resist its supernatural power. The women took great pleasure in watching the youth succumb to powers that were beyond their control, as though such a moment had been long in the making. The older women knew that it was only a matter of time before the girls would be brought under subjection, just as they themselves had been in years past. This ritual event reminded me of a surgeon getting a kick out of a patient under the influence of anesthesia making silly utterances that he or she would not remember after awakening. I felt like an audience member watching some helpless soul behave out of character while under the spell of a hypnotist. Church members believe and have great respect for the Holy Spirit; they are in awe of its otherworldly power. Yet this respect does not preclude their capacity to find humor in the situation. Simply put, it is okay for it to be funny. The humor of the event in no way diminishes its ritual efficacy. On the contrary, it renders it more memorable and reinforces its "holy" affect.

The heavenly army service I attended in Haiti was markedly different from the church services I attended in the United States. The playfulness of it, however, was not entirely unusual. In fact, in African American Pentecostal churches, some of the most powerful manifestations of the Holy Spirit are at times accompanied by laughter. This occurs in several ways. For example, it takes the form of casual banter among congregants, especially when they observe "holy dancing" (sometimes called "shouting") to lively music. Even those who participate in holy dancing may smile and laugh while doing so. I have seen many instances when a pastor or other minister will begin to dance with a congregant, enjoying the felt presence of the Spirit and the opportunity to celebrate a spiritual victory. There are also numerous cases of "holy laughter" that have become ritualized among various Christian congregations and Spirit-filled churches in the United States and beyond.[3]

[3] In his historical study of nineteenth-century Shakers in the United States, Stephen J. Stein describes instances in which believers were "obsessed with the gift of laughter" (1992, 173). See also Poloma (2003).

Through ethnographic research in religious settings, I have gained the opportunity to observe and participate in many types of playful transcendence. The heavenly army services in Haiti are only one of many examples.[4] Let me now turn to another type play, one that involves my own grappling with what it means to be both a scholar and a performing musician in today's academic marketplace.

Double Play

I remember very well a time when I enjoyed being able to play freely in both sacred and secular contexts—a time in the early 1990s, when it seemed I would be able to cross the boundaries between jazz club and church service without controversy. But one evening after a church service in Boston, a conversation with a visiting preacher shattered my illusions of spiritual invincibility and hassle-free travel between sacred and secular domains. Not only was playing jazz "sinful," the preacher warned, but it would also lead to my eternal damnation. By continuing to embrace secular music, I would be living outside of divine purpose and thus walking on treacherous spiritual ground. "Music is worship," he matter-of-factly declared, "so don't listen to jazz and don't have anything to do with it." I was then instructed to read aloud a passage of scripture, "No man can serve two masters: for either he will hate the one, and love the other; or else he will hold to the one, and despise the other. Ye cannot serve God and mammon" (Matthew 6:24, King James [Authorized Version] Bible). Music, I was told, could only serve one of two functions: It either glorified God, or it amounted to devil worship. To my chagrin, jazz fit in the latter category. Although I knew that some Christians considered certain genres of secular music unhealthy, I'd never expected labels such as "sin" and "devil worship" to be applied to the jazz art form I was trying to master. I would discover that such sentiments are by no means unusual among Pentecostal leaders, who sometimes claim that certain rhythms,

---

[4] In *From Ritual to Theatre: The Human Seriousness of Play*, Victor Turner describes ritual as "both earnest and playful." He draws on case studies from around the world to problematize conceptual boundaries between work and play as they apply to ritual events. Summarizing Milton Singer's synopsis (1972, 160) of the Indian religious tradition known as "the Krishna dance," Turner writes that the dance "is called *lila*, 'sport,' in which the participants 'play' at being the 'Gopis' or cowherdesses who 'sport' in a variety of ways with Krishna, Vishnu incarnate, reliving the myth. But the Gopis' erotic love-play with Krishna has mystical implications, like the *Song of Solomon*—it is at once serious and playful, God's 'sport' with a human soul" (1982, 35).

melodies, and timbres are inappropriate or sinful because of their perceived similarity to sounds associated with secular dance hall spaces.

One of the most stinging accusations of a Pentecostal church musician is that he or she may have secretly performed in a secular nightclub the night before a Sunday morning service. Skeptics from within a congregation may raise this issue as a means of casting doubt on the spiritual sincerity of a gospel soloist, mocking the perceived naïveté of unsuspecting churchgoers, or criticizing church leaders for preaching vehemently against nightclubs only to look the other way when their most gifted musicians frequent them. In the African American musical and social contexts that I'm most familiar with, sacred/secular boundaries have a long history, wherein the blues and other genres, such as jazz, R&B, and hip-hop, were highly controversial within African American religious communities. The blues, in particular, was considered "the devil's music," characterized as "the music of immorality, licentiousness, eroticism, whisky-drinking, juke joints, low-life, violence, a source of corruption and the harbinger of social disruption" (Oakley 196–197). Yet secular genres have never monopolized contentious debates. The history of gospel music is replete with debates over the appropriateness and authenticity of artists such as Thomas Dorsey, Rosetta Tharpe, Andrae Crouch, the Winans, and others who dared to blend the sounds of the sanctuary with those of the nightclub (Ramsey 191).

Much of the motivation for my interest in music and human flourishing stems from my personal experience with traversing sacred-secular boundaries and navigating the twists and turns of my career path. This project also presents for me an opportunity to bring into conversation two aspects of my identity as a creative professional. Before and during the process of becoming a card-carrying scholar, trained in the ways of ethnomusicology, I knew music as a maker of it. And over the past thirty years, I have sustained a career as both an academic and a jazz saxophonist. My *scholarship* (in the conventional sense of the term) explores music and religious experience, with a focus on Spirit-filled, Pentecostal, or charismatic Christian music-making in African American and African Caribbean ritual contexts. As a *musician*, I have had wonderful opportunities to tour and record with numerous jazz artists, Caribbean dance bands, and pop singers with whom I continue to perform. As Todd Decker explains in his own exploration of the dual character of the music scholar/performer in Chapter 6 of this volume, I often feel as though I have a secret identity—like a mild-mannered Professor Clark Kent by day, and a musical Superman by night.

I tend not to tell my students when and where I am performing. Sometimes it simply doesn't occur to me to mention it. But my reticence stems mostly from a deeply ingrained sense that making my playing self visible will render my scholarly identity less believable. Indeed, the history of media representation of Black people, along with our perpetual underrepresentation in elite academic spaces, fuels my insecurities and heightens the anxieties I carry with me into each classroom I enter. Allowing my students to believe I am a "regular professor," pure and simple, is a strategy of self-presentation I deploy in hopes of evading the painful threat of confirming a stereotype. "Oh, of course!" I imagine my students thinking. "He's *really* a jazz musician. He's only *pretending* to be a professor!" As silly as it seems, and as vulnerable as I feel putting those fears into words, I know I am not alone. All scholars harbor at least some concerns about what others think of their work. Those of us from marginalized and minoritized communities work to safeguard the integrity of our intellectual identities from those who doubt our ability to excel as analysts of music and see musical "play" and mental "work" as mutually exclusive.

Every now and then, I'm caught off guard, and a student shows up at one of my local gigs in Miami. My mask has fallen off; my cover has been blown. It feels as if I've been "made," "busted," "found out." But when I'm honest with myself, I acknowledge that there is something about those instances that gives me pleasure. Perhaps it's the look of surprise on the faces of those who see me. Or maybe it's the risk involved—the thrill of going "off script" (in the eyes of my students, at least) while possibly getting "caught" that keeps me coming back for more. As it turns out, this is also, for me, a way of flourishing. Maybe it's the mischievousness of it all that I like—the thrill of imagining myself as a double agent—undercover as a jazz artist masquerading as a professor to some, while also undercover as a professor performing the role of a jazz artist to others. I rather enjoy those moments when an audience member, either in a classroom or a jazz club, is shocked to discover my other life. And it is probably also the nature of academic life—or simply the need to make a living—that prompts me always to represent this duality as a means of being in the world while constantly on the move. In ways that feel both pleasurable and precarious, I am bouncing around, hopping to and fro, juggling responsibilities, spinning plates, balancing occupations, enacting roles, dancing in different domains, playing the field, wrestling with musical meanings, and, at times, skating on thin ice. These playful metaphors seem particularly apropos to the two-track career I have carved out for myself.

In this context, the notion of "transcendence" works for me by connoting activities that cut across boundaries of occupation within which most other card-carrying scholars I know reside. I have come to realize—I should say, embrace—the joyful challenge of being someone who both "plays" and "transcends." I see my career as a creative and improvisatory journey, and I hope it also serves as a useful analogy for thinking about playful transcendence as a characteristic of the musical and religious practitioners I study.

"The Sound of God Laughing"

A few years ago, a commentator on National Public Radio's *All Things Considered* defined jazz as "the sound of God laughing" (Shaddox n.p.). "The devil's music," E. Taylor Atkins noted, "has clearly changed hands" (Atkins 384). In thinking about the role of improvisatory music-making as a vehicle for spiritual transcendence, this quote prompts me to elaborate on the intersections of jazz and gospel music—or perhaps I should say the interpenetration of these socially constructed categories. Much has been written about legendary jazz saxophonist John Coltrane—the fact that he was the son of a Methodist preacher and that he explored a variety on spiritualities and religious beliefs throughout his career. In some ways, he resembles many other jazz musicians who, in the 1950s, "drew consistently from the gospel genre in order to differentiate and reclaim their music from that of the [mostly] white 'cool school'" of jazz (Berkman 43). But as Franya Berkman notes, "by the mid-to-late 1960s . . . jazz musicians [like Coltrane] drew not only from African American spiritual traditions, but also from non-Christian, non-Western, even idiosyncratic, spiritual concepts." In some respects, Berkman asserts,

> . . . such musical and spiritual explorations of "the East," of Africa, and of various cosmic realms distanced jazz from the traditional Protestant church as the locus of black ethnicity. Yet many of the same "functional dimensions" of African American sacred music persisted. . . . The new spiritual jazz continued to provide what Mellonee Burnim calls "a means of cultural affirmation, individual and collective expression, and spiritual sustenance." (Burnim 11; Berkman 43)

Coltrane nevertheless stands out during this era insofar as he "imbued modal and avant-garde jazz improvisation with spiritual significance, and, in many respects, succeeded in creating a new religion for jazz musicians based on what [his second wife Alice Coltrane] described as, 'the entire experience of the expressive self'" (Berkman 43). These observations resonate with me in the present day, as they make clear the experiential and theological linkages between the spaces of church worship and those of jazz improvisation. Indeed, these spaces are not mutually exclusive. Rather, they overlap for me whether I'm positioned as a worshipper, a saxophonist, and/or a participant observer.

Much has changed over the years, even as much has remained the same—in terms of how I perceive tensions between the sacred and secular. Yet it remains all too clear that such dichotomies have always been problematized in scholarly, musical, and religious realms. I should point out that although my perspective is mostly informed by the loose aggregate of assemblies often referred to as "the Black church," the religious realms I have in mind are not exclusively Christian. Saxophonist Marvin "Doc" Holladay famously stated that before he became a member of the Baha'i faith, "I was convinced that the only people I knew who seemed to understand God as I understood Him were jazz musicians." Indeed, it now feels passé to assert that jazz was "once condemned as 'the devil's music'" (Atkins 383). In a 2006 article on John Coltrane, E. Taylor Atkins notes that "jazz music has [now] assumed a sacred aura." He adds that since the 1950s,

> many prominent jazz artists have infused their music with an overt spirituality, and have been met by listeners turning to jazz for a sacred experience. The release of John Coltrane's majestic *A Love Supreme* (1965), which paid unabashed tribute to God, "To Whom All Praise Is Due," was but the culmination of a broader trend. (383)

Moreover, recorded works by Duke Ellington, Horace Silver, Charles Mingus, Mary Lou Williams, and Jimmy Smith "paid musical homage to the African American church, while other musicians, such as Art Blakey, ... Yusef Lateef, and Kenny Clarke ... converted to Islam. Pharoah Sanders, Tony Scott, and Alice Coltrane explicitly evoked Asian mysticism and spiritual practice in their music" (Atkins 383).

The tension between sacred and secular can be a source of consternation for church members, particularly skilled musicians who feel creatively confined. I think this tension can also provide a sense of satisfaction that makes rituals cohere and gives musicians and congregants a sense that they are doing something "risky"—something that is even "dangerous," but in a pleasurable kind of way. In African American contexts, a dialogic relation between blues and jazz has historically served this purpose. We certainly see this in the case of blues musicians who have used alter egos to record gospel songs and gospel artists who have drawn on the blues. The latter include Washington Philips, along with a variety of elders and reverends who recorded on race records during the 1920s and 1930s. Within the realm of sacred Black musical expression, contemporary debates still center on what Timothy Rommen (2007) refers to as "the ethics of style," as musical performances incorporate an ever-widening pool of expressive resources. In many Pentecostal contexts, the use of hip-hop-influenced gospel music in worship services can be a way of pushing against conventional notions of what constitutes "religious music" and bringing about what some might consider a "guilty pleasure." In other contexts, it is the idea of pushing against a spiritual boundary, of accessing the divine, of transcending the human/spiritual line of demarcation in order to touch that which is numinous, holy, extraordinary, and "wholly Other" (to use Rudolf Otto's famous formulation). This kind of pushing of the boundaries—stretching oneself to access the holy—is also, I argue, a type of "play" that involves exploring what it means to be human and how we relate to the divine.

Another way that music is connected to human flourishing in Black church services is through the art of preaching. The musicality of African American "chanted sermons" has been examined by several scholars.[5] Braxton Shelley uses the phrase "tuning up" not only to denote this type of preaching but also to theorize various modes of "homiletical musicality" that encompass performances of gospel music (175). Lerone A. Martin explains that in the 1920s, the "chanted sermon" was described as part of the "frenzy" of Pentecostal practice, in which "the expressive worship of the congregation, and the chanted sermon all merged to create an ecstatic worship experience." He adds, "Pentecostals believed this brand of euphoric experience was a must for true Christian experience" (115). Thérèse Smith provides detailed transcriptions of chanted preaching, calling it "the most powerful expression of the African American church" (204). Recordings of African American preachers during the 1920s and 1930s also reveal an attitude of playfulness with regard to boundaries, not only those between song and speech, but

---

[5] Braxton Shelley (2019) synthesizes much of the extant scholarly literature on the topic. See also Jackson (1981), Davis (1985), Spencer (1987), Pitts (1993), Simmons (2010), and Martin (2014).

also between religious expression and comedic entertainment. The subversiveness of the boundary-crossing featured on these "race records," as they were called, was a source of annoyance for some listeners. Jonathan Walton captures the sense of moral outrage that some middle-class Black people expressed. Despite the "politics of respectability" that governed boundary construction in some quarters, "religious race records . . . undercut African American bourgeois obsessions with such expressivity and decorum. Many African Americans believed the program of bourgeois social uplift came with too high of a cultural price tag as southern migrants were not willing to toss out the baby of African American cultural creativity with the bathwater of slavery and racial oppression" (205).

In more recent Christian church contexts, secular forms of hip-hop, rock, and R&B provide grist for the mill of play. Take Kirk Franklin's recordings of the 1990s and the following decade, where he challenges his listeners, "If you think that gospel music has gone too far . . ." before beginning the song "Stomp." Other examples from Kirk Franklin, along with gospel recordings by Fred Hammond, Tye Tribbett, and a variety of "holy hip-hop" artists, also shed light on this phenomenon, wherein artists "play" on their recordings in ways that are anathema to the members of more theologically conservative churches. These forms of gospel play are a source of pleasure for youth and other fans of secular music who want to "get their groove on" in a Christian setting.

One of the things that surprises some outsiders about Pentecostal church services is the extent to which playfulness, humor, and ritual transcendence intertwine to produce a worship experience that is both spiritually fulfilling and entertaining to participants. The notion that any religious service could be "fun" strikes many as oxymoronic, although scholars have recognized such phenomena in a variety of global contexts. Deborah Smith Pollard's aptly titled book, *When the Church Becomes Your Party*, underscores how gospel musicians and their fans dissolve conceptual boundaries between holy work and worldly play. Pollard contends that "holy hip hop" is best understood as "an authentic part of a continuum that includes all other sacred music and speech traditions" (137–138). Contemporary African American gospel music builds on a legacy of embodied spirituality that has nevertheless been regarded as sacrilegious by those who espouse conservative views on what constitutes an appropriate style of worship. Even instrumental jazz remains a source of controversy in some Pentecostal churches.

Music-making is often a contentious issue within other faith traditions as well. What I am describing as "playful transcendence" would be experienced by some religious practitioners as an unwelcome blend of spiritual work and earthly play. Such is the case for one of Jeffrey Summit's interviewees, who spoke at length about her annoyance with parts of the liturgical worship in her Jewish synagogue.

One woman said, "I like that tune . . . [but] I often don't like what happens in the group dynamic. That's like 'play time.' . . . I come to services one Friday night a month to have my jolt of mysticism and . . . people get silly. That's the only way I can put it." She continued, "[People are] . . . throwing teddy bears in the air, doing the can-can, stuff like that. I sound very 'stick-in-the- muddy' . . . I find it breaks the unity. I find usually what happens in the service is that it's got this . . . soft glow to it and this is like . . . people get frisky. . . . There are certain melodies where I feel like we're singing camp songs and it doesn't work. . . . People will bring in these little songs . . . sometimes we'll do little dances . . . and it feels too workshop-y, it feels too campfire-y. And it's fine to have a campfire and it's fine to have a workshop but I want my prayer space to be just mystical and full of grace." While asserting that she was "not a puritan," she explained, "I don't like blueberries in my yogurt and I don't like frivolity in my spirituality." (Summit 50)

Summit adds that for this woman, the ritual "walked a thin line between meaningful spiritual expression and a hodgepodge of experiential exercises." She felt the dancing and frivolity "diminished the seriousness and intensity" of the service and failed to create an atmosphere sufficiently distinct from "party time." Within the same congregation, however, there were no doubt worshippers who derived a sense of fulfillment and joy from the freedom to express themselves unabashedly. Differences of opinion result in a "struggle to create a worship service." In the words of one member: "It feels like true talking to God." Summit explains:

In their creative efforts to achieve that goal, these Jews push the limits to explore how music, dance, and meditative exercises can help them transcend regular prayer and transform the worship experience. However, this experimentation requires careful monitoring. If it crosses the line and is seen as silly or out of control, its power is diminished. (50)

The intra-congregational tensions within this Jewish synagogue bear a striking resemblance to what I experienced as a music minister at Emmanuel Temple in Brooklyn, where negotiations of musical style helped me to understand how the cultural and generational identities of African American and Caribbean Pentecostals shaped their ritual needs and expectations.[6]

Throughout my career as a saxophonist, I have often visited the intersections of jazz and gospel. Since the mid-1990s, I have worked with drummer and composer Brian Blade as a member of his group, the Fellowship Band. Touring with this group has prompted me to explore the relation between what I do musically and what I do as a scholar and worshipper. I note, in particular, band members' frequent remarks about improvisation as a means of tapping into something beyond ourselves. Alto saxophonist Myron Walden, with whom I share the bandstand, speaks of relaying or being a conduit for the messages that he's being sent. And we often experience what I can only describe as transcendent moments during the course of a performance. An especially moving reaction to one of our concerts in Denver was expressed via email in a letter to Brian, who shared it with us. Discussing his close friend, (whom I'll call "Lloyd"), the email author wrote at length about the transformative effect of the music. What follows is an excerpt from that message:

> To give you a little back story on Lloyd. He has been a very close friend of mine for fifteen years now. He did three tours in Iraq and during his second tour he was stationed at Abu Ghraib prison during the time of all the torture and abuse by American troops. Lloyd has always been a very caring and compassionate soul but in that culture, under orders he was witness to some unimaginably traumatic events. As with many veterans Lloyd has experienced significant post-traumatic stress and during the past year his family and friends have watched him deteriorate dramatically and we have all been very scared for Lloyd. He had consistently been backing out of plans with me for months and it literally took daily phone calls and emails over the past month to get him to come to [the concert]. Lloyd has seen many jazz performances with me over the years, and has always enjoyed them. What we all saw on Saturday was something very different. I say this without hyperbole: It was the most profound musical, soulful, and spiritually fulfilling experience of our lives. Lloyd called me on Sunday with a cheerful tone in his voice I hadn't heard in years and asked me how to get

---

[6] See Butler (2000).

in touch with you and Brian. What the Fellowship shared really provided the avenue for healing in Lloyd that nothing else in almost ten years has been able to do. I had to wait a few days to collect myself after this weekend to even begin to form some words that described my personal experience from both nights. Everyone I invited to the shows left speechless and just glowing. I have received several emails from friends just raving about what they experienced. I knew we were all going to experience something special, but I simply could not imagine ahead of time that the Fellowship would share something so life affirming and spiritually profound. Another close friend of mine stated, "That was the most soulful music I've ever heard in my life." Please tell Brian and everyone in the Fellowship thank-you from the bottom of my heart for what they do and for what they brought to Denver last weekend. It was something I will never forget and I can't wait to see them again whenever life permits. They quite literally may have saved Lloyd's life.

These types of reactions are a source of encouragement for all members of the band. Brian's wife, Lurah, often expresses awe at the spiritual power she experiences when watching the group perform. "It's like going to church," she once explained, adding that the Fellowship Band's concerts *are* church for many listeners. In some respects, the spiritual connection listeners experience is unsurprising. Brian's father, Rev. Brady Blade, has for over thirty-five years pastored Zion Baptist Church in Shreveport, Louisiana. Brian learned to play drums in this spiritually charged atmosphere, in which the Holy Spirit's manifestations were invited through a variety of tempos and genres from the African American sacred music tradition. Hymns are often "lined out," such that a deacon sings a highly ornamented line of text that is then echoed heterophonically by the congregation. Congregational and solo singing requires flexibility on the part of accompanying instrumentalists, and Brian Blade's fluid sense of time is largely informed by the rhythmic give-and-take of worship services he experienced growing up. According to Brian, playing music is necessarily a matter of listening to one's surroundings—the sounds and potential soundings of other musicians. As a composer, Brian allows his church background to come through—even in song titles such as "Omni," "Alpha and Omega," and "Most Precious One." And he has also been leading a series of performances titled, "The Hallelujah Train," featuring his father and members of Zion Baptist presenting traditional gospel songs in what will become a full-fledged documentary film and album. Whether musical performances are characterized as sacred or secular, and perhaps especially when they fit in both categories, I maintain that playful transcendence encapsulates the experiences of those on and off stage.

Conclusion

I believe there is much to gain by examining music-making in relation to the rich concepts of play and transcendence. In sacred and secular ritual settings, music often becomes a means through which practitioners strive to transcend the self and tap into supernatural joy, deliverance, and power. My discursive juxtaposition of ritualized musical spaces has sought to shed light on what makes each type of transcendent performance unique, as well as the ties that bind them together. I think "transcendence" is an apt description of what happens when a "believer" yields body and mind to a divine Other or to the power of music to effect transformation in their lives. Thinking of performances as playful transcendence helps to make sense of the transformative, boundary-crossing endeavors we witness as researchers, religious practitioners, and musicians. Playful transcendence occurs when human beings step into spiritually charged spaces and allow themselves to be moved. If transcendence of this sort doesn't reveal alternative ways of feeling a holy touch, then perhaps it at least inspires a newfound appreciation for how spiritually and epistemologically diverse groups access the divine through a variety of feelings and performative modes. One of the ways musicologists and other scholars have historically performed their scholarly roles is by supposing that solid boundaries exist between fieldwork and homework, and between the practice of one's faith and the practice of everyday life. By continuing to make explicit the fragility of such dichotomies, I hope we can continue to wonder about the multifaceted performances that define who we are, who we hope to become, and how we relate both musically and spiritually to those we study.

The scholarly writing that most inspires me pushes boundaries and reflects a sense of playfulness with regard to human behavior and our efforts to understand it. What we might label "ethnographic play" refers to a kind of academic experimentation whereby one adopts controversial or out-of-the-ordinary research topics or methods that bend the rules of conventional scholarship. In some cases, this might involve the use of reflexive writing, sometimes termed "auto-ethnography," as a means of drawing from the deeply personal to connect with a unit of study with which one may have much or very little in common. Although this type of ethnographic writing, which often goes hand in hand with "insider ethnography," has become more widespread in recent decades, there remains a stigma attached to research and writing that comes across as overly subjective. I have spoken with many students and scholars of music and religion who express frustration at the pressure they feel to abide by epistemological rules of engagement that they feel run counter to their faith. Moreover, scholars writing about religious music must take extra care, it seems, to remain dispassionate in their description and analyses, lest they be accused of sacrificing intellectually objective analysis for a slippery subjectivity that hardly qualifies as scholarship. Karen Brown's *Mama Lola* (2011) is highly reflexive and experimental in terms of how the author allows the voice of her primary interlocutor to have primacy of place. The boundary between researcher and informant collapses, and Brown allows her own subjectivities to count as "data" and to inform the readers' understanding of her topic. Brown also interposes semi-fictional historical narratives between each chapter, allowing recounted memories of Haitian ancestors to structure the book while yielding space for the Vodou spirits, known as the *lwa*, to speak. The *lwa* embody the full gamut of human emotions and perform their identities with playfulness, eroticism, obscenity, and humor, without undermining the seriousness of their mission. The *lwa* are brought into being by serious ritual and musical work designed to effect spiritual and social transformation in the lives of those who serve them. Other examples of ethnographic play are labeled "experimental" or "auto-ethnographic" writing and research. I submit that studying these forms of play helps us to flourish as scholars, even or perhaps especially within intellectual spaces where methodological orthodoxies are continually reasserting themselves.

As George Marcus has suggested, it is often only after scholars have climbed the academic ranks and acquired job security that they feel safe enough to conduct research that is groundbreaking, experimental, and, I would add, "fun" (233–234). It appears we must prove our ability to "work" in the fields before we are permitted to "play" in them. The "field" of fieldwork also comes "into play" when scholars refuse to confine themselves to the traditional "fly on the wall" perspective and instead become fully engaged participants in the activities they are observing. I believe we must allow ourselves to live and flourish not simply as "field workers" but also as committed "players" who act for the physical, emotional, and spiritual well-being of those around us and for ourselves. In times past, this type of fieldwork was considered anathema to respectable research; it was akin to "going native," "losing oneself," and forsaking one's objectivity. This critique relies, of course, on dichotomous ways of thinking that have long been considered outdated among most social scientists. However, the remnants of this high-minded perspective are still discernible in academia, as is a mindset that labels some types of field research as unserious or rejects research activities that register as unfaithful to "the field." I have only begun to realize the many benefits of being myself in the academy, of allowing myself to shine as both an ethnomusicologist and a performer. Success in this dual endeavor has been hard won and, at times, frustrating. But finding joy as a scholar-performer has been worth the journey, as it has led to a greater capacity to flourish within and beyond academic spaces.

Works Cited

Atkins, E. Taylor. "Sacred Swing: The Sacralization of Jazz in the American Bahá'í Community." *American Music*, vol. 24, no. 4, December 1, 2006, 383–420.

Averill, Gage. "Anraje to Angaje: Carnival Politics and Music in Haiti." *Ethnomusicology*, vol. 38, no. 2, 1994, pp. 217–247.

Baudrillard, Jean. *Simulacra and Simulation*. Ann Arbor: University of Michigan Press, 1994.

Becker, Judith. *Deep Listeners: Music, Emotion, and Trancing*. Bloomington: Indiana University Press, 2004.

Berkman, Franya J. "Appropriating Universality: The Coltranes and 1960s Spirituality." *American Studies*, vol. 48, no. 1, 2007, pp. 41–62.

Brown, Karen McCarthy. *Mama Lola: A Vodou Priestess in Brooklyn*. 3rd ed., with a new foreword by Claudine Michel. Berkeley: University of California Press, 2011.

Burnim, Mellonee. "Functional Dimensions of Gospel Music Performance." *The Western Journal of Black Studies*, vol. 12, no. 2, 1988, pp. 112–121.

Butler, Melvin L. "'Nou Kwe Nan Sentespri'(We Believe in the Holy Spirit): Music, Ecstasy, and Identity in Haitian Pentecostal Worship." *Black Music Research Journal*, vol. 22, no. 1, 2002, pp. 85–125.

Butler, Melvin L. "In Zora's Footsteps: Experiencing Music and Pentecostal Ritual in the African Diaspora." *Obsidian*, vol. 9, no. 1, 2008, pp. 74–106.

Butler, Melvin L. "Musical Style and Experience in a Brooklyn Pentecostal Church: An 'Insider's' Perspective." *Current Musicology*, vol. 70, 2000, pp. 33–50.

Davis, Gerald L. *I Got the Word in Me and I Can Sing It, You Know: A Study of the Performed African-American Sermon*. Philadelphia: University of Pennsylvania Press, 1987.

Droogers, André. *Religion at Play: A Manifesto*. Eugene, OR: Cascade Books, 2014.

Gupta, Akhil, and James Ferguson. "Discipline and Practice: 'The Field' as Site, Method, and Location in Anthropology." *Anthropological Locations: Boundaries and Grounds of a Field Science*, edited by Akhil Gupta and James Ferguson. Berkeley: University of California Press, 1997, pp. 1–46.

Hagedorn, Katherine J. *Divine Utterances: The Performance of Afro-Cuban Santería*. Washington, DC: Smithsonian Institution Press, 2001.

Hinson, Glenn. *Fire in My Bones: Transcendence and the Holy Spirit in African American Gospel*. Philadelphia: University of Pennsylvania Press, 2000.

Jackson, Joyce M. "The Black American Folk Preacher and the Chanted Sermon: Parallels with a West African Tradition." *Discourse in Ethnomusicology II: A Tribute to Alan P. Merriam*, edited by Caroline Card, Jane Cowan, Sally Carr Helton, Carl Rahkonen, and Kay Laura Sommers. Bloomington, IN: Ethnomusicology Publication Group, 1981, pp. 202–225.

Marcus, George E. *Ethnography through Thick and Thin*. Princeton, NJ: Princeton University Press, 2010.

Martin, Lerone A. *Preaching on Wax: The Phonograph and the Shaping of Modern African American Religion*, vol. 5. New York: New York University Press, 2014.

McAlister, Elizabeth A. *Rara!: Vodou, Power, and Performance in Haiti and Its Diaspora*. Berkeley: University of California Press, 2002.

Oakley, Giles. *The Devil's Music: A History of the Blues*. 2nd ed. New York: Da Capo Press, 1997.

Otto, Rudolf. *The Idea of the Holy*, vol. 14. New York: Oxford University Press, 1958.

Pitts, Walter F. *Old Ship of Zion: The Afro-Baptist Ritual in the African Diaspora*. New York: Oxford University Press, 1993.

Pollard, Deborah Smith. *When the Church Becomes Your Party: Contemporary Gospel Music*. 1st ed. Detroit: Wayne State University Press, 2008.

Poloma, Margaret M. *Main Street Mystics: The Toronto Blessing and Reviving Pentecostalism*. Walnut Creek, CA: AltaMira Press, 2003.

Ramsey, Guthrie P. *Race Music*. Berkeley: University of California Press, 2004.

Rommen, Timothy. *"Mek Some Noise": Gospel Music and the Ethics of Style in Trinidad*. Berkeley: University of California Press, 2007.

Shaddox, Colleen. "Jazz Is the Sound of God Laughing." *This I Believe* (blog), June 13, 2005. https://thisibelieve.org/essay/16/.

Shelley, Braxton D. "Analyzing Gospel." *Journal of the American Musicological Society*, vol. 72, no. 1, 2019, pp. 181–243.

Simmons, Martha J. "Whooping: The Musicality of African American Preaching Past and Present." *Preaching with Sacred Fire: An Anthology of African American Sermons, 1750 to the Present*, edited by Frank A. Thomas and Martha J. Simmons. New York: Norton, 2010, pp. 864–884.

Singer, Milton B. *When a Great Tradition Modernizes: An Anthropological Approach to Indian Civilization*. New York: Praeger, 1972.

Smith, Thérèse. *Let the Church Sing!: Music and Worship in a Black Mississippi Community*. Rochester, NY: University of Rochester Press, 2004.

Spencer, Jon Michael. *Sacred Symphony: The Chanted Sermon of the Black Preacher*. New York: Greenwood Press, 1987.

Stein, Stephen J. *The Shaker Experience in America: A History of the United Society of Believers*. New Haven, CT: Yale University Press, 1992.

Summit, Jeffrey A. *The Lord's Song in a Strange Land: Music and Identity in Contemporary Jewish Worship*. Pap/Com ed. New York: Oxford University Press, 2000.

Trost, Wiebke, Thomas Ethofer, Marcel Zentner, and Patrik Vuilleumier. "Mapping Aesthetic Musical Emotions in the Brain." *Cerebral Cortex*, vol. 22, no. 12, December 15, 2011, pp. 2769–2783.

Turner, Victor W. *From Ritual to Theatre: The Human Seriousness of Play*. Performance Studies Series, vol. 1. New York: Performing Arts Journal Publications, 1982.

Van Gennep, Arnold. *The Rites of Passage*. Translated by Monika B. Vizedom and Gabrielle L. Caffee. London: Routledge and Kegan Paul, 1960.

Walton, Jonathan L. "The Preachers' Blues: Religious Race Records and Claims of Authority on Wax." *Religion and American Culture: A Journal of Interpretation*, vol. 20, no. 2, 2010, pp. 205–232.

Zentner, Marcel, Didier Grandjean, and Klaus Scherer. "Emotions Evoked by the Sound of Music: Characterization, Classification, and Measurement." *Emotion*, vol. 8, no. 4, September 1, 2008, pp. 494–521.

11

Music for the Masses

Finding a Balance between Emotional Labor and Human Flourishing

Anna Harwell Celenza

In this day and age, it is hard to imagine a world without recorded sound. Music permeates our lives. Thanks to technology, it is always with us: via our smartphones, the radio, film scores, TV commercials, even the streamed music at our favorite stores and restaurants. Modern technology has made music more accessible to the masses. It has also given listeners the ability to connect directly, via social media, with the performers creating the music. But what about human flourishing? Have these societal changes influenced the way we value music? Has technology influenced the psychological benefits of music performance? How have the rituals that have developed around music performance affected the relationship between the musicians and audiences discussed in the previous chapters of this volume? Even more importantly, what happens to music flourishing when the relationship between performers and their fans is commodified?

In an effort to address these questions, this chapter contemplates the changing dynamics between professional performers and their audiences over the past two centuries. Previous studies about the connections between music and human flourishing have tended to focus on music as a pastime (i.e., amateur performance or music consumption). In this volume, the life of professional musicians has been touched upon by Jonathan Coopersmith, Wendy Heller, and Todd Decker, but not in reference to their changing relationships with audiences. Specifically, this chapter explores the working conditions of professional musicians, specifically the ways that technological advances in recorded sound and social media have influenced, for good and for bad, the complex nature of the professional performer's connection to his/her/their listening audiences. As I hope to show, technological advances

Anna Harwell Celenza, *Music for the Masses* In: *Music and Human Flourishing*. Edited by: Anna Harwell Celenza, Oxford University Press. © Oxford University Press 2023. DOI: 10.1093/oso/9780197646748.003.0012 in the realm of recorded sound have changed the role of the performer, especially with regard to his/her/their participation in emotional labor.

"Emotional labor," a term coined by sociologist Arlie Hochschild, refers to the management of one's feelings and expressions based on the emotional requirements of a job. According to Hochschild, this type of labor is distinctive, in that it requires the worker "to induce or suppress feeling in order to sustain the outward countenance that produces the proper state of mind in others" (7). Hochschild does not include music performance among the service professions shaped by emotional labor, but the requirements for such service-industry jobs, as she and others have defined them, are applicable to professional musicians. They include: adapting one's emotional activities in response to feedback from one's employer, producing an emotional state in the consumer/public through one's labor, and regular and direct contact with the consumer/public. These three requirements for emotional labor have existed, in varying degrees, in the work of professional musicians ever since the early modern era. And since the introduction of recording technology at the beginning of the past century, the relationship between professional musicians and their audiences has undergone a series of consequential changes that, among other things, has complicated the correlations between professional music-making and human flourishing. But in order to fully understand the impact of recording technology on the performer/audience relationship, we must first outline how the concept of emotional labor applied to professional musicians prior to the arrival of recorded sound.

For most musicians, performance is an avocation, an activity that they participate in outside their main occupation as a means of personal fulfillment. For others, it is also a vocation, an activity one participates in for financial reward. Although human flourishing occurs in both instances, for professional musicians a significant part of their labor—the activity for which they are being paid—involves their engagement with a live audience. This, in effect, is emotional labor. In the realm of music, evidence of emotional labor can be traced back to the earliest descriptions of professional performance. There are countless anecdotes in music history reflecting the effects of emotional labor on working musicians. During the early modern era, most professional musicians worked under the patronage system. Considered little more than servants, these musicians were expected to perform, without complaint, at their patron's pleasure. In return, they received a moderate salary and pension, and housing for themselves and their families. Their "audience" was their employer, and their obligation as servants was to adapt their emotional activities in response to feedback from said employer. As one can imagine, such working conditions could lead to high levels of stress and thus diminish human flourishing. Nonetheless, musicians regularly found methods to circumvent the stress of their emotional labor—methods that enabled them to thrive. Take for example the story of Franz Joseph Haydn's creation of his Symphony No. 45 (*Farewell*), composed in 1772 for Prince Nikolaus I of Esterházy.

Prince Nikolaus was a great fan of music, and like many wealthy noblemen of his era, his household included a retinue of highly trained musicians. Haydn regularly composed works for the prince that were performed at court. His Symphony No. 45 was composed in November 1772, at Prince Nikolaus's summer palace, Esterháza, in rural Hungary. Haydn and the musicians had accompanied the prince to Esterháza earlier that spring, leaving their families behind in Eisenstadt. As the months passed, the musicians grew restless, but dared not voice their displeasure. In an effort to alleviate the situation, and thus contribute to the wellness of his fellow musicians, Haydn composed his Symphony No. 45, which in addition to articulating the emotions of the musicians (anger, melancholy, etc.) used a structural format in the final movement that symbolically replicated the act of departure: one by one, each musician stops playing and exits, leaving an empty stage at the end. The prince understood the musicians' direct, yet diplomatic, message, and the next day they returned to Eisenstadt. In short, the emotional labor required of the musicians working for Prince Nikolaus inhibited their ability to flourish at court, but the creative act of music-making itself offered a solution. Haydn's Symphony No. 45 enabled the musicians to adhere to the strictures of emotional labor required by their employment, while simultaneously communicating effectively with their audience (the prince) in a way that produced a positive outcome for everyone. But such positive outcomes were rare for working musicians in the eighteenth century.

Haydn's generation was the last to be fully dependent on the patronage system. At the turn of the century, the conditions of musical labor began to change. As public concerts with paying audiences became regular events, the social status of musicians rose, leading to the concept of the independent, "genius" musician, whose artistic talent set him/her apart from the servant-class status of previous generations. By the mid-nineteenth century, this "star" status (which had previously only applied to select opera singers) was conferred upon professional instrumentalists, such as Niccolò Paganini, Franz Liszt, Frédéric Chopin, and Clara Schumann (to name just a few).

Often described as the age of the virtuoso, this was an era when many professional performers chose to reject the patronage system (with its single employer/audience) and to attempt instead a career in the entrepreneurial system we today call the gig economy, with its inherent financial risk and constantly shifting employer/audience.

The gig economy expanded the audience base of working musicians and gave them greater freedom and autonomy as artists, but with this freedom came the loss of financial security offered by the patronage system and the stress of constantly having to make connections with new audiences. Consequently, many performers—even the most successful—suffered regularly from burnout. A case in point was the pianist Franz Liszt.

As a soloist, Liszt went on grueling, transcontinental concert tours, where he connected with thousands of fans directly. As a contemporary observer noted, Liszt's personal connection with his audience, his ability to mesmerize them, was one of the things that made his live performances stand out:

> Liszt is a complete actor who intends to carry away the public. . . . [He] subdues the people to him by the very way he walks on to the stage. He gives his proud head a toss, throws an electric look out of his eagle eye, and seats himself with an air as much as to say, "Now I am going to do just what I please with you, and you are nothing but puppets subject to my will." (Fay 207)

To the audience, Liszt appeared to have the upper hand in the artist/audience relationship. For Liszt, the perception of these encounters was often quite different. This is perhaps most clearly revealed in a letter he wrote to his close friend, George Sand, in 1837, wherein he described his life as a concert artist: "I have spent the past six months living a life of shabby squabbles and virtually sterile endeavors. I have willingly laid my artist's heart open to all the bruises of an active public life" (Liszt 30–31). As Liszt explained, the rewards of such a life were only financial. For artists like him, the peripatetic existence of a touring performer led to a sense of isolation and despair:

> It behooves an artist more than anyone else to pitch a tent only for an hour and not to build anything like a permanent residence. Isn't he always a stranger among men? . . . What then can he do to escape his vague sadness and regrets? He must sing and move on, pass through the crowd, scattering his works to it without caring where they land, without listening to

the clamor with which people stifle them, and without paying attention to
the contemptible laurels with which they crown him. What a sad and great
destiny it is to be an artist! (Liszt 28)

With regard to emotional labor, Liszt noted that the demands made on professional musicians were different from practitioners of other art forms, because the musician was forced to interact directly with the public:

> In this sort of relationship [of the artist with his audience] it is the musi-
> cian, without doubt, who suffers the worst fate of all. The poet, painter, or
> sculptor, left to himself in his study or studio, completes the task that he
> has set for himself; and once his work is done, he has bookshops to dis-
> tribute it or museums to exhibit it. . . . [But with regard to] the musical
> performer . . . how many times, except for those rare instances when he
> is understood, must he prostitute himself to an unresponsive audience,
> must he scoff at his own most intimate feelings and toss his soul out, so to
> speak, to stir up some applause from the inattentive crowd? Even then, a
> tremendous effort is required if the flame of his fervor is to reflect even a
> pale glimmer on those icy faces or to strike a few sparks from those loveless,
> apathetic hearts. (Liszt 31)

Part of what troubled Liszt as a performer were the rituals of performance
as he encountered them in the early nineteenth century. Audience members
came and went at their leisure during performances. They clapped and
cheered when the music pleased them, and hissed when it didn't. Today,
audiences attending performances of classical music are expected to remain
in their seats and listen attentively. They wait until the conclusion of a performance to show their approval or disapproval. These new rituals create
a hierarchy between the performer(s) (on stage and in the spotlight) and
the audience (silently observing from the darkened hall). They also make
the musical composition (and through association, its composer) the focal
point of the experience. As the philosopher Lydia Goehr once so eloquently
explained, in the realm of classical music performance, the concert hall has
become a sacred space, an "imaginary museum of musical works." And
the rituals that enforce this concept have contributed to the applications of
adjectives such as elitist and highbrow to classical music (Goehr).

Of course, attaching such appellations to a musical genre is stereotyping.
And such stereotyping occurs, for better or worse, with all genres of music.

Take jazz, for example. Although performed in a variety of venues, including the Kennedy Center and Carnegie Hall, the music is often perceived as less formal and more spontaneous than classical music. This stereotyping is largely tied to the rituals of performance in jazz and the impact such rituals have on the interactions between the performer(s) and audience. In jazz, the focus is not so much on the works themselves, but rather the way in which they are performed. There is an intimacy to jazz that is tied to its reliance on improvisation. When listening to jazz, it is standard practice to listen attentively, but also to respond physically to the music as it is being performed—to applaud, or call out, when an improvised solo is especially good. The rituals of jazz encourage a dialogue of sorts, a call and response, not only among the musicians performing, but also between the musicians and listeners. Such interactions often create a deep sense of community and inclusion among listeners.

Each genre has its own rituals, be they singing in unison during a church service or crowd surfing at a rock concert. For audience members, knowing the performance rituals of live music can create a sense of inclusion (if one is in the know) or exclusion (if one is experiencing the rituals for the first time). All of which is to say: listening to music as part of an audience can encourage or discourage human flourishing. It all depends on one's familiarity with the expected norms of behavior. These practices also influence profoundly the relationships between performers and their audiences. And in each instance, maintaining these relationships requires a certain level of emotional labor from the performer.

In his book *Musicking: The Meanings of Performing and Listening*, Christopher Small notes how the act of performing music establishes a set of relationships between the performer(s) and listener(s), and that in many cases, these are not *real* relationships that "actually exist in our lives," but rather imagined experiences tied to one's own desires and experiences (183). In live performances, such as those described above, this sense of a relationship (whether it be fulfilling or not) is experienced by both the performer and his/her audience. But with the inception of recording technology, the dynamic between performers and their audiences began to change.

The invention of recorded sound at the turn of the twentieth century transformed the concept of emotional labor and music. It also added new revenue streams, and a new form of the patronage system, through the rise of recording contracts with major labels. Recordings turned music into a commodity. A musical performance was no longer simply a service paid for by a listener; when captured as recorded sound and preserved in physical form (i.e., on a disc, cassette, CD), the musical performance became a commodity, an object created to be bought and sold. Recording technology raised the value of music in the minds of listeners who were willing to invest a significant amount of money into recordings and the machines needed to play them. Through recordings, a musical performance became a commodity that one could purchase and enjoy again and again. Human flourishing, as experienced through music listening, expanded exponentially with the advent of recorded sound. Performers benefited as well. In addition to being blessed with new revenue streams, they were given the ability, as recording and editing techniques improved, to create technically "perfect" performances. With each new advance, from the gramophone to the CD, recording technology increased the "value" of music—both monetarily and culturally—in the minds of musicians and their audiences. It also changed the relationships between musicians and their listeners.

For musicians who found it difficult to participate in the emotional labor required when performing in front of a live audience, the recording studio offered a new work venue, a different career path, and an alternative means of human flourishing. Recording technology enables performers to disengage with the emotional labor connected to live performance. Gone is the stress of playing to a new crowd each night and all that it entails. In its place is the ability to focus on the music, to make multiple takes and edits, all toward the goal of artistic excellence. For musicians who suffer under the strains of emotional labor, recording technology strengthens their ability to flourish both professionally and psychologically. Such was the case with Glen Gould and Miles Davis, to offer just two examples from the realms of classical music and jazz. Although both performed live, they preferred the recording studio. Gould enjoyed getting lost in performances, and he often found audiences to be distracting. For him, the high standards that had been achieved through the recording process made performing live all the more frustrating. He noted that the rise of recording technology had turned the live concert into an "anachronistic" exercise and a "force of evil" (Hozer and Raymont n.p.). The perfection achieved through the recording process had raised audience expectations to impossible levels, and for Gould, this destroyed his ability to flourish during live performances. In his mind, the audiences at live concerts had become more critical, focusing not on the performer's successes, but rather on his/her errors or failure to meet expectations. For this reason, Gould jokingly suggested creating GPAADAK: the

Gould Plan for the Abolition of Applause and Demonstrations of All Kinds (Hozer and Raymont). Gould found audience engagement and audience re-action distracting. He grew to dislike the rituals of live performance, because the audience's response, be it positive or negative, took him out of the zone he tried to inhabit when performing. As Gould explained it, he couldn't help but react to audience response during live performances, and this, in effect, negatively affected his ability to create performances that were fully his own, performances that created within himself a sense of human flourishing.

Miles Davis harbored similar views, but for different reasons, and this had to do with the makeup of the audience itself. For Davis, the stresses of emotional labor in live performance were intensified by issues of race and the fact that when he looked out into the audience, many of the faces staring back at him were white. For Davis, and countless other African Americans, the legacy of performing for white audiences, and the obvious links to minstrelsy, added new meaning to the concept of emotional labor. From its inception in the 1840s, when it became the predominant form of popular entertainment in the United States, minstrelsy promoted offensive, burlesque depictions of African Americans. As Yuval Taylor and Jake Austin have noted, "black minstrelsy" was "based precisely on the adoption of the most slanderous fictions that white people have used to characterize black men" (14). And as African Americans struggled to establish careers as performers, a "double-consciousness" arose. W. E. B. Du Bois described this double-consciousness in *The Souls of Black Folk* (1903): it is "this sense of always looking at one's self through the eyes of others, of measuring one's soul by the tape of a world that looks on in amused contempt and pity" (quoted in Taylor and Austen 14). Davis rebuffed the expectation that he should interact with listeners at live performances. He had a reputation of turning his back to audiences as he played. The reasons for this were complex, but revolved around the inter-section of emotional labor and race relations. Davis abhorred the fact that African American musicians he admired, like Louis Armstrong and Dizzy Gillespie, still felt the need to play the role of "entertainer" when performing in front of a live audience. As he described, in no uncertain terms, this was a service he was unwilling to provide his listeners:

> I wasn't about to kiss anybody's ass and do that grinning shit for no-body . . . I didn't look at myself as an entertainer like they both did. I wasn't going to do it just so that some non-playing, racist white motherfucker could write some nice things about me. Naw, I wasn't going to sell out my

principles for them. I wanted to be accepted as a good musician and that didn't call for no grinning, but just being able to play the horn good. (Davis 81, 84)

The psychological anguish here is palpable. And there have been countless musicians over the past century who have felt the same way. But the pain of emotional labor was not necessarily relieved in the recording studio for some musicians of color. In 1951, sociologist Howard Becker noted the tensions that could arise between performers and label executives in recording studios, when the goal was to create works that adhered to the desires of the imagined consumer, as opposed to the performer:

> The most distressing problem in the career of the average musician is the necessity of choosing between conventional success and his "artistic" standards. In order to achieve success, he finds it necessary to "go com- mercial," that is, to play in accord with the wishes of the non-musicians for whom he works [the label executives]. (Becker 136; Hesmondhalgh and Baker, 206)

Davis eventually circumvented this problem by taking control of the re- cording process himself, and by collaborating with musicians who were willing to dedicate countless hours in the recording studio and to follow his lead in the creative process.

But not everyone is Gould or Davis. Some performers, many in fact, thrive on the emotional labor of live performance. They enjoy direct contact with listeners and prefer the instant feedback of a live audience over the delayed response of published music reviews. For them, the isolated existence of the recording studio is detrimental to human flourishing.

For listeners, the pros and cons of recording technology are equally compli- cated. Although recordings enable fans to enjoy their favorite performances, time and again, whenever and wherever they choose, gone is the real-life, face-to-face connection and shared experience of live performance. In its place is the bodiless voice of recorded sound. But as David Suisman notes in *Selling Sounds: The Commercial Revolution in American Music*, the loss of a face-to-face interaction between the fan and performer does not necessarily result in a loss of connection, at least from the side of the listener. Recordings have enabled listeners to feel a new sense of intimacy with performers. As re- cording technologies have improved, "countless anonymous listeners" have been able to "cultivate relationships with performers that approximated real intimacy, knowing the rhythms of another human being's breath, registering the grain of another's voice in one's own body, and perhaps experiencing genuine feelings of exaltation or ecstasy" (Suisman 184). All of this contributes to human flourishing. Through recordings, listeners are able to expand their knowledge of different regions, ethnicities, and cultures. And performers have discovered that their music has the ability to connect with audiences, across time and location, that they never imagined possible. Music recordings often outlive their performers, offering musicians a rare chance at immortality. For professional musicians, especially, the knowledge of such possibilities adds a sense of permanence to an otherwise transitory art form.

But what has become of the permanence of music recording now that we've entered the age of streaming? Although streaming offers, quite literally, a world of music at the click of a button, it has also transformed the process of music curating. Gone are the disc jockeys of regional radio, replaced by data streams and algorithms that suggest new music based on what listeners have previously heard. Streaming services have made listening to music more convenient, for sure. But in exchange for that convenience, listeners have been forced to give up the commentary and cultural context that was included in the liner notes and cover art of LPs and CDs. In some ways, this loss of context has led to a loss of identity and personal ownership for listeners. A recording is no longer something one owns, but rather something that is offered to listeners, temporarily, as part of a service. Streaming has also changed music composition, at least with regard to pop songs. When listeners stream a song, they must listen to it for at least thirty seconds for the stream to register. In other words, for a songwriter and performer to receive payment for their song, they must hold the listener's attention for at least half a minute. This phenomenon has led to a change in the way many pop songs are structured. Composers are now frontloading songs with musical elements designed to grab the listener's interest. Gone are the long instrumental introductions and opening narrative verses. The beginning of most pop songs today features a catchy hook or sing-along chorus (Seabrook).

Streaming has also made music more affordable, and this has changed the "value" of music in the minds of some listeners. In fact, many casual listeners now consider music recordings to be free, open-source commodities, since basically every commercially recorded piece of music can now be heard at no cost, on services like Spotify and YouTube, in exchange for giving up a little personal data and exposing oneself to targeted advertisements. And for less than ten dollars a month, listeners can gain access to any music they want, twenty-four hours a day/seven days a week, commercial free (Witt).

This change in the monetary value of music recordings has proven financially disastrous for many musicians. Gone are the days when a professional musician could make a living working in the recording studio alone. A million streams of a performance on Spotify nets a performer less than $5,000 today—and that's only if he/she/they are both the performer and composer.

But music streaming has also proven beneficial to professional musicians. As the monetary value of recorded music has dropped, the value of live music has grown exponentially, especially among millennials. Although Generation Z spends dramatically less money each month on recorded music than members of Generation X did at the same age, they spend dramatically more on attending live performances. In a world of virtual relationships, they prefer spending their money on "experiences" rather than "things." And they often discover which experiences to invest in through their contacts on social media.[1] Consequently, the professional musician's social capital has risen in the digital age. And this has largely been achieved by performers interacting directly with their fans through apps like Twitter, Facebook, YouTube, TikTok, and Instagram. Social capital allows performers "to better license themselves, sell merchandise," and "bring crowds to concerts." As Tim Anderson has noted, musicians have had to create new relationships with fans:

> This has meant that artists and acts have had to experiment with opening themselves and their work online so that users could make them topics around which connections could be formed. The proposition to the fan is that an act's online presence, the work, and the activities can be used as a source through which community can be formed and explored. (Anderson 169)

With streaming, recorded music is no longer only a commodity that listeners buy, it is also a service to which they subscribe. And this service has created a new form of emotional labor—having a presence on social media—for those performers who care to engage in it. As Nancy Baym explains in *Playing to the Crowd: Musicians, Audiences, and the Intimate Work of*

---

[1] Information on listening habits among various demographic groups is published each year in the Nielsen Music 360 Report. For this chapter, the 2015, 2016, 2017, and 2018 reports were consulted. To access summaries go to: https://www.nielsen.com/?s=Music+360&market=us&language=en.

Connection, the concept of audiences as undifferentiated masses mediated through record labels and the press is disappearing as the emotional connection between musicians and their fans migrates to various social media platforms. Through social media, audiences connect with the performers they are listening to, and performers reach out in search of new audiences. The emotional labor is now more intimate and more constant as the stream of messages range from the thoughtful and uplifting, to the shocking and banal (Baym). Human flourishing is far from guaranteed under such circumstances, but it is possible, if professional musicians take the time and effort to communicate with their fans in a thoughtful, art-focused way.

In discussions of music and social media, great focus has been placed on artists who have suffered under the strain of sharing too much (e.g., Justin Bieber and Ariana Grande) and those who consciously remain something of an enigma through social media (e.g., Beyoncé and Adele). The intersection of social media and music, however, is not limited to pop stars. In recent years, musicians associated with classical music and jazz have taken on the emotional labor of connecting with audiences through social media, some in especially effective and creative ways.

Opera baritone Lucas Meachum has gained attention in recent years for *The Baritone Blog* and his regular presence on social media platforms like Twitter and Instagram. "To reach so many people with the click of a button is amazing," he notes. Meachum uses social media as more than merely a tool for self-promotion. For him, it's a way to build community and to grow as an artist. "I receive so many questions from young singers and find that connecting with them helps me stay fresh and in the know as a singer myself" (*Classical Post*).

Meachum works hard on developing his online presence. "I put in at least an hour every day of thinking, strategizing, producing content, responding to messages, etc. It doesn't seem like a chore, though, because the reward of connecting with people is so gratifying." For Meachum, the key is staying on target when connecting with fans and colleagues. "Your brand is integral to your social media accounts," he notes, "so each post is carefully crafted with that in mind. I imagine what my followers want to see from an opera singer, and I try to inform them about music, entertain them, or inspire them" (*Classical Post*).

Jazz musician Esperanza Spaulding has a markedly different approach to social media: "I respond to the pressure that you have to have a social media presence, but I don't feel very proud or inspired by it," she admits.

I try to spend my time away from my phone to do my job, which is making things for people to experience live. Partially, I'm a little torn about the thought of encouraging people to look at their phones for the sake of something I put up there. I'd rather encourage everyone I know and love, and [even those I] don't know, to go outside and take a walk or have a conversation or read a book or listen to music. I don't know if these phones are enhancing our compassion, or creativity or expression. (Nodjimbadem n.p.)

For Spalding, the best use of social media is as a window to the creative process. Instead of spending hours interacting with followers, she simply lets them witness her rehearsals and recording sessions. This practice is perhaps best exemplified by the making of her 2017 album, *Exposure*, which was recorded, from scratch, over several days, and streamed live on the internet using Facebook. When asked what motivated her to pursue this particular project using social media, she responded that she wanted "to have an experience and share the experience of doing one thing without any agenda." She wanted to see if she could use social media as "purely an exposition of creativity and imagination" (Nodjimbadem n.p.). She wanted her audience there with her as witnesses of the creative process. For Spalding's fans, being given the opportunity to observe the creation process enhanced their interest in and appreciation of her work. Watching the recording process live supplied a new level of artistic and cultural context. In short, it served as a direct communication link between Spalding and her listeners.

"Music is communication that does social work," explains Nancy Baym. "Its energy moves from artists to audience, among audiences, and back from audience to artists" (52). For professional musicians, successful, sustainable careers often depend upon a performer's comfort and willingness to participate in emotional labor, be it through live performance or via social media. New technologies in music have continuously complicated the professional performer's relationship with his/her/their fans. Each new innovation has brought rituals, which in turn have created new challenges and opportunities. In today's music economy, musicians must remember to focus on those things they can actually control. They have myriad channels of communication that they can choose to engage in or reject when it comes to the emotional labor of their work. Social media can be an appealing tool for some, but a stress-inducing burden for others. Consequently, human flourishing among professional musicians is dependent upon their willingness to reflect deeply on the forms of communication that work best for them and their fans. Performers can connect through their music—be it live performance or recordings—and social media. All the options of the past are still available to performers today. To put it simply, the commodification of the performer/ fan relationship has always existed in professional music performance, be it under the patronage system, as part of the gig economy, or through the recording and social media industries. So, when it comes to contemplating the connections between emotional labor and music performance in the twenty-first century, the key question isn't so much: What happens to human flourishing when the relationship between performers and their fans is commodified? But rather: How can an awareness of human flourishing facilitate healthier commodified relationships between performers and their fans?

Works Cited

Anderson, Tim J. *Popular Music in a Digital Music Economy: Problems and Practices for an Emerging Service Industry*. New York: Routledge, 2014.

Baym, Nancy K. *Playing to the Crowd: Musicians, Audiences, and the Intimate Work of Connection*. New York: New York University Press, 2018.

Becker, Howard. "The Professional Dance Musician and His Audience." *American Journal of Sociology*, vol. 57, no. 2, 1951, pp. 136–144.

Classical Post. "Why Baritone Lucas Meachem Thinks Social Media is Necessary for Classical Musicians of Today." August 31, 2018. https://classicalpost.com/read/2018/8/30/why-baritone-lucas-meachem-thinks-social-media-is-necessary-for-classical-musicians-of-today.

Davis, Miles. *Miles*. New York: Simon & Schuster, 2009.

Fay, Amy. *Music-Study in Germany in the Nineteenth Century*. New York: A. C. McClurg, 1880. Reprint, New York: Dover Publications, 1965.

Goehr, Lydia. *The Imaginary Museum of Musical Works*. Oxford: Oxford University Press, 1994.

Hesmondhalgh, David, and Sarah Baker. *Creative Labour: Media Work in Three Cultural Industries*. London and New York: Routledge, 2011.

Hochschild, Arlie R. *The Managed Heart: Commercialization of Human Feeling*. Berkeley: University of California Press, 1983.

Hozer, Michèle, and Peter Raymont, directors. *Genius Within: The Inner Life of Glenn Gould*, 2009. https://www.youtube.com/watch?v=jIc_USZtIiE.

Liszt, Franz. *An Artist's Journey*, translated and annotated by Charles Suttoni. Chicago: University of Chicago Press, 1989.

Nodjimbadem, Katie. "Esperanza Spalding's Pop Culture Loves." *Smithsonian Magazine* [expanded interview online], September 2017. https://www.smithsonianmag.com/arts-culture/esperanza-spalding-pop-culture-loves-180964396/.

Seabrook, John. *The Song Machine: Inside the Hit Factory*. New York: W.W. Norton, 2016.

Small, Christopher. *Musicking: The Meanings of Performing and Listening*. Hanover, NH: Wesleyan University Press, 1998.

Suisman, David. *Selling Sounds: The Commercial Revolution in American Music*. Cambridge, MA: Harvard University Press, 2012.

Taylor, Yuval, and Jake Austen. *Darkest America: Black Minstrelsy from Slavery to Hip Hop*. New York: W. W. Norton, 2012.

Witt, Stephen. *How Music Got Free: A Story of Obsession and Invention*. New York: Viking, 2015.

Index